BATMAN
ARKHAM CITY

P9-CJP-836

A YEAR HAS PASSED

It's been a year since riots at Arkham Asylum practically destroyed the facility. Between the damage caused there and to Blackgate Prison, there are no facilities to place the criminals of Gotham City. Threatened with the untenable option of releasing dangerous criminals, the citizens of Gotham have chosen another option. Newly elected Mayor Quincy Sharp is leading the charge to use the old slums of Gotham as its own prison. The region has been walled off and dubbed "Arkham City."

The desperate blocks of Arkham City are practically a lawless land. Ostensibly protected by TYGER guard forces, the reality of the situation is much more grim. Prisoners rally to the most powerful and charismatic of their numbers, violence is commonplace, and literally no one on the outside seems to know—or care—what's going on.

Hugo Strange, a psychiatrist, is in charge of all TYGER guard forces. Few know what this man is capable of and his motives are unclear as well.

From the shadows, Batman watches. Something is changing inside Arkham City and he'll be there when it all starts to unravel. The ravages of TITAN. The mystery of Protocol 10. The identity of Batman himself. Where will it all lead?

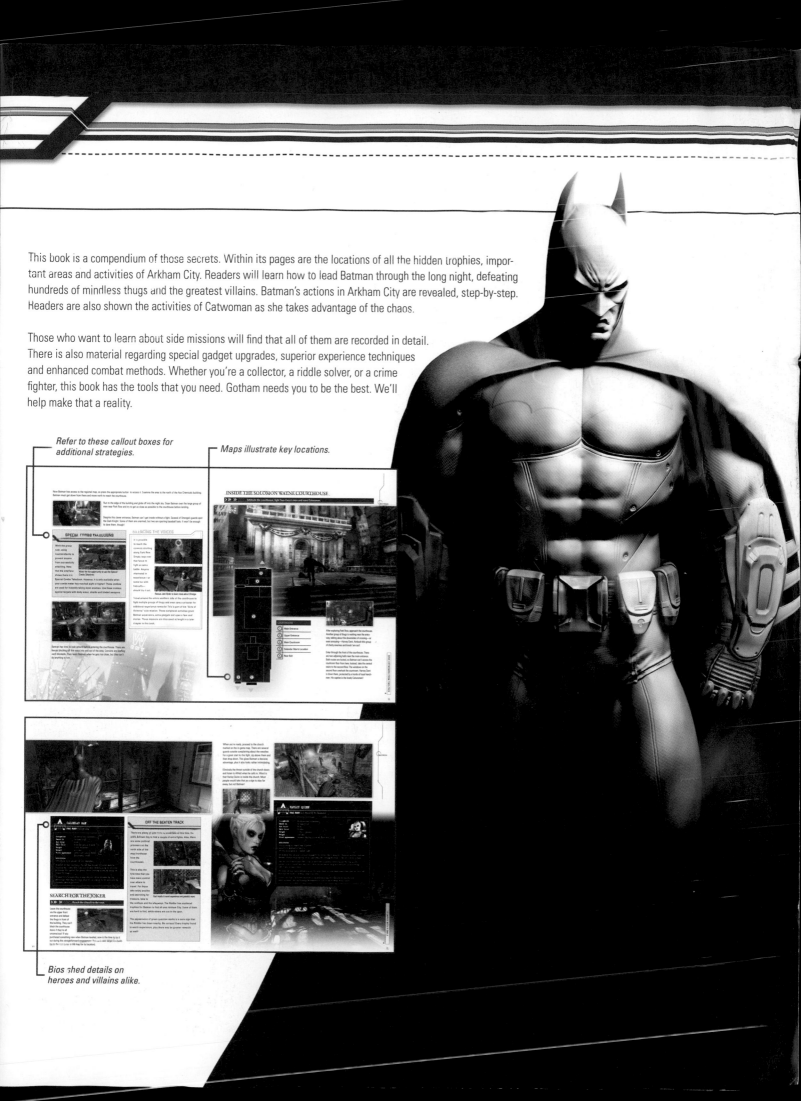

This book is a compendium of those secrets. Within its pages are the locations of all the hidden trophies, important areas and activities of Arkham City. Readers will learn how to lead Batman through the long night, defeating hundreds of mindless thugs and the greatest villains. Batman's actions in Arkham City are revealed, step-by-step. Readers are also shown the activities of Catwoman as she takes advantage of the chaos.

Those who want to learn about side missions will find that all of them are recorded in detail. There is also material regarding special gadget upgrades, superior experience techniques and enhanced combat methods. Whether you're a collector, a riddle solver, or a crime fighter, this book has the tools that you need. Gotham needs you to be the best. We'll help make that a reality.

Refer to these callout boxes for additional strategies.

Maps illustrate key locations.

Bios shed details on heroes and villains alike.

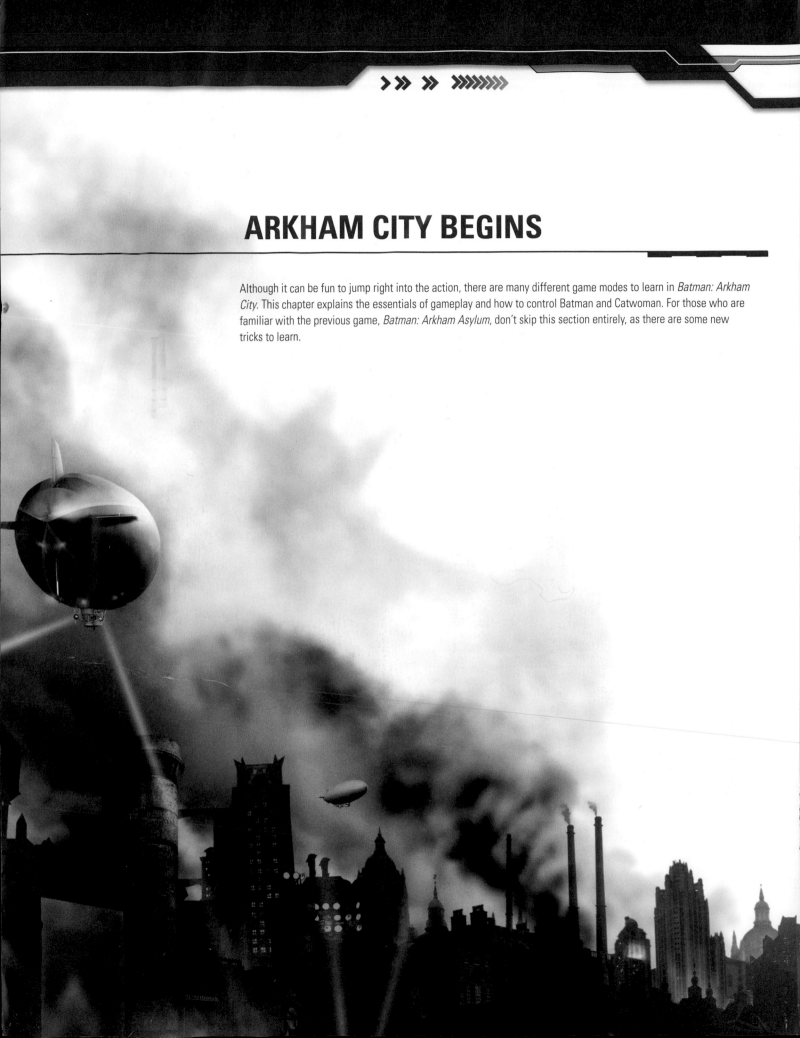

ARKHAM CITY BEGINS

Although it can be fun to jump right into the action, there are many different game modes to learn in *Batman: Arkham City*. This chapter explains the essentials of gameplay and how to control Batman and Catwoman. For those who are familiar with the previous game, *Batman: Arkham Asylum*, don't skip this section entirely, as there are some new tricks to learn.

① There isn't much to see in the Heads Up Display (HUD). At the top of the screen is a compass. A small wedge indicates the direction that the camera is facing. Waypoints or primary objectives appear above the compass and show the direction in which they're located. Note that the HUD only appears when outside and not in an interior location.

② The health bar (shown in gray) appears in the upper-left corner of the screen. It diminishes as Batman takes damage from melee, gunfire or dangerous objects/terrain. Health is restored when Batman gains experience or wins fights.

③ Above the health bar is a green bar that fills to note Batman's "growth." When this XP Meter is full, you can enter the WayneTech menu and spend a point on at least one new upgrade.

BASIC CONTROLS

You can't get very far in a game without knowing the basics. To learn more about the control scheme and get a visual representation, load the game and select the Options menu. The Controls submenu loads a picture of your system's controller. The following sections describe what each button press does in detail. For button pressing specifics, please refer to the game's manual as this section is written to cover all platforms.

MOVEMENT

The most basic function of all is movement. This control allows Batman to move forward or backward, left or right. It's quite direct. Batman normally moves at a walking pace, but there are ways to speed him up. That is covered later in this section.

LOOKING AROUND

Another intuitive function is looking. Press the appropriate button to pan the camera around and see the area from different angles. This becomes quite useful when fighting a room full of thugs, or scoping an area from high above. This is also a good function for discovering hidden Riddler puzzles or other items that may otherwise go unnoticed.

Look around to get the drop on unsuspecting enemies.

CENTER CAMERA

Use this command to snap the camera back into place. The camera will auto-fix itself in Batman's normal line of sight. After thoroughly exploring an area, press this button to return the camera view back to its default position.

ZOOMING

To get a better view of something off in the distance, utilize the zoom command. This feature is invaluable during some of the Riddler's puzzles when a distant target may be difficult to hit with Batarangs or just plain hard to make out. Also, some of the Riddler's puzzles involve snapping pictures and the zoom function will be needed on occasion.

When solving the Riddler's puzzles, use the zoom feature to get a really good view of an object to make the picture count!

RUNNING/EVADING

This button command should be fairly obvious to all gamers. When held down, it causes Batman to run in a particular direction. The main  downside to running is that Batman makes a small amount of noise. This allows him to reach places much faster, plus he doesn't tire!

 When the appropriate button is double tapped, this command causes Batman to Evade (a leaping dodge). Evade is fast, safe and allows the Dark Knight to avoid some attacks. Use it to avoid blade users, thrown objects and some boss attacks.

SLIDING

Once running, Batman can slide underneath low objects and into thugs. Press the same button as crouch to engage the slide function. Not only does this help Batman to avoid certain obstacles, it's also needed to obtain a few Riddler Trophies!

STRIKING

Press this button command to perform Batman's basic punch attacks. Continue tapping the button to trigger a combo of hits.

Combos are extremely important in combat potential, because it earns the player extra experience and special moves that are quite powerful.

Use the strike command in conjunction with movement to direct Batman toward different targets. Batman automatically swings directly in front of himself, so push the movement stick in a different direction to shift the position of the attack. To enter Free-flow against a foe, it requires landing three successive hits.

COUNTERING

Often, several foes attack Batman at the same time which makes it quite difficult to defeat them in a timely manner. During such instances, these foes unleash their own attacks and inflict damage against the Dark Knight. The counter command lets you turn the tables on almost anyone who attempts to hit Batman. Attacks that can be countered appear as a series of blue lines over the attacker; this is their giveaway.

As soon as the blue lines appear, press the Counter button to stop the attack and deal damage to the enemy instead.

When trying to counter multiple attacks at the same time, press the Counter button once for each enemy. There is no penalty for countering too many times, but there is one for not countering enough. Thus, it's better to err on the side of caution; pound the Counter button repeatedly if there is any doubt.

CROUCHING

This command causes Batman to crouch low to the ground. It enables him to get underneath most obstacles and move quietly.

If the obstacle is too low to crouch under, use the slide technique instead.

BLADE DODGE

Enemies with blades or stun sticks will have yellow lines above their heads when they attack, which require a Blade Dodge. To start a Blade Dodge, hold the movement button away from the attacking thugs through the entirety of the attack. Also, make sure to hold the Counter button for the duration of the attack. Repeat this each time that the opponent attacks, as they oftentimes swing three times. Note that enemies with red lines cannot be countered.

CAPE STUNNING

Stuns aren't used as often as strikes and counters, but they're extremely effective. This command slaps the target in the face with Batman's cape, leaving them stunned and unable to move for a period of time. Use Cape Stuns to disrupt more foes wearing body armor or enemies using stun sticks, blades, swords, and heavy shields. Batman can follow a stun with a variety of special moves.

BEATDOWN

Immediately after a stun, tap the strike button repeatedly to initiate a Beatdown. Use this technique to defeat enemies sporting body armor. It's also a great way to raise

Batman's combo meter. A drawback when using Beatdown is that Batman is exposed while focusing on a lone enemy. Watch his back and break off to attack other targets if they start getting too close.

ULTRA STUN

Use an Ultra Stun, or Triple Stun Combo, to really addle an opponent. Extremely large thugs are susceptible to an Ultra Stun attack. Afterward, they're ripe for a major combo of strikes.

AERIAL ATTACK [CAPE STUN, EVADE, EVADE]

Hit an enemy with a Cape Stun and then evade twice to leap over the attacker. Press attack again and push the movement stick toward other foes to perform a redirected aerial attack. This gives Batman the advantage in the fight, allowing him to wail on the thug from their blindside. This is perfect to use against foes with heavy shields and stun sticks, because both are immune to standard frontal assaults.

REDIRECTING

Press toward an enemy and evade twice to redirect an opponent. This lets Batman escape harm's way when fighting multiple enemies.

NORMAL TAKEDOWNS

It's possible to quickly defeat many targets as long as you get the drop on them. Enemies caught unaware can be knocked out from behind or above.

It's also possible to catch them while Batman is suspended below them on a ledge, hiding around a corner and so forth. Almost any means of hiding can provide an opportunity for a Takedown.

There's no need to guess if Batman is within range for a Takedown. As soon as one of these methods is applicable, the command appears on-screen.

One of the best types of Takedowns occurs when Batman is standing behind a target, called Silent Takedowns. Although they take longer to complete, no noise is made during the process. Because of this, it's possible to walk behind an entire line of guards; Batman can bring down one foe after another using Silent Takedowns and not alert anyone in the area.

SPECIAL COMBO TAKEDOWN [CAPE STUN + COUNTER]

The Special Combo Takedown is a move that is available from the start of the game. When Batman's combo meter climbs above x7, this attack becomes an option. Use it against any thug to instantly knock him out. To perform this move, the Cape Stun and Counter buttons must be pressed simultaneously. Special Combo Takedowns are ideal against enemies with heavy shields, body armor, stun sticks and other high-end weaponry. (Note that controls for the PC version may vary.)

SELECTING A GADGET

Use the command to move around Batman's Gadget list. The chosen gadget is the one that is used when Batman attempts to Aim Gadget. Think of this as selecting your default gadget.

AIMING A GADGET

Batman prepares to use his currently selected gadget when this command is chosen. Hold down the button and see what happens. With Batarangs, Batman starts to aim the device before throwing it. Other tools, such as the Explosive Gel or Sequencer, are held at the ready and should be directed toward an applicable area or device.

Batman can still move slowly while aiming a gadget. Use this as a way to look for consoles to hack or potential Batarang targets.

USING A GADGET

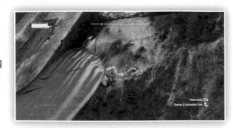

When a gadget is at the ready, this command uses it. That means throwing a Batarang, applying Explosive Gel and so forth.

DETECTIVE MODE

Detective Mode is an alternate viewing system that highlights a variety of important targets. Batman's eyepiece draws his attention to living people, Riddler Trophies, damaged flooring/walls and other points of interest.

Thugs without firearms are shown in blue, while thugs with guns appear in orange.

SCANNING

Sometimes Batman scans evidence to track targets across Arkham City. This is easy to do because the necessary commands are shown on-screen any time that Batman gets close to a clue.

Some Riddler Trophies are achieved by scanning an object or a hidden Riddler question mark. To do this, hold down the same button as used for Detective Mode. Objects can be scanned when looking at them in a normal fashion or while in Detective Mode. The latter

is necessary when attempting to find the hidden question marks. They are somewhat difficult to line up, so try to find the proper angle.

GRAPPLING

The Grapnel tool is used to pull Batman to rooftops, balconies, hanging statues and other distant locations. The Grapnel is much faster than running, so a mix  of grappling, gliding and diving cuts down traveling time quite a bit.

The grapple command appears on-screen when a viable surface is within range. Change the viewing angle to select different grappling targets if multiple ones are nearby.

To cancel a grapple, use the Stun Cape Command.

DROP ATTACK

Batman can drop onto thugs that are beneath him. These drop attacks are extremely effective. They're loud, but the person who gets squished won't stand back up without first taking a long snooze. This command appears whenever Batman gets into position, much like a Takedown.

GLIDING

Press and hold the run button to let Batman glide through the air. During a glide, press forward to gain speed or pull back to get more distance while gliding.

The grapnel can still be used from this position, which means it's possible to leap off a building, glide toward another, and grapple to safety as soon as the target building is within range.

DIVE BOMB

While gliding, press and hold the Crouch button to send Batman into an aggressive dive. If an enemy is already a target, the action turns into  an attack. The dive distance determines the amount of damage an attack causes, so a long dive can bring down an enemy instantly.

Dive bombing is also a good way to pick up speed during a long flight. Dive just long enough to get moving, then release the button (while pulling up) to return to a standard glide. Mastering this technique takes a little bit of practice; hone this skill in the "Augmented Reality" side missions for an awesome reward.

GLIDE KICK

Another aerial attack is the Glide Kick. An enemy with a bat icon over his head indicates that he is marked as a target. Press the strike button  to glide toward that person and nail him when the opportunity arises. The damage from a Glide Kick isn't as much as a Dive Bomb, but isolated enemies are still easy to finish off afterward.

WAYNETECH

The WayneTech button brings up a variety of submenus. These explain Batman's gadgets, armor and moves. It's also a place to see maps of the city, look at Riddler Trophies and read biographies about the main characters. After leveling, come here to spend points on Batman's suit, attacks or gadgets.

WayneTech Submenus: Map of Arkham City

Shows a map of the local area. Batman is identified by a white blinking icon. Objectives are shown as green exclamation points. Look for side missions in blue. The map also reveals any marked Riddler Trophies that have been left behind, which appear as question marks.

Move the cursor over the map and set custom waypoints, but note this can be done only while outside. These waypoints show up on the HUD when you resume the game,.

The extra controls at the bottom of the map provide some fun features, like the game's multitude of Side Missions.

Batcomputer Data

Character biographies and Arkham City Stories are unlocked throughout the game. Some of these come from meeting characters, while others are unlocked by finding various trophies. Read through the biographies and stories and select anything that piques your interest. This is a great place to find out more about the region and its people.

WayneTech

All features of Batman's suit, gadgets, combat moves and predator techniques appear here. Select them to learn more about their commands and effects. Locked moves can be purchased with points that are earned by leveling. There is also a section with Catwoman's moves! Some of the more essential combat techniques have tutorials, so check them out if you're new to the game.

Riddles

After finding Riddler Trophies, this submenu unlocks. Almost all of the hidden items in the game show up here. Combat trophies, hidden objects and puzzles are part of the Riddler's game. Find them to access other game features and earn additional experience. Trophies are divided by region, which makes it much easier to track the missing ones.

THE MAIN MENU

Select the mode of play that you want after the game loads. Some of these options won't be available until after you've achieved certain milestones in the main story.

PLAY THE MAIN STORY

This is the main game. Batman takes on the problems of Arkham City during one very dangerous evening!

STATISTICS

See how well you're doing in side missions and Trophy collection. The statistics screen contains information about all the game's major features.

RIDDLER'S REVENGE

Exciting combat challenges are unlocked as Batman uncovers more of Riddler's Trophies. This mode pits Batman against deadly foes in preset encounters.

Learn various fighting techniques to win medals and become the master of Riddler's Revenge!

STORY SYNOPSIS

If you didn't play Arkham Asylum or want to get a refresher about the story, select this option.

CHARACTER TROPHIES

Special models are unlocked by completing major objectives, such as the ones found in the game's side missions.

OPTIONS

This is similar to the in-game pause menu. Come here to modify game options, audio options, controls or 3D effects.

NEW GAME PLUS

After completing the main story, players can start anew. Secondary playthroughs are necessary to unlock many of the game's rewards. New Game Plus allows you to

keep all of the upgrades and experience earned from your previous game, but the enemies are much stronger.

CATWOMAN EPISODES

Those who download Catwoman's DLC content can play through the story with a few extra objectives. Catwoman's story is interwoven with the game's main storyline, so her missions come before, during and after Batman's involvement in Arkham City.

CONCEPT ART

Environment and character concept art is unlocked when you find Riddler trophies.

CREDITS

Take a look at all the people who helped make this game a reality.

GLOSSARY

The following list contains game terminology that should be familiar to anyone who plays the game. Take a moment to review these terms, as they appear throughout this guide book.

Bat-Vault: Containers dropped off by the Batwing.

Batarang: Thrown at enemies, causing them to be disoriented for a very short time.

Batclaw: Pulls enemies up to 30 feet away toward the player. Can be used to pull rafts, icebergs, open vent covers and collect unreachable Riddler pick-ups.

Beatdown: Rapid Strikes following a Stun Attack, increments Combo Meter for every hit after a short build-up of speed.

Blade Dodge: Counter action against a Sharp Object (Knife, Bottle, Sword).

Bolas: Similar to Batarangs; used by Catwoman.

Caltrops: Sets up a trap; when enemies path over the Caltrops they are initially disoriented, then become incapacitated.

Counter: Basic counter from being hit, counters do not do damage unless the player's Combo Meter is at or above 3.

Cryptographic Sequencer: Use to decode radio frequencies and unlock security panels.

Custom Room: Challenge Rooms that do not post scores or times to the Leaderboards.

Detective Mode: A visual mode that lets you look through walls and detect enemies.

Dive Boost: Performed when holding Dive during a prompted Glide Kick.

Dodge Roll/Evade: Performed when tapping the Sprint Button twice.

Drop Attack: Performed when prompted from a higher elevation, ledge or Vantage Point.

Enemy States: Detective Mode allows Batman to see an enemy's status; active or calm enemies follow their normal patrol paths, while other modes will react with confusion or aggression.

Environmental Counter: Performed when Countering with a Combo Meter of 2 or more and player and thug are near a wall or railing, the Counter needs to be performed near a wall or railing.

Expire: In relation to the Combo Meter, when the player misses, becomes hit or too much time passes between actions.

Explosive Gel: Detonates weak walls and floors.

Fire Extinguishers: In combat, fire extinguishers carried by enemies can be detonated with Batarangs to the effect of a Smoke Pellet. In predator, fire extinguishers placed in the environment can be detonated with Batarangs for distractions

Flawless Freeflow: Bonus points for completing a Round in a Combat Challenge with a single combo.

Freeflow: Act of remaining in combat without the Combo Meter expiring.

Freeze Blast: Can create floating platforms in open water. Used in Freeflow combat and Predator mode to freeze thugs in place.

Freeze Cluster Grenade: Causes an area of effect snare; enemies in the effect are disoriented for focus on freeing themselves. Can freeze enemies and create floating platforms in open water.

Gadget Variation Bonus: Bonus points for using a variety of gadgets during a fight or round in a Combat Challenge.

Glide Kick: Performed when prompted from a higher elevation, ledge or Vantage Point, as Batman or Robin.

Glyph: Scannable design left by Azrael, the Watcher in the Wings side story.

Ground Takedown: Performed on an incapacitated enemy; nearby enemies will attempt to hit you off (increments Combo Meter +1 upon completion). Enemy is defeated upon completion.

Jump Kick: Use while running and greater than 5-7 feet away; increments Combo Meter +2.

Knockout Smash: Performed by pressing the Strike Button during a Silent Takedown; finishes the takedown faster but alerts enemies in the room.

Line Launcher: Launches a line between two points, allowing the player to traverse gaps.

Medals: Medals are awarded in Riddler's Revenge for meeting goals within a Challenge Room.

Modifier: Changes to Challenge Rooms to either increase or decrease the difficulty.

Perfect Round Bonus: Bonus points for completing a Round in a Combat Challenge without taking damage.

Predator: A section of gameplay that requires the player to be stealthy.

Quick-Use: Act of using the quick version of a gadget.

Ranked Room: Challenge Rooms that post scores and times to Leaderboards.

REC: Deploys a high current charge to power generators and electromagnets. Can be used and quick-used on enemies in Freeflow combat and Predator Mode.

Remote Controlled Batarang: Player controls the direction the Batarang flies.

Riddler Trophies: Collectible objects that are worth experience and unlock artwork and Riddler challenges.

Security Panels: Player can interact with these consoles using the Cryptographic Sequencer to input passwords.

Shimmy: Used when the player is hanging from a ledge and wants to move along the ledge.

Silent Takedown Smash: Performed when prompted on an unaware enemy, usually from behind; does not alert nearby enemies.

Simultaneous Counters: Counter multiple attackers; increments Combo Meter 1 x number of Countered enemies.

Slide Kick: While running, tap crouch to slide; increments Combo Meter +2.

Smoke Pellet: Creates a large smoke cloud, that disorients enemies; enemies inside the area will attack randomly and can hit other enemies.

Sonic Batarang: Can be used to lure enemies in predator mode.

Strike: A basic attack for hitting; increments Combo Meter +1.

Stun Attack: The basic disorientation effect (Cape Stun).

Telephones: Contact point for Zsasz, the Cold Call Killer side story.

Thief Vision: Catwoman's version of Detective Mode.

Thrown Counter: Counter action against thrown objects; thrown direction can be altered.

Titan Containers: Objectives for Bane in the Fragile Alliance side story.

Ultra Stun: Use three Stun Attacks in a row.

Uncounterable: These attacks appear as red Counter prompts (shields and stun sticks)..

Vantage Point: A gargoyle or support that is at a high elevation.

Variation Bonus: Bonus points for performing a variety of actions during a fight or round in a Combat Challenge.

Whip: Similar to the Batclaw but instead trips enemies.

WHERE DOES HE GET ALL THOSE WONDERFUL TOYS?

Batman has so many special moves and gadgets that it takes some time to master his fighting style. This chapter covers advanced gameplay elements, including combat dynamics! Learn how to use gadgets, attack combos and planned movements to succeed under almost any combat condition. This makes it easier to gain experience, win across any difficulty setting and look intimidating while doing it!

DIFFICULTY MODES

There are three difficulty settings in story mode (Easy, Normal and Hard). It is strongly suggested that you try Normal or Hard during a first attempt at Arkham City. Easy works well for people who are new to games of this type, but an experienced gamer should enjoy the challenges of the tougher modes. In addition, there is a reward for completing the game in Normal or Hard mode—New Game Plus!

EFFECTS OF DIFFICULTY

Enemies gain better weaponry sooner on higher difficulty modes. Batman fights tougher goons , which leads to higher possible combos. This also means there is a chance to gain more experience earlier in the game at higher difficulty levels. Lower difficulty modes reduce enemy health in larger fights, too.

Hang and wait for an ideal target to arrive

Enemies are smarter in Hard mode and in New Game Plus. For example, they can destroy Vantage Points such as gargoyles. If they see Batman hiding somewhere, they will destroy other points of refuge throughout the room.

THINGS THAT DON'T CHANGE

The size of each encounter is exactly the same, regardless of the chosen game mode. There are never more enemies or fewer. There are no novel weapons or challenges on higher difficulty modes either. Although the enemies are stronger sooner

in the game, they don't gain access to anything that you wouldn't eventually encounter in any run through the story.

NEW GAME PLUS

New Game Plus has a few additional changes that make it unique right from the start of the game.

 Enemy difficulty is set to the max.

 Enemies are armed with all types of weapons and equipment.

 Armored thugs appear in Predator rooms, making it impossible to take down all enemies silently.

 Counter prompts are not displayed.

 Ninja can perform their counter move right away.

 Some bosses get additional perks. For example, a boss's swing attack may switch between high and low-mid swing, another boss will fire more attacks, while a third may use his more difficult shield configuration throughout the entire fight.

COMBAT

Combat is one of the great tests of a superhero. Batman avoids any weapon that may prove deadly against his opponents, so much of his fighting relies on strikes that wound and weapons that disable. Let's find out how to use them both to their fullest.

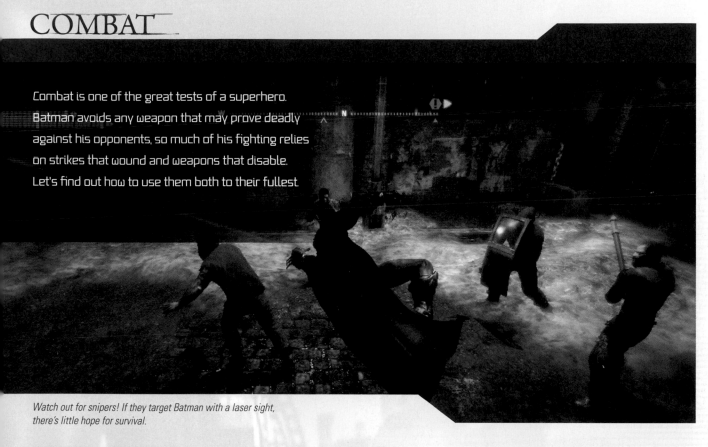

Watch out for snipers! If they target Batman with a laser sight, there's little hope for survival.

ENTERING COMBOS

Batman enters his combos by making several initial strikes. These first three blows occur at a slower rate than the following attacks, so try to start the combo against an unprepared enemy. Once the third successive blow lands, Batman enters Freeflow, which means his damage and speed increase. You can trigger this combo by attacking several different enemies. The timing of the attacks is what matters. You can't delay very long between each swing!

MAINTAINING COMBOS

Batman doesn't fight like a landslide. He doesn't pound down against single targets with unstoppable force. Instead, he fights like water, flowing from target to target without stopping to make himself more difficult to hit.

The combo system is in place to reward players for correctly using Batman's abilities. High combos result in experience at the conclusion of a battle and they're tied to all of Batman's special moves. It's extremely important to maintain a combo because this improves Batman's damage, mobility and potential for high-damage moves.

Counters and Special Combo Takedowns offer a moment of calm during a melee bout.

TIMING IS EVERYTHING!

The first trick in combo maintenance is to master the timing. The initial victim in a group is often good to pound with three hits. The damage escalates after the combo gets going, so it doesn't take multiple strikes to knock down regular thugs after that. Instead, jump back and forth between targets by pressing toward a new victim each time to cover ground quickly.

Make sure to tap the counter button each time a thug lights up with a blue "telegraph" symbol. Counters result in combo points, deal damage to enemies, avoid the attacks in question, and temporarily make Batman immune to additional attacks.

Another advantage of counters is that they're slow. Batman spends more time on the individual who was attacking him, which gives enemies on the ground time to stand back up. After finishing a victim, there should be several targets within striking distance. Get back into the combo as soon as possible! This makes it easier to achieve extremely high combos.

KEY UPGRADES

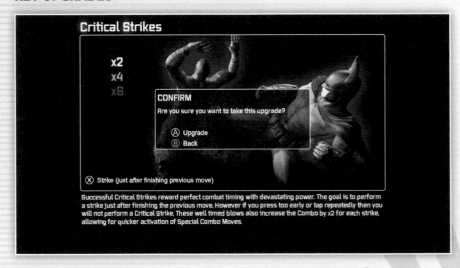

While leveling up, try to gain upgrades that make it easier to get high combo points and more special attacks. It's wise to invest in these early in the game because Batman accrues more experience once he's using critical strikes and a higher degree of special moves.

Key combat upgrades include:

- Critical Strikes (faster combos)

- Special Combo Boost (more special moves)

- Freeflow (major combat upgrade)

Critical strikes are somewhat hard to master, as they're another factor of proper timing. Don't just tap the strike button repeatedly and hope to hit everyone in sight. Taking an aggressive approach will likely result in taking more damage, because the enemies will surround Batman and strike from the flanks or rear.

Instead, time strikes so that each button press is its own attack. If you press the button more than Batman attacks, then slow down! There is absolutely a sense of flow in the game's battle system, so adhere to it!

The interface also indicates if you're going too fast or slow with critical strikes. Once the upgrade is purchased, a message appears if the timing isn't correct.

If you don't master proper timing for critical hits and counters, it could be lights out.

USING GADGETS TO EXTEND COMBOS

Quickfired gadgets don't break combos. If a target isn't within range, use a Batarang (or another gadget) to nail an enemy farther away while waiting for another opportunity to present itself. Evasion works this way, too. Try to evade toward a distant enemy to stop the combo timer briefly and get a second chance to hit another foe before the timer ends.

The ideal time to press the strike button occurs at the exact moment that Batman hits the previous target.

SPECIAL MOVES

Now it's time to learn about special moves. Even before gaining any levels, Batman has the Special Combo Takedown. This special move automatically knocks out a single thug! That's how powerful special moves are; they inflict extreme damage, stun multiple enemies, or otherwise give Batman an advantage in a fight.

Special moves don't take up resources and most of them don't cancel combos. A combo must reach x8 for them to become active, but after that it's possible to trigger a special move at any time. The only limitation is that once a move is unleashed, the combo must continue for several hits before another special move can be used.

Special moves include the following:

 Special Combo Takedown (Counter + Stun): Knocks out one enemy.

 Batswarm (Evade + Strike): Disorients all enemies nearby.

 Disarm and Destroy (Strike + Counter): Destroys the target's weapon permanently.

 Multi-Ground Takedown (Evade + Stun): Knocks out all enemies who are already incapacitated.

Always look for enemy targets who are worthy of special attacks. The Special Combo Takedown is one of the best ways to knock out enemies sporting heavy shields, bladed weapons and other dangerous goodies. There is also a Disarm and Destroy attack that trashes guns, which is another way to use special moves to keep enemies at bay.

If you upgrade Batman's special moves early on, he levels faster and can still pick up suit upgrades later. This forces players to master proper fighting techniques from the beginning because there is less health to work with but more attack options. The beginning stages of the game may be slightly harder, but later levels will be easier.

USING GADGETS IN COMBAT

Gadgets are fun for a variety of reasons: they disable foes, grant bonus experience, and all of them look awesome! All of Batman's gadgets have a point, so learn each one's capabilities and integrate them into your combat style.

THE BATCLAW

 Pulls enemies forward if they are over 10 feet away.

 Pushes enemies away and pulls them closer if they are less than 10 feet away.

 If enemies hit environmental objects or Batman while stumbling, they become incapacitated.

Pull specific targets away from their friends to keep fights more manageable.

 Can be upgraded to disarm guns.

The Batclaw is a ranged tool used for pulling around and disarming opponents. It's one of the slower gadgets to deploy, so avoid its use when multiple enemies are nearby. It's better to use at medium range to pull a thug away from a group.

BATARANGS

- Thrown at enemies, causes them to become disoriented for a short time.

- When the Combo Meter is three or more, Batarangs incapacitate their target.

Batarangs are quite powerful. It takes very little time to throw them, so Batman isn't exposed for long. He can flick between one and three of them in the blink of an eye! Use them to disable ranged enemies (with the Batclaw Disarm upgrade, it's possible to do more). These gadgets also help to slow down a large group of thugs. After hitting a few enemies, they stop their approach. Batman can take out their buddies next, then return to hitting the initial targets.

Remote Batarangs take more time to use, but they're still quite useful. Use them to hit enemies who are at a distance. The remote feature even allows for movement around corners, hitting objects behind Batman, and so forth. Batarangs are a vital tool for fighting in rooms with multiple ranged gunmen.

REMOTE ELECTRICAL CHARGE (REC)

Batman receives the REC fairly early in the game. This weapon can stun enemies or trigger them to go into a frenzy. Foes with larger, heavier weapons sometimes knock down their own friends while reeling from the effects of the REC.

Special REC effects include the following:

◉ Armored thugs are sent flying.

◉ Mister Hammer and other lieutenants spin around, hitting nearby allies.

◉ Bat/Pipe/Shield/Stun Stick thugs flail around, hitting other enemies.

◉ Knife/Bottle/Ninja thugs tense up but don't hit other enemies.

EXPLOSIVE GEL

Explosive Gel takes more time to use than other gadgets because its quickfire form must be deployed *and* detonated. Lure enemies onto gel and listen for the "beep," which signifies that someone is in the area of effect. That's when it's time to detonate the gel! After the explosion, Batman can finish the foe and disarm them without even throwing a punch.

Anyone carrying shields, guns, or melee weapons drop their toys when the gel explodes.

FREEZE BLAST

The Freeze Blast is acquired late in the game. This gadget disables an enemy for a moderate period of time. It's a way to remove a foe from a fight and still focus on other enemies. It works best against armed thugs by quickly removing them early in an encounter.

Attacking a frozen enemy incapacitates the foe, so try to slam the cold thug to bring him down right away. A Ground Takedown provides a permanent follow-up, as long as no one else is attacking at that time.

SMOKE PELLETS

 IMPORTANT! Do not affect Ninja or shield thugs!

Smoke Pellets are defensive in nature and, therefore, most of their applications are for that purpose. Deploy the pellet and let the smoke conceal Batman's location. Smoke pellets work best in Predator Mode when gunmen are present. In fact, it's possible to trick gunmen into doing some silly things.

GETTING MORE EXPERIENCE

One way to get maximum experience from a fight is to use all of Batman's gadgets before the action gets too serious, which ensures the highest gadget bonus. Then, try to hit every enemy in one fluid combo while performing special moves and counterattacks. This union can increase the amount of battle experience by a large margin.

LINE LAUNCHER

 While on the Line Launcher, Batman kicks enemies who get in the way, incapacitating them in the process.

 It's possible to perform a prompted Takedown on a thug while riding the Line Launcher.

The Line Launcher lets Batman cross from one side to another. Use it to get above an enemy and zip over his head, then drop and land behind the foe and finish off the opponent unaware. As with Smoke Pellets, this is a better tool for Predator Mode than for direct melee combat.

THE FINAL THUG

Thugs without a group become isolated, so they are easier to take out. This is also true of the final thug from a group of enemies. In either case, the solo victim is known as the "final thug."

Final thugs are defeated under the following circumstances:

 Any counterattack results in defeat.

 Three strikes without a combo, or a single strike with a combo greater than three, knocks out the thug.

 Normal strikes and gadgets cause damage as well.

 Defeating a final thug always triggers a brief cinematic attack. That's how you know that a fight is over! Batman heals and gains experience when this occurs.

PREDATOR MODE

Predator Mode is an entirely different type of challenge from melee combat. In some rooms, it's possible to eliminate thugs without being seen or detected. This is when Batman enters Predator Mode. Oftentimes, these challenges are made more dangerous by the inclusion of firearms. It's possible to complete certain Predator Rooms with keen combat skills, but it's much safer to hunt silently and slip away into the darkness.

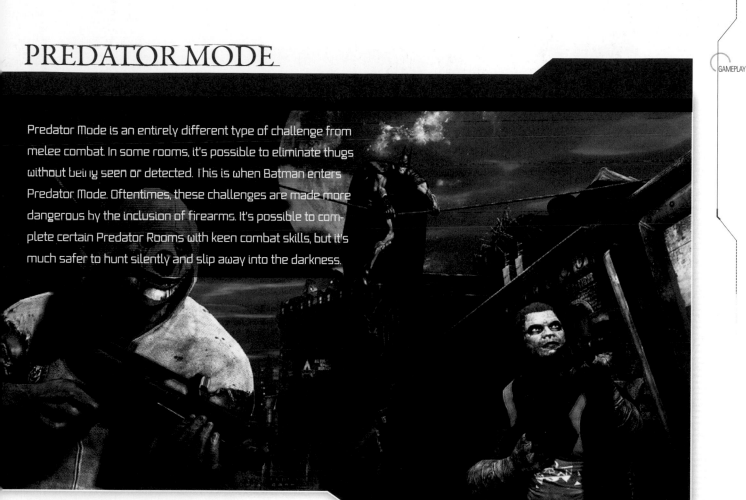

HUNTING ARMED FOES

Thugs are always dangerous, but guns bring things to a whole new level. These weapons can result in instant death if Batman tries to stand and take the hits. That's why caution is one of Batman's best allies!

Watch gunmen from a distance before making a move.

DETECTIVE MODE

In Detective Mode, it's possible to see through walls to learn how many foes are in the next area. This mode also reveals who has guns and who doesn't; orange indicates an armed foe while blue means an unarmed opponent.

In addition, Batman can track his victims while hiding behind cover. Watch for enemies to move into vulnerable positions, then attack from behind for Silent Takedowns.

It's often wise to switch between normal vision and Detective Mode during a predator run. Normal vision is good for seeing which direction an enemy is facing. It's also a good way to examine the general layout of a room. Detective Mode is superior for tracking. Rely on both types of vision.

SIGNAL JAMMERS

On rare occasions, Batman enters a room with a signal jammer. These devices prevent Detective Mode from working. The only person visible is the guy with the jammer. Use Detective Mode to track the target, but switch to normal vision to ensure that you don't encounter other thugs!

Watch the patrols before going after someone in a signal jammer room.

Before starting your run, stay in the safety of the shadows. Detective Mode sometimes blinks in for just a second, so try to count the enemies in the room and memorize their placement. Knock out a signal jammer to restore Detective Mode before clearing the remainder of the enemies in the room.

PATROL ROUTES & CHATTY GUARDS

 After watching a room, reset the game to restore patrol routes to their original status.

If enemies fail to notice that Batman is in the area, they stay fairly relaxed. Expect the thugs to wander around and patrol the area for trouble. Most thugs stay on a preset path that goes through the room they're assigned to guard. Watch the path and find a way behind the target. Crouch, stay quiet, and approach from the rear for a Silent Takedown.

Occasionally, guards may wander close to one other. Talking guards don't look around much, so if two guards are sharing the same blind spot, approach them and unleash a Takedown against them both. Double Takedowns are perfect if the goons are close together. If they're not, use a Takedown on one guy and creep up to his buddy before the other person realizes that they're in danger.

FAST & SLOW TAKEDOWNS

Slow Takedowns are usually quite effective. When attacking from the rear, Batman can disable a thug in just a few seconds. The thug won't make any noise, so no one else in the room will come running.

Other Takedowns are much faster, but all of them make some noise, which attracts other guards. Instead of waiting for them to arrive, hide and look for opportunities to attack. Thugs from a distance may not have anyone watching their backs, so bring them down while the others are distracted!

THE HIT-AND-RUN

When Batman gets spotted (or if guards are alerted), it may be time to get aggressive. Wary enemies look around more, making it tougher to get the drop on them. When pure stealth isn't an option, try speed and aggression. Sneak up on a target and use a fast Takedown or an  attack that knocks the target to the ground. Ground Takedowns are extremely fast, making it easier to flee the situation.

The point of a hit-and-run tactic is to silence one enemy without getting into a prolonged firefight. Have Smoke Pellets at the ready, because they are often a great follow-up. Take out the enemy in question, drop a Smoke Pellet, and grapple to safety higher in the room. Find things to hide behind and wait for the enemies to give up.

BODY ARMOR IS PROBLEMATIC

In New Game Plus, enemies with body armor appear during Predator Mode battles. This is a major thorn, because a normal Takedown isn't possible against armored opponents.

Yeah, he's going to be a pain! Give the guy a Beatdown when no one is looking

Use standard predator techniques to thin the other enemies in the room first. Isolated thugs with body armor are no more dangerous than anyone else because you can attack them at leisure and make lots of noise.

If it's necessary to knock out an armored thug sooner, wait until no one is watching and then attack at high speed. Give them a Beatdown, knock 'em out and flee!

USE HEIGHT TO YOUR ADVANTAGE

Unless there is a compelling reason to stay on the ground, get high up as quickly as possible. It's not as easy to spot Batman near the ceiling. Guards usually look up when they're searching for Batman. In addition, there are more opportunities to attack someone down below than compared to hitting people above.

When it's safe, watch the room and take note of the guards' patrol patterns. Look for vulnerable enemies, hiding places, and so forth. Vents, grates and ledges are all useful ways to get around without being seen.

DISTRACTIONS ARE EFFECTIVE

Sonic Batarangs, detonated mines and any normal noises get the attention of guards. Use intentional distractions to make enemies look the wrong way or move in the wrong direction. After exhausting all opportunities for normal stealth attacks, these misdirected techniques become prominent.

DISCOVERED!

There will be times when the enemies get the drop. Predator Rooms take practice and some of them are extremely difficult to complete without resorting to combat tactics in conjunction with predator Takedowns. Don't get anxious when enemies start closing in; instead, get some distance and turn a problem into a solution.

SMOKE PELLETS

As noted previously, Smoke Pellets are extremely effective in Predator Rooms. Armed enemies can't see into or out of smoke, so dropping these pellets ensures free passage.

HEARTBEAT MONITORS

Some enemies are monitored, meaning their allies are alerted when they get knocked out. Don't stay near fallen thugs; instead, find a safe spot and spy on anyone who approaches the downed man. If there are only a couple of guards left in a room, leave some Explosive Gel on top of a fallen thug and detonate it when his buddies arrive. Before they recover, drop down and use Ground Takedowns to finish the job.

THERMAL GOGGLES

Thugs with thermal goggles appear in Detective Mode when they scan the area for heat signatures. Be wary of these foes, because they can spot Batman even when he's in the shadows. However, there is an upgrade to purchase that can conceal Batman's heat signature. If it's not available, use hard cover to block line of sight between scanning enemies and Batman.

VANTAGE POINTS

Use hiding spots such as gargoyles to scour the room and ambush enemies. However, the enemies in Hard and New Game Plus difficulty won't stand for this. Once they realize that Batman is using Vantage Points, they'll shoot at these targets and actively destroy them.

Use the Vantage Points early on, but abandon them once the guards catch on.

THE RETREAT

Once spotted by the enemy, it's imperative to seek cover as soon as possible. Find a vent or a grate to slip into, or grapple away and continue to swing from point to point until the enemies lose sight.

EXPLORING ARKHAM CITY

The walkthrough section of this strategy guide reveals how to complete the game in its entirety. In addition, it identifies how to hunt for Trophies/Achievements, collect goodies from the Riddler, spot cameos from various people, and so on.

COLLECTIBLE ITEMS

Once unlocked, it's possible to invest hours of gameplay into the Riddler's hunt for Trophies. Finding them is fun by itself, plus there are a number of rewards for your effort. Batman gains experience and various pictures and Challenge Rooms are unlocked in the process.

Cameras are easy to spot while in Detective Mode.

The WayneTech submenus contain a section for Riddler Trophies. Go there often to determine what is left to collect. These sections are divided by region in most cases, although there is a tab for combat-related trophies.

After obtaining all the gadgets in the game, start a massive hunt for Riddler Trophies and try to collect them all! It takes a long time, but that's perfect for anyone who wants even more to do in Arkham City.

SIDE MISSIONS

There are 12 missions in Arkham City that are not essential to the main plot. However, it's possible to unlock upgrades by completing them and there are several Trophies/Achievements tied to them. Play through the side missions to learn more about the residents of Arkham City. Refer to the chapter titled "The Hero Gotham Needs" to learn more about the side missions.

DOWNLOADABLE CONTENT

Batman isn't the only person who can fight against the bad guys. DLC for Arkham City lets you play portions of the game as other heroes. Catwoman's combat techniques and content is covered in full detail in this book.

CATWOMAN'S MOVES

Catwoman has several unique aspects of play. The first one involves the way she moves around Arkham City. Instead of gliding between buildings, Catwoman lashes out with her Whip and pulls herself over to distant areas. When she lands, Catwoman can quickly scamper up a vertical surface. Look for the on-screen prompt and press the corresponding button to climb. If the timing is off, a message appears that indicates whether to speed up or slow down your actions.

In addition, Catwoman can climb on the underside of grates and other surfaces. When underneath such an area, a button appears on-screen that indicates when she can hop up. Once there, she can jump back down at will or move about freely to explore.

Catwoman's Toys

Catwoman's gadgets include her Whip, Caltrops, and Bolas. These are partially analogous to some of Batman's equipment. The Whip is similar to the Batclaw. This gadget pulls attackers closer to Catwoman, making it possible to separate enemies from their buddies or pull them behind cover.

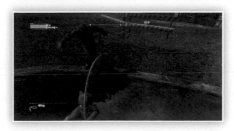

The Caltrops are ground traps that hamper movement for anyone who walks over them, making them perfect for leading groups into an ambush. Catwoman can deploy up to three groups of them before or during a fight. The Bolas act just like Batarangs.

Upgrades

When you gain levels, check out Catwoman's area in the WayneTech menu. This is where you can spend points to upgrade her abilities. The following is a list of things that can be upgraded:

 Ballistic Armor (two slots)

 Combat Armor (two slots)

 Special Combo Whiplash (an area of effect combo attack)

 Special Combo Whip Trip (a special combo that lays out the enemies)

Although Batman's Batsuit and gadget upgrades don't carry over to Catwoman, some of his Combat upgrades do! Purchase reliable upgrades like Critical Strikes, Special Combo Boost and Freeflow Focus to ensure that Batman and Catwoman receive equal benefits.

THE PEOPLE OF GOTHAM

Gotham City has a history that spans generations. Its people are as diverse as any in the world and it has some of the greatest heroes—and worst villains—that anyone could imagine. Batman has files on practically everyone of importance. These entries help him keep an edge against his enemies and allow him to safeguard the innocent citizens of Gotham.

BRUCE WAYNE

REAL NAME
BRUCE WAYNE

OCCUPATION: WORLD'S GREATEST DETECTIVE
BASED IN: GOTHAM CITY

When his parents were gunned down in front of him, young Bruce Wayne resolved to rid Gotham City of the criminal element that took their lives.

He trained extensively to achieve mental and physical perfection, in addition to mastering martial arts, detective techniques and criminal psychology.

Dressing as a bat to prey on criminals' fears, Batman fights crimes with the aid of specialized gadgets and vehicles, operating out of his secret Batcave below Wayne Manor.

As Batman, Bruce Wayne can stop many of the worst criminals of Gotham. He has to work hard to maintain his secret identity, though, because many enemies would love to strike at Batman through the people he cares about. In addition, Batman's vigilantism would be directly called to question if a face could be put to his name.

The events at Arkham Asylum occurred roughly a year ago. Batman arrested the Joker, but it all turned out to be a trap. The ensuing violence damaged many structures on the island and left the Asylum completely unfit for use. That is why sections of Gotham have been militarized and are being used to house the criminally insane and violent members of the city. Batman can't allow this to continue!

BATMAN

REAL NAME
BRUCE WAYNE

OCCUPATION: WORLD'S GREATEST DETECTIVE
BASED IN: GOTHAM CITY

Hair Color: Black

Eye Color: Blue

Height:
6 ft. 2 inches

Weight: 210 lbs.

ALFRED

REAL NAME

ALFRED PENNYWORTH

OCCUPATION: BUTLER
BASED IN: GOTHAM CITY

After a varied career, Alfred Pennyworth was employed as the Wayne family's butler. When Bruce Wayne's parents were killed, Alfred raised the young orphan and reluctantly aided him in his quest to become the Batman.

Alfred's many skills—ranging from cooking to combat medicine—make him Batman's staunchest ally, along with a formal demeanor that grounds the Dark Knight and deflects those who might otherwise suspect Bruce Wayne's true identity.

Hair Color: Gray [formerly black]

Eye Color: Blue

Height:
6 ft 0 inches

Weight: 180 lbs

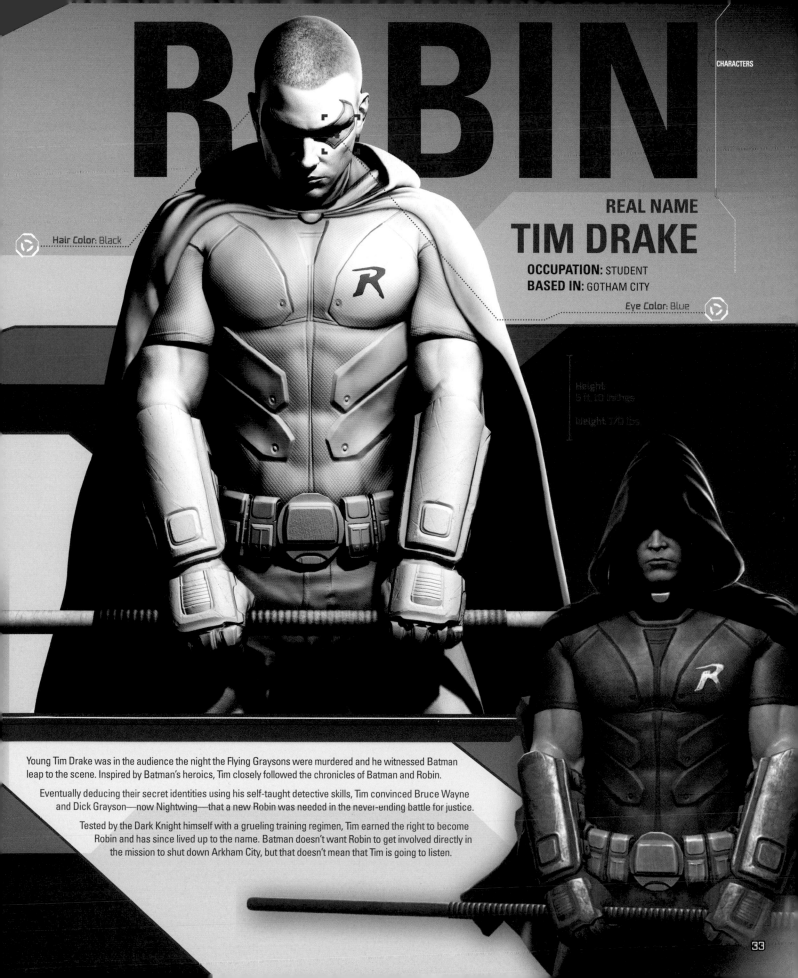

ROBIN

Hair Color: Black

REAL NAME
TIM DRAKE

OCCUPATION: STUDENT
BASED IN: GOTHAM CITY

Eye Color: Blue

Height
5 ft. 10 inches

Weight 170 lbs

Young Tim Drake was in the audience the night the Flying Graysons were murdered and he witnessed Batman leap to the scene. Inspired by Batman's heroics, Tim closely followed the chronicles of Batman and Robin.

Eventually deducing their secret identities using his self-taught detective skills, Tim convinced Bruce Wayne and Dick Grayson—now Nightwing—that a new Robin was needed in the never-ending battle for justice.

Tested by the Dark Knight himself with a grueling training regimen, Tim earned the right to become Robin and has since lived up to the name. Batman doesn't want Robin to get involved directly in the mission to shut down Arkham City, but that doesn't mean that Tim is going to listen.

ORACLE

REAL NAME
BARBARA GORDON

OCCUPATION: INFORMATION BROKER

BASED IN: GOTHAM CITY

The daughter of Gotham City's Police Commissioner James W. Gordon, Barbara Gordon was forbidden by her overprotective father from joining the GCPD.

Instead, she took on the identity of Batgirl and became a crime-fighting partner of Batman for years. But that all ended when Joker shot her through the spine.

Paralyzed from the waist down and confined to a wheelchair, Barbara adopted the new identity of Oracle. She now aids the Dark Knight with her computer expertise, providing Batman with a constant stream of information in the field to aid his battle against crime. Her ability to scour Arkham City and locate problems is crucial for solving a number of cases in the beleaguered area.

Hair Color: Red

Eye Color: Blue

Height: 5 ft 11 inches

Weight: 126 lbs.

Hair Color: White (formerly brown)

JIM GORDON

REAL NAME
JAMES W. GORDON

OCCUPATION: POLICE COMMISSIONER

BASED IN: GOTHAM CITY

Height: 6 ft. 0 inches

Weight: 180 lbs.

Eye Color: Blue

Police Commissioner James W. Gordon dedicated his career to cleaning up the corruption in the Gotham City Police Department, a goal he has come a long way towards accomplishing.

He has been equally tough on crime and, in the pursuit of making Gotham City safe for all its citizens, Gordon has forged an uneasy alliance with Gotham's other top crime fighter, the mysterious vigilante known as Batman.

In the wake of Mayor Sharp's establishment of Arkham City and TYGER guards assuming most law-enforcement roles, Gordon has been increasingly marginalized—but he remains an ally to the Batman.

Jim has his hands full keeping everything outside of Arkham City contained during this chaotic time. As long as he keeps the rest of Gotham under control, things should work out for the best.

JACK RYDER

REAL NAME

JACK RYDER

OCCUPATION: INVESTIGATIVE REPORTER

BASED IN: GOTHAM CITY

Hair Color: Black

Eye Color: Blue

Height:
6 ft. 0 inches

Weight: 194 lbs.

Jack Ryder is an investigative reporter turned controversial talk show host, well-known for his aggressive manner and his relentless determination to get to the truth.

With the opening of the controversial Arkham City at hand, Ryder hopes to discover the roots of this dangerous stronghold and expose them for the good of Gotham.

However, Mr. Ryder's efforts have not gone unnoticed. What will TYGER guard forces do if they have a chance to "talk" to this difficult reporter?

VICKI VALE

Hair Color: Blonde

REAL NAME

VICKI VALE

OCCUPATION: INVESTIGATIVE JOURNALIST
BASED IN: GOTHAM CITY

Height
5 ft. 7 inches

Weight: 121 lbs.

Investigative reporter Vicki Vale got her start at the Gotham City Gazette, where she quickly rose to fame for her unwavering commitment to rooting out the ugly truths behind Gotham's corruption and poverty.

Focusing more and more on Batman's feats, Vicki has recently turned her attention to the opening of Arkham City.

She risks life and limb to portray the danger this prison city poses to the public, perhaps overly confident that Batman will be there to catch her when she falls.

Civilians aren't supposed to be anywhere near Arkham City and all the ground routes into the area are strictly off limits. Will Vicki Vale miss her scoop this time?

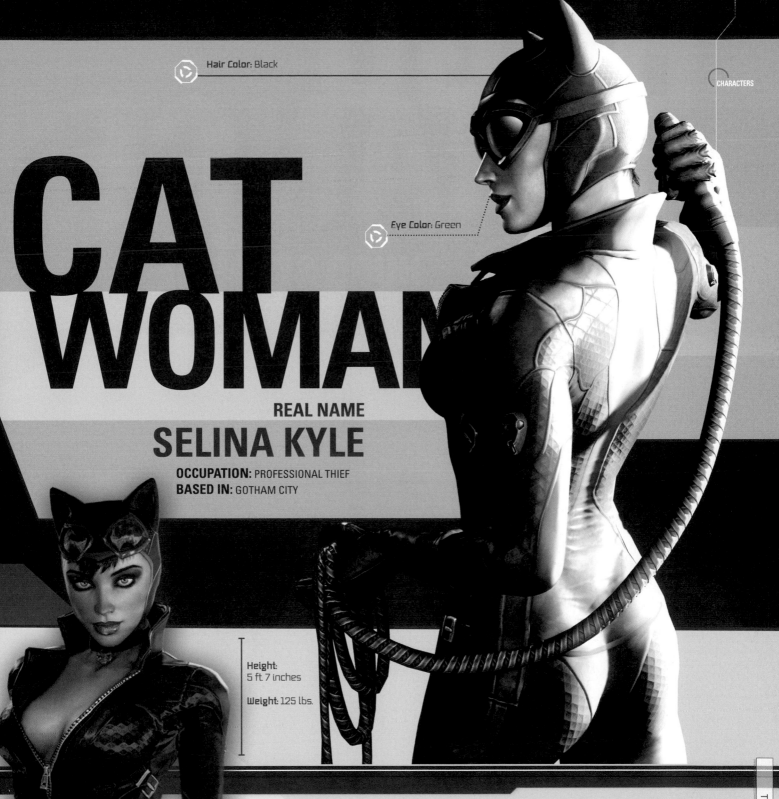

Hair Color: Black

Eye Color: Green

CAT WOMAN

REAL NAME

SELINA KYLE

OCCUPATION: PROFESSIONAL THIEF
BASED IN: GOTHAM CITY

Height:
5 ft 7 inches

Weight: 125 lbs.

An orphan who learned to survive on the mean streets of Gotham, Selina Kyle turned to thievery to survive. Determined to do it with style, she learned martial arts and trained in gymnastics to perfect her skills.

Her criminal activities are tempered by a reluctant altruism, making her an inconstant villain and occasional hero. She maintains a complicated, adversarial relationship with Batman that frequently turns flirtatious and occasionally romantic.

Since the opening of Arkham City, reports of Catwoman burglaries are down, although underworld rumors have her hunting down Two-Face for an unknown reason. Maybe the clever girl is on to something. Is her presence going to make things easier for Batman? Somehow that seems doubtful.

HUGO STRANGE

REAL NAME
HUGO STRANGE

OCCUPATION: PSYCHIATRIST
BASED IN: GOTHAM CITY

Height
6 ft 10 inches

Weight 180 lbs

Infamous psychiatrist Hugo Strange claims to have unique insight on the criminal mind from years of clinical study. He persuaded Mayor sharp that the Arkham City project was the only way for Gotham City to eliminate crime and "rogue vigilantes" like Batman.

Rumors persist of Strange performing ethically dubious experiments on inmates without consent, but unless hard proof comes to light, the Gotham public is happy to credit Strange with their dramatically reduced crime rate. Strange knows that Batman will hunt him down. He's counting on it.

Clearly, Hugo Strange has had plans in motion for years. Even during the assault in Arkham Asylum, there was something sinister in the air that Batman couldn't fully unravel. This could be the culmination of years of effort, but to what end?

MAYOR QUINCY SHARP

REAL NAME
QUINCY SHARP

OCCUPATION: MAYOR OF GOTHAM CITY
BASED IN: GOTHAM CITY

 Hair Color: Gray

 Eye Color: Blue

Quincy Sharp was the warden of Arkham Asylum on the night that Joker broke free 18 months ago. Unknown to most, but discovered by Batman, Sharp suffered from a split personality disorder and had been committing atrocities in the asylum, believing himself to be possessed by the Spirit of Amadeus Arkham.

In reality, he was being influenced by Hugo Strange, who provided Sharp with powerful mind control drugs that allowed him to manipulate Sharp's behavior, enabling him to plant the seed that led to the creation of Arkham City.

Hugo Strange used the evidence of the atrocities committed by Sharp as collateral to make sure that, whatever happened, Sharp must remain loyal to him.

Height:
5 ft. 8 inches

Weight: 190 lbs.

THE PEOPLE OF GOTHAM

THE JOKER

REAL NAME
UNKNOWN

OCCUPATION: PROFESSIONAL CRIMINAL
BASED IN: GOTHAM CITY

Hair Color: Green

Eye Color: Green

Height:
6 ft. 0 inches

Weight: 160 lbs.

The self-styled Clown Prince of Crime has no superpowers beyond a capacity for incredible violence and the skill of creating deadly mayhem.

Since his last encounter with the Dark Knight, the Joker has been transferred to Arkham City. Eye witnesses claim he is stricken with a serious disease, possibly caused by his Titan overdose on Arkham Island.

He has been lying low, delivering orders through Harley Quinn, so no one can confirm if the Joker is actually in poor health or playing another sick joke.

Either way, the Joker has a huge gang of loyal followers throughout the Industrial District of Arkham City. His thugs and snipers have a reputation for killing first and taking names, well, never. They aren't to be taken lightly.

HARLEY QUINN

REAL NAME
DR. HARLEEN F. QUINZEL

OCCUPATION: PROFESSIONAL CRIMINAL
BASED IN: GOTHAM CITY

Hair Color: Blonde

Eye Color: Blue

Height
5 ft 7 inches

Weight 140 lbs

An Arkham Asylum psychiatrist assigned to treat the Joker, Dr. Harleen Quinzel instead became obsessively fixated on her patient, believing herself to be in love with him.

She helped him escape and took on her own criminal identity as Harley Quinn. Quinn is a violent and unpredictable felon whose only motivation is achieving the Joker's approval.

Because of his cruel and mercurial nature, this in some ways makes her just another one of his victims—albeit a very dangerous one.

Since Joker's Titan overdose in Arkham Asylum, Harley's mind has further deteriorated. She is blindly determined to put a smile back on his face.

Harley knows that she can't beat Batman in a fight. Expect her to use any advantage to keep Batman on the ropes. Stay calm and look for ways to minimize the chaos that follows in Harley's wake.

THE PEOPLE OF GOTHAM

MISTER FREEZE

REAL NAME

DR. VICTOR FRIES

OCCUPATION: PROFESSIONAL CRIMINAL
BASED IN: GOTHAM CITY

Hair Color: None

Eye Color: Blue

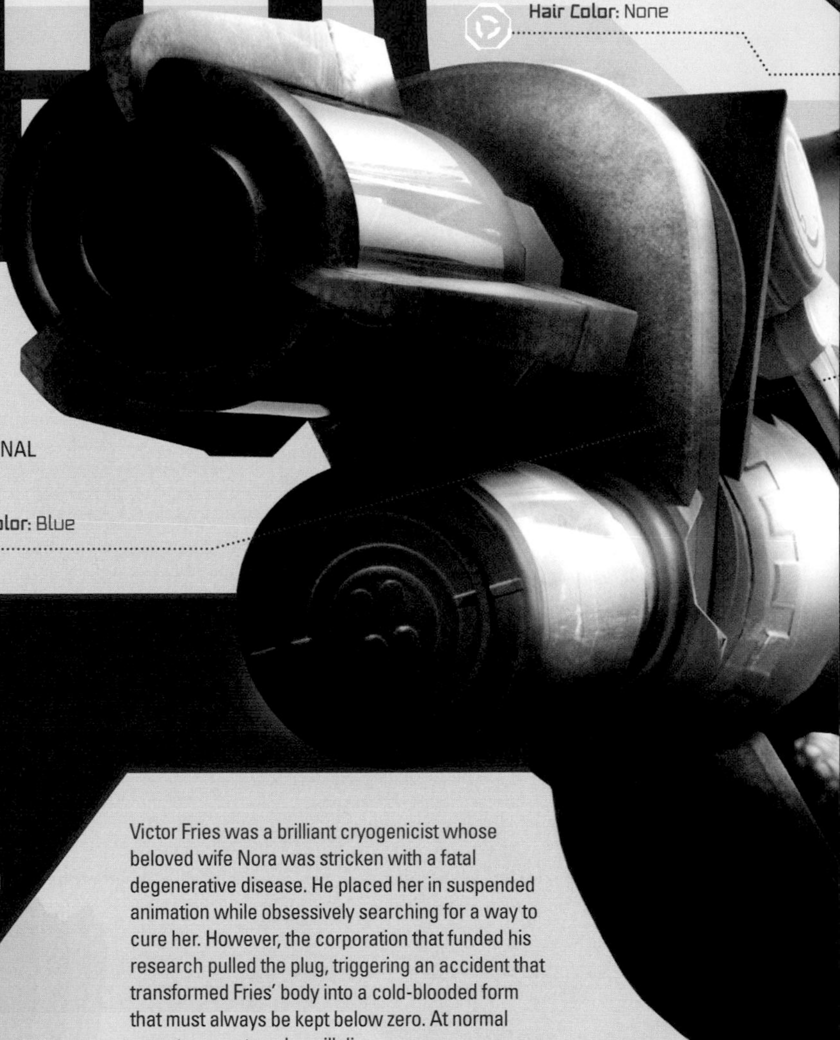

Victor Fries was a brilliant cryogenicist whose beloved wife Nora was stricken with a fatal degenerative disease. He placed her in suspended animation while obsessively searching for a way to cure her. However, the corporation that funded his research pulled the plug, triggering an accident that transformed Fries' body into a cold-blooded form that must always be kept below zero. At normal room temperature, he will die.

Wielding a number of freezing weapons, he wears protective armor in his quest to somehow bring back his lovely wife and avenge her fate. Since the opening of Arkham City, Mr. Freeze has seemingly disappeared.

One thing about Victor is that he's almost reasonable—for a major villain, that is. Batman already has a lot of trouble on his hands. Maybe he can convince Mr. Freeze to hold off on fighting for another night. Or maybe not.

Height:
6 ft 3 inches

Weight: 190 lbs

NORA FRIES

REAL NAME
NORA FRIES
OCCUPATION: N/A
BASED IN: N/A

Beautiful Nora Fries found undying love when she married the shy but brilliant cryogenicist, Victor Fries. After she was struck with a rare disease, Victor used his lab to freeze Nora in a state of suspended animation until he could find a cure. Since then, Nora has been trapped between life and death. Victor became Mister Freeze, willing to break every law in his desperate search for a means to cure Nora.

Surveillance cameras saw some goons securing a massive block of ice inside a building in the Industrial District. They've barricaded the front door to the building and won't let anyone in. This might have relevance to Mister Freeze.

Hair Color: Blonde

Eye Color: Blue

Height:
5 ft. 6 inches

Weight: 145 lbs.

THE PENGUIN

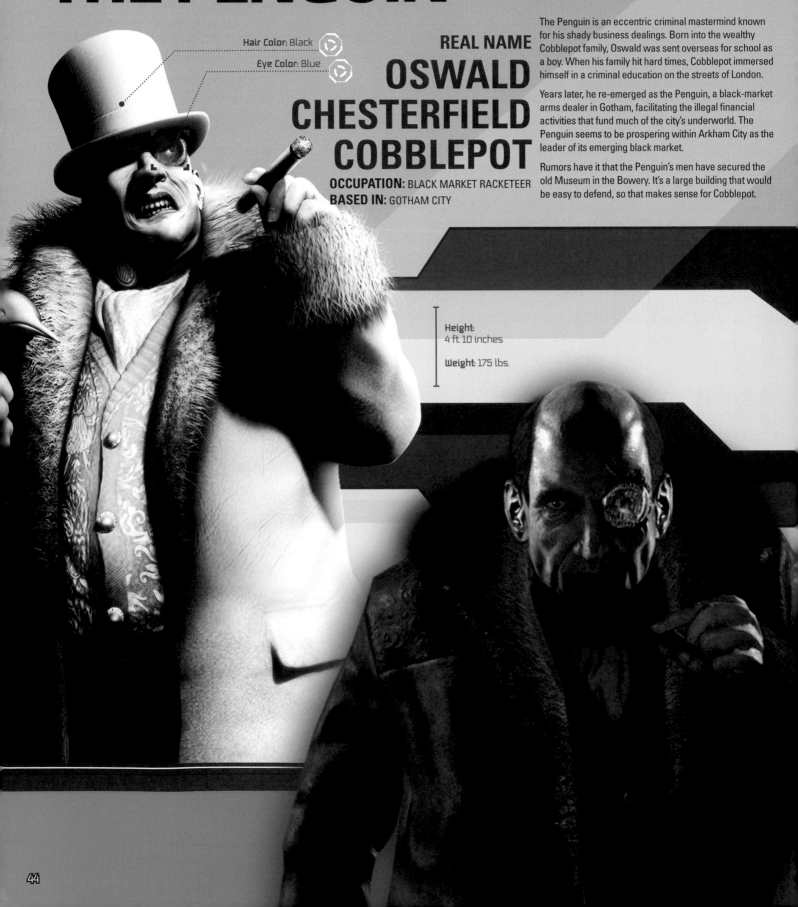

Hair Color: Black

Eye Color: Blue

REAL NAME

OSWALD CHESTERFIELD COBBLEPOT

OCCUPATION: BLACK MARKET RACKETEER
BASED IN: GOTHAM CITY

The Penguin is an eccentric criminal mastermind known for his shady business dealings. Born into the wealthy Cobblepot family, Oswald was sent overseas for school as a boy. When his family hit hard times, Cobblepot immersed himself in a criminal education on the streets of London.

Years later, he re-emerged as the Penguin, a black-market arms dealer in Gotham, facilitating the illegal financial activities that fund much of the city's underworld. The Penguin seems to be prospering within Arkham City as the leader of its emerging black market.

Rumors have it that the Penguin's men have secured the old Museum in the Bowery. It's a large building that would be easy to defend, so that makes sense for Cobblepot.

Height:
4 ft 10 inches

Weight: 175 lbs.

TWO-FACE

REAL NAME

HARVEY DENT

OCCUPATION: PROFESSIONAL CRIMINAL
BASED IN: GOTHAM CITY

Eye Color: Blue

Hair Color: Brown/Gray

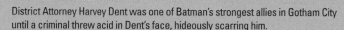

District Attorney Harvey Dent was one of Batman's strongest allies in Gotham City until a criminal threw acid in Dent's face, hideously scarring him.

The wounds fractured his psyche and he was reborn Two-Face, a schizoid criminal mastermind obsessed with duality. His former good-luck charm, a "two-headed" trick silver dollar, was damaged on one side in the attack, and Dent has seized on it as a reflection of his half-scarred visage. He flips it to decide the fates of his victims.

Two-Face is thriving in Arkham City, rallying inmates to join his gang using tried-and-true campaign tactics. Some of his posters appear in Park Row. The Courthouse is near there, which is probably where Dent spends most of his time.

Height:
6 ft. 0 inches

Weight: 182 lbs.

RĀ'S AL GHŪL

Hair Color: Gray with white streaks

Eye Color: Green

REAL NAME
UNKNOWN

OCCUPATION: INTERNATIONAL TERRORIST
BASED IN: MOBILE

Little is known about the early years of the nearly immortal Rā's al Ghūl, leader of the League of Assassins, whose name means "the Demon's Head."

He has lived for many centuries due to the Lazarus Pits, mystical and alchemical brews that restore his youth. A brilliant master of strategy and organization, Rā's goal is to save the Earth from eventual ecological devastation by destroying most of its population.

He recognizes Batman as both a worthy foe and a possible ally—except that Batman cannot accept Rā's dystopic worldview. To bring Batman to his side, Ra's has even orchestrated a relationship between Batman and his beautiful daughter, Talia al Ghūl.

Rā's al Ghūl won't appear out in the open; that's not the way of an assassin. If Batman is to find him, he must look somewhere in the shadows.

Height:
6 ft. 0 inches

Weight: 210 lbs.

TALIA AL GHŪL

REAL NAME
TALIA AL GHŪL

OCCUPATION: ASSASSIN
BASED IN: MOBILE

The headstrong daughter of Rā's al Ghūl and on-again/off-again lover of Bruce Wayne, Talia al Ghūl is second in command of the League of Assassins.

A master of hand-to-hand combat and swordplay, Talia has dueled with Batman on several occasions and considers him an honorable opponent.

Despite Batman's elusiveness, her attraction to him has only increased—an attraction that her father encourages in his made quest for a male heir.

Talia knows that one day she may be forced to choose between her father and her beloved.

Hair Color: Brown

Eye Color: Green

Height:
5 ft. 7 inches

Weight: 141 lbs.

THE RIDDLER

With an obsessive-compulsive need for attention, Edward Nigma is determined to be the cleverest of Gotham City's criminals, plotting elaborate trails of clues and riddles around his crimes.

Batman has proven a worthy opponent, capable of unraveling the Riddler's most intricate plans, but Nigma is dedicated to creating a mystery that will stump the Dark Knight, even if he has to kill someone to do it.

Humiliated by Batman on Arkham Island, Nigma is more determined than ever to bring the Caped Crusader to his knees.

Not many people in Arkham City admit to knowing where the Riddler is hiding, but it's whispered that he has several hideouts. His question marks and riddles litter the city. The Riddler also has informants in quite a few gangs. If they could be caught and intimidated, maybe they'll give up some information.

REAL NAME

EDDIE NASTHON A.K.A. EDWARD NIGMA

OCCUPATION: PROFESSIONAL CRIMINAL
BASED IN: GOTHAM CITY

Hair Color: Brown

Eye Color: Blue

Height: 6 ft. 1 inches

Weight: 183 lbs.

POISON IVY

REAL NAME

PAMELA LILLIAN ISLEY

OCCUPATION: PROFESSIONAL CRIMINAL
BASED IN: GOTHAM CITY

Hair Color: Red

Eye Color: Green

Botanist Pamela Isley was transformed by a science experiment gone wrong into a plant-human hybrid. With chlorophyll flowing through her veins instead of blood, she developed a toxic touch and a pheromone-fueled talent for seduction.

Her unique brand of eco-terrorism often puts her into conflicts with Batman, whose iron will usually protects him from her seductive powers. Since her encounter with the Dark Knight on Arkham Island, Ivy has been transferred to Arkham City.

Taking refuge in a vine-covered stronghold, Ivy would rather keep humanity away than participate in the gang wars of Arkham City. If anyone needs to find her, there are vines and other strange plants growing in the northeastern part of town.

Height:
5 ft. 8 inches

Weight: 115 lbs.

SOLOMON GRUNDY

REAL NAME

CYRUS GOLD

Hair Color: Gray

OCCUPATION: N/A
BASED IN: SLAUGHTER SWAMP

Over a century ago, murderer Cyrus Gold sought to escape justice by hiding in Slaughter Swamp where he met a fate worse than death. Mysterious forces doomed the now immortal Grundy to an endless cycle of death and rebirth.

Robbed of his memories, he adopted the name of a nursery rhyme. "Solomon Grundy, Born on a Monday, Christened on Tuesday, Married on Wednesday, Took ill on Thursday, Grew worse on Friday, Died on Saturday, Buried on Sunday. This is the end of Solomon Grundy."

Eye Color: Gray

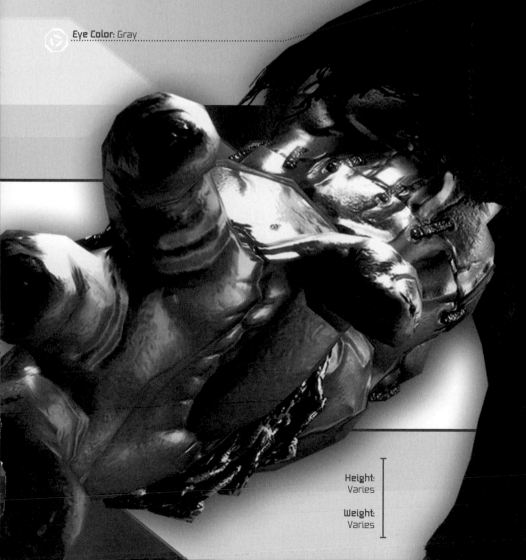

Height: Varies

Weight: Varies

CLAYFACE

REAL NAME
BASIL KARLO
OCCUPATION: PROFESSIONAL CRIMINAL
BASED IN: GOTHAM CITY

Horror film icon Basil Karlo went mad when he uncovered plans for his most classic film to be remade with a different actor in the lead role. He took on the mark of the film's villain, Clayface, and killed several of the remake's cast and crew before being stopped by Batman and Robin.

Later, Karlo stole and injected himself with experimental compounds that transformed him into a mass of living clay who can alter his composition to mimic anything…or anyone.

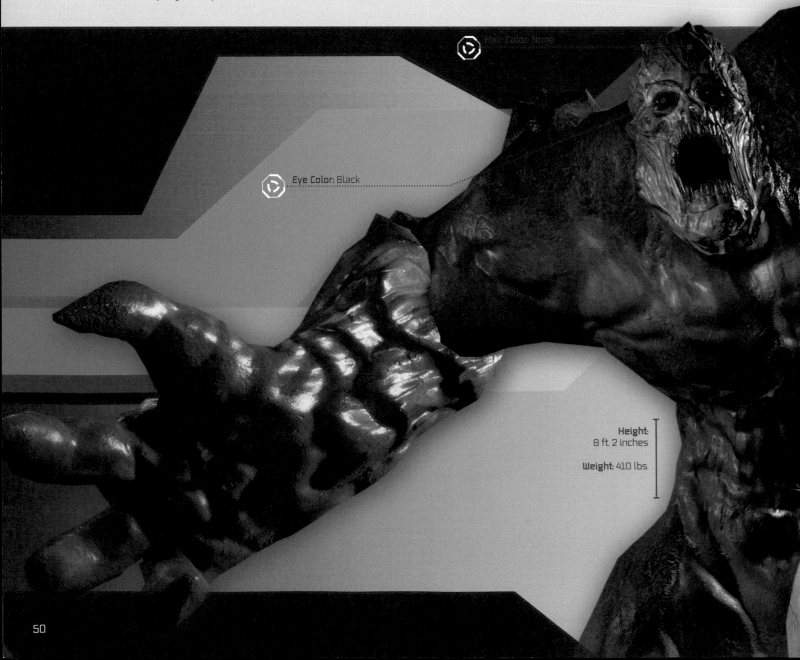

Hair Color: None

Eye Color: Black

Height:
8 ft. 2 inches

Weight: 410 lbs.

DEADSHOT

REAL NAME

FLOYD LAWTON

OCCUPATION: MERCENARY
BASED IN: GOTHAM CITY

Hair Color: Brown

Eye Color: Blue

He never misses a shot, especially with his pair of silenced, wrist-mounted 9mm cannons. Deadshot disdains himself almost as much as his corrupt targets; several prison psychologists have diagnosed him with "suicidal tendencies."

Batman is the only person who has made Deadshot miss, a distinction that puts the Dark Knight at the top of Deadshot's hit list.

If Deadshot starts killing anyone in Arkham City, Batman can use his tools to scan for clues. Though a gifted sniper, Deadshot can't clean up his crime scenes perfectly every time.

ZSASZ

Hair Color: None
(formerly blonde)

REAL NAME

VICTOR ZSASZ

OCCUPATION: PROFESSIONAL CRIMINAL
BASED IN: GOTHAM CITY

Eye Color: Blue

A true sociopath, Zsasz grew up in a life of ease, but nonetheless became a serial killer. Indiscriminate in his prey, body count is the only thing that matters to Zsasz. He carves a mark for each of his victims into his own body and is saving a special spot for the Batman.

Since being thrown into Arkham City, his whereabouts are unknown, although reports of rising body counts fit his modus operandi. There could be a way to track Zsasz. Surely he'll make a mistake of some sort.

Height:
5 ft. 8 inches

Weight:
150 lbs.

THE PEOPLE OF GOTHAM

MAD HATTER

REAL NAME
JERVIS TETCH

OCCUPATION: PROFESSIONAL CRIMINAL
BASED IN: GOTHAM CITY

 Hair Color: Blond

 Eye Color: Blue

Obsessed from a young age with Lewis Carroll's book "Alice's Adventures in Wonderland," Jervis Tetch, an expert hypnotist, embraced a delusion that he was the incarnation of a character in the story, the Mad Hatter.

Using his skills for mesmerism, the Mad Hatter has committed many crimes, often themed-based around the book that inspired him and his love of hats and headgear, going so far as to implant his hats with mind-control chips to amplify his hypnosis skills.

Above all other headwear, however, he covets Batman's distinctive cowl and will stop at nothing to acquire it.

Height:
4 ft 11 inches

Weight:
115 lbs.

HUSH

Hair Color: Reddish-brown

REAL NAME
THOMAS "TOMMY" ELLIOT

OCCUPATION: SURGEON, SERIAL KILLER
BASED IN: GOTHAM CITY

Eye Color: Blue (formerly brown)

Height:
6 ft. 3 inches

Weight:
235 lbs.

Tommy Elliot and Bruce Wayne were childhood friends and, unknown to Bruce, dark reflections of each other. A childhood sociopath, Elliot tried to kill his parents so he could control their fortune. When his plan failed due to the surgical skills of Thomas Wayne, Bruce's father, Elliot blamed the Wayne family for his problems.

An incredibly gifted surgeon as an adult, Elliot has spent decades planning an elaborate revenge scheme to destroy Bruce Wayne.

THE PEOPLE OF GOTHAM

BANE

REAL NAME

UNKNOWN

OCCUPATION: PROFESSIONAL CRIMINAL
BASED IN: GOTHAM CITY

Hair Color: Brown

Eye Color: Brown
(altered on Venom: Green)

Height:
5 ft. 6 inches (9 ft. 2 inches on Venom)

Weight:
140 lbs. (350 lbs. on Venom)

Imprisoned from birth to serve his dead father's sentence, Bane was raised inside the horrific environs of a Senta Priscan prison. Subjected to military experiments with the experimental ultra-steroid Venom, his superhuman strength and iron-forged will helped him to escape. Determined to build a criminal empire, he sought out Batman and broke the Dark Knight's spine. But Batman recovered and managed to best Bane, cutting off Bane's precious Venom supply.

Since the events at Arkham Asylum, it's rumored that Bane has turned over a new leaf in an effort to save others from similar addiction.

CALENDAR MAN

Hair Color: None
(formerly brown)

REAL NAME
JULIAN DAY

OCCUPATION: PROFESSIONAL CRIMINAL
BASED IN: GOTHAM CITY

Fixated on the calendar, Julian Day became Calendar Man, a villain who timed and tied his crimes thematically to certain holidays throughout the year, often leaving clues by which he could be caught.

Gotham City's hopes for a day off are often clouded by the knowledge that any holiday of note is likely to be shadowed by Calendar Man's presence.

The last sighting of Calendar Man was near the Courthouse in Arkham City. He was taken inside, but no one reported seeing him leave. Maybe he's still there…

Eye Color: Blue

Height:
5 ft. 9 inches

Weight:
215 lbs.

KILLER CROC

REAL NAME

Eye Color: Yellow

WAYLON JONES

OCCUPATION: ALLIGATOR WRESTLER, GANGSTER, MURDERER
BASED IN: MOBILE

Born with a rare mutation that made his skin green and scaly and grew his body to grotesque proportions, Waylon Jones was raised by an alcoholic aunt and bullied relentlessly for his appearance.

He briefly worked as a carnival freak under the name Killer Croc, but his misanthropy grew with his animal nature, pushing him to a life of crime. As his physical condition and mental state deteriorate, Killer Croc becomes a more bestial foe, increasingly detached from humanity.

His whereabouts are unknown since his escape from Askham Asylum. If Killer Croc is anywhere in Arkham City, it would likely be somewhere dank. Maybe he'd take refuge in the sewers…

Height:
9 ft. 0 inches

Weight:
310 lbs.

BLACK MASK

REAL NAME
ROMAN SIONIS

OCCUPATION: PROFESSIONAL CRIMINAL
BASED IN: GOTHAM CITY

Eye Color: Brown

Hair Color: Brown

Height:
6 ft. 1 inches

Weight:
195 lbs.

Following the suspicious death of his wealthy parents in a fire, Roman Sionis inherited their fortune and went on to bankrupt their company. Saved with a buyout by Bruce Wayne, Sionis came to resent and hate his rescuer.

Fixated on the concept of masks, Sionis carved one from his father's black coffin and sought revenge on Wayne. His ensuing battle with the Dark Knight caused his mask to be burnt into his skin, remaking him as the Black Mask.

Sionis is now a feared gang leader and one of the most powerful mob bosses in Gotham, with a burning hatred of the Batman.

TYGER guards have done a keen job of grabbing a variety of criminals. They might have Roman Sionis in custody as well. Rumors abound that some guards were seen beating a man who matches Roman Sionis' description.

THE PEOPLE OF GOTHAM

SOLVING THE PROBLEM OF CRIME

They told the people of Gotham that Arkham City would help cure the crime issue that plagued its streets. When Arkham Asylum didn't fulfill its promise, this was supposed to be the answer. Now prisoners are overrunning the area and Hugo Strange's minions are making a nightmare of the situation. To help calm matters and give people direction, Bruce Wayne has called a press conference. During the proceedings, though, a group of armed men attack and kidnap Bruce Wayne in front of the press and all of Gotham. As the smoke fades, we're all left to wonder what will happen next. Who will stop this insanity?

BRUCE WAYNE
REAL NAME Bruce Wayne

Real Name	Bruce Wayne
Occupation	CEO/Philanthropist
Based In	Gotham City
Eye Color	Blue
Hair Color	Black
Height	6 Ft. 2 Inches
Weight	210 Lbs
First Appearance	Detective Comics #27 [May 1939]

Attributes
-Billionaire playboy by day, Batman by night
-Gotham's most eligible bachelor

Born into the wealthy Wayne family, Bruce Wayne had an idyllic childhood. But after witnessing his parents' violent murder in Crime Alley, Bruce dedicated his life to battling criminals.

He circled the globe for years, training his mental and physical abilities to their peek. Gotham City welcomed him home, not knowing that high society's favorite billionaire playboy is also the Batman.

Bruce has never been into politics but Batman alone has not been able to stop Arkham City's construction. He has no choice but to use his alter ego and invest millions to bring enough political pressure to bear to force its closure. He knows it is a ticking time bomb waiting to explode onto the streets of Gotham.

HUGO STRANGE
REAL NAME Hugo Strange

Occupation	Psychiatrist
Based In	Gotham City
Eye Color	Grey
Hair Color	Grey
Height	5 Ft. 10 Inches
Weight	180 Lbs
First Appearance	Detective Comics #36 [February 1940]

Attributes
-Trained to physical perfection
-Brilliant psychological analyst
-Extensive knowledge of psychoactive substances
-Obsessed with Batman and Batman's secret identity
-Plagued by schizophrenic episodes

Infamous psychiatrist Hugo Strange claims to have unique insight on the criminal mind from years of clinical study. He persuaded Mayor Sharp that the Arkham City project was the only way for Gotham City to eliminate crime and "rogue vigilantes" like Batman.

Rumors persist of Strange performing ethically dubious experiments on inmates without consent, but unless hard proof comes to light, the Gotham public is happy to credit Strange with their dramatically reduced crime rate. Strange knows that Batman will hunt him down. He's counting on it.

AND SO THE STORY BEGINS...

▓▓ PRIMARY OBJECTIVE: Make contact with Alfred; acquire Batman's suit and equipment.

Bruce Wayne wakes up inside a cell, tied to a chair. To free him from captivity, slowly move the left analog stick from side to side. Maintain the proper speed to match the movement of the chair until Bruce topples over, setting off an alarm.

A guard enters the room to stop Bruce from fleeing. Counter his attack by following the on-screen icon that appears. This prevents the guard from kicking Bruce!

Counter the TYGER guard's attack to get an Encrypted Data Chip.

Although this works well, Bruce cannot break free in time to save himself. Another guard charges him and nothing will prevent this assault. Wounded, Bruce is shoved into an open yard. Direct him toward the staging area on the right while looking around at the other prisoners. The processing center is a grim location.

Walk toward the fenced area on the right. Hugo Strange is there, along with several waiting guards. They give Bruce some rough treatment, but Hugo doesn't let them take it too far. Eventually, Bruce bumps into Jack Ryder, a reporter who was covering the press conference before everything went awry.

Bruce and Jack talk until a large door opens in front of them. The next walkway is fenced off, but the inmates surrounding it are riled up. As Jack runs forward, men climb over the fences and attack him. Bruce is soon a target as well.

THE FIGHT IN THE YARD

>>> >> GOAL: Stay alive and look for an opportunity to escape.

It's time to practice counters again, as they're a vital move when fighting multiple enemies. Using them in this situation disables each attacker. Rush toward Jack as soon as the thugs are dispatched and attack the creep who keeps hitting him.

Stand next to Jack after the fight and use the on-screen command to help him get to his feet. Wayne tries to help him, but another attacker comes forward and this fight doesn't go so well…

THE PENGUIN & HIS MEN

>>> >> GOAL: Defeat the Penguin and his five men.

The Penguin and five of his goons surround Bruce and escort him into a side yard. After hearing the Penguin rant, get ready to fight him. Counter his initial attack and he pulls away to let his cronies take the damage. Bruce fights all five foes. Slap at the goons until they get up enough courage to launch attacks of their own. Once this happens, counter them until Bruce breaks free of his handcuffs.

THE PENGUIN

REAL NAME Oswald Chesterfield Cobblepot

Occupation	Black Market Racketeer
Based In	Gotham City
Eye Color	Blue
Hair Color	Black
Height	4 Ft. 10 Inches
Weight	175 Lbs
First Appearance	Detective Comics #58 December 1941

Attributes
- Criminal and financial mastermind
- Expert hand-to-hand combatant
- Driven to prove himself
- Employs various weapons

The Penguin is an eccentric criminal mastermind known for his shady business dealings. Born into the wealthy Cobblepot family, Oswald was sent overseas for school as a boy. When his family hit hard times, Cobblepot immersed himself in a criminal education on the streets of London.

Years later, he re-emerged as the Penguin, a black-market arms dealer in Gotham, facilitating the illegal financial activities that fund much of the city's underworld.

The Penguin seems to be prospering within Arkham City as the leader of its emerging black market.

FIGHTING BASICS

Get a feel for the flow of combat during this encounter. Bruce doesn't fight a single target at a time; instead, he crashes from foe to foe, smacking each one while countering anyone who attempts to nail him from the sides or rear. Rely on counters quite a bit, even if it seems like it breaks up the rhythm of the fight. The damage from counterattacks is considerable and these moves become more intuitive over time.

This is your chance to try out freeform fighting.

Don't leave immediately after the fight. Make sure to slap the Penguin around for what he just did. Bruce doesn't kill him, but he leaves the Penguin with a heck of a bruise!

TAKE TO THE ROOFTOPS

>>> >> GOAL **Find a place with enough reception to contact Alfred.**

Bruce needs to contact his butler, Alfred, but the reception on his communicator doesn't work down in the yards. Bruce must scale upward to get a message out. The on-screen indicator illustrates which command to use to climb. Follow the commands while directing Bruce toward the garbage dumpster on the side of the yard.

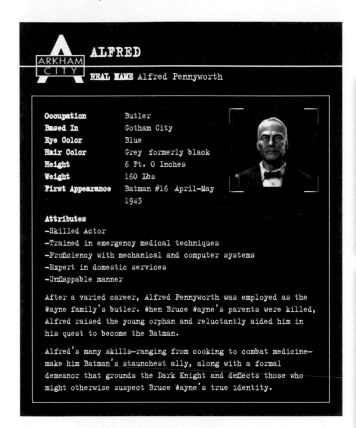

ALFRED

REAL NAME Alfred Pennyworth

Occupation	Butler
Based In	Gotham City
Eye Color	Blue
Hair Color	Grey formerly black
Height	6 Ft. 0 Inches
Weight	160 lbs
First Appearance	Batman #16 April-May 1943

Attributes
- Skilled Actor
- Trained in emergency medical techniques
- Proficiency with mechanical and computer systems
- Expert in domestic services
- Unflappable manner

After a varied career, Alfred Pennyworth was employed as the Wayne family's butler. When Bruce Wayne's parents were killed, Alfred raised the young orphan and reluctantly aided him in his quest to become the Batman.

Alfred's many skills—ranging from cooking to combat medicine—make him Batman's staunchest ally, along with a formal demeanor that grounds the Dark Knight and deflects those who might otherwise suspect Bruce Wayne's true identity.

Continue to hold the button and press toward the ladder that leads up from the dumpster. The same command is used for climbing and jumping, so you'll need to use it almost constantly while moving forward.

At the top of the ladder there is a small ledge. There doesn't seem to be a way up, but there is. Jump from the end of the ledge to the far side of the area to make Bruce pull himself onto some ductwork. Use the next ladder to continue upward.

Head for the rooftops for better reception and a great vantage point.

THE PEAK OF THE ACE CHEMICALS BUILDING

GOAL Find Batman's equipment.

Bruce calls Alfred after reaching the roof. The trusting butler can now get a fix on his location. While standing on top of the building next to the Ace Chemicals building, leap across the gap to access a small recess below a glowing "E" sign. Bruce grabs the recessed ledge and uses it to shimmy along the outer edge of the structure.

Move right until Bruce reaches more ductwork. Climb the next ladder and listen as Bruce and Alfred discuss Hugo Strange's plans.

Crawl underneath another pipe and let Bruce take a ladder toward the top of the building. Alfred's package arrives just as Bruce nears the top. Get onto the roof and use the Bat-Vault to suit up. With the change of clothes, Bruce Wayne becomes…Batman!

Once at the summit, Bruce learns a new command. Use it to crouch down while moving underneath obstacles. Watch the open sky on the right while Bruce crawls through this short section.

Crouch to maneuver underneath obstacles.

Don't leap off the far end of the passage. There's a long fall below and that's not where you want to go. Instead, use the commands for crawling and jumping together. Doing so enables Bruce to hang off the side of the building. Shimmy to the right and climb back up on the opposite side.

Press the appropriate buttons to hang off the side of the building.

BATMAN

ARKHAM CITY

REAL NAME Bruce Wayne

Occupation	World's Greatest Detective
Based In	Gotham City
Eye Color	Blue
Hair Color	Black
Height	6 Ft. 2 Inches
Weight	210 lbs
First Appearance	Detective Comics #27 May 1939

Attributes

-Trained to physical and mental peak
-Arsenal of gadgets, vehicles, and advanced technology
-Inventor, detective, genius-level intelligence
-Expert in most known forms of martial arts
-Trained in all aspects of criminology

When his parents were gunned down in front of him, young Bruce Wayne resolved to rid Gotham City of the criminal elemental that took their lives.

He trained extensively to achieve mental and physical perfection, in addition to mastering martial arts, detective techniques, and criminal psychology.

Dressing as a bat to prey on criminals' fears, Batman fights crimes with the aid of specialized gadgets and vehicles, operating out of his secret Batcave below Wayne Manor.

FINDING A TARGET

>>> >> GOAL Use Batman's Sequencer to listen to the TYGER broadcast.

Now that Batman has access to some of his toys, it will make a huge difference in what he can accomplish. A TYGER Encryption Key that he took from one of the enemies was useless before, but the equipment from the Bat-Vault lets Batman decode the broadcast.

Batman uses the transmitter/receiver to hone in on a strange signal. There are also two normal signals that are un-encoded. Position the cursor over the green signals to hear any un-encoded signal. The transmission on the left is the Gotham FM broadcast. Listen to the GCPD Dispatch on the right if you want to learn how the police are handling the events of the evening. At the top of the grid is an anomalous signal.

When ready to proceed, use the decoder on the upper-right signal. Keep using the decoder until the signal is completely compromised. It's at this point that Bruce learns about the location of two dangerous enemies.

THE SEQUENCER

Batman's Sequencer is a multi-purpose tool. When used alone, the device unfolds and allows Batman to receive radio broadcasts. Later, he'll uncover codes and use the device to hack into municipal security consoles and then eventually TYGER consoles.

SAVE CATWOMAN FROM TWO-FACE

PRIMARY OBJECTIVE: Save Catwoman from Two-Face.

Decode the broadcast to gain access to TYGER Communications.

PARK ROW

1	Courthouse
2	Apartments (Catwoman and Identity Thief Mission)
3	Church/Medical Center
4	Enigma Conundrum Building
5	Mad Hatter's Apartment
6	Crime Alley
7	Entrance to Confiscated Goods Vault (Catwoman)
8	Azrael Symbol Location
9	Completion of Azrael Symbol Mission

Now Batman has access to the regional map, so press the appropriate button to access it. Examine the area to the north of the Ace Chemicals building; Batman must get down from there and move north to reach the courthouse.

Run to the edge of the building and glide off into the night sky. Steer Batman over the large group of men near Park Row and try to get as close as possible to the courthouse before landing.

Despite this clever entrance, Batman can't get inside without a fight. Several men spot the Dark Knight. Some of them are unarmed, but two are sporting baseball bats. It won't be enough to save them, though!

SPECIAL COMBO TAKEDOWNS

Work the group over, using counterattacks to prevent anyone from successfully attacking. Note that the interface shows there is a

Watch for the opportunity to use the Special Combo Takedown.

Special Combo Takedown. However, it is only available when your combo meter has reached eight or higher! These combos are used for instantly taking down enemies. Use these combos against targets with body armor, shields and bladed weapons.

SILENCING THE VOICES

It is possible to reach the convicts strolling along Park Row. Simply leap over that fence to fight an extra battle. Anyone interested in experience—or some fun with fisticuffs—should try it out.

Rescue Jack Ryder to learn more about Strange.

Travel around the entire southern side of the courthouse to fight multiple groups of thugs and even save a prisoner for additional experience rewards! This is part of the "Acts of Violence" side mission. These peripheral activities grant Batman experience, extra gadgets and open a few cool stories. These missions are discussed at length in a later chapter in this book.

Batman has time to look around before entering the courthouse. There are fences blocking off the ways into and out of the area. Convicts are staffing each blockade. They taunt Batman when he gets too close, but they can't do anything to him.

INSIDE THE SOLOMON WAYNE COURTHOUSE

>>> >> GOAL: Infiltrate the courthouse, fight Two-Face's men and save Catwoman.

COURTHOUSE

1. Main Entrance
2. Upper Entrance
3. Main Courtroom
4. Calendar Man's Location
5. Rear Exit

After exploring Park Row, approach the court-house. Another group of thugs is waiting near the entryway, talking about the downsides of crossing—or even annoying—Harvey Dent. Ambush this group of chatty enemies and knock 'em out!

Enter through the front of the courthouse or via the balcony. There are two adjoining halls near the main entrance. Both routes are locked, so Batman can't access the courtroom floor from here. Instead, take the central stairs to the second floor. The windows on the second floor overlook the courtroom. Harvey Dent is down there, protected by a horde of loyal henchmen. His captive is the lovely Catwoman!

TWO-FACE

REAL NAME Harvey Dent

Occupation	Professional Criminal
Based In	Gotham City
Eye Color	Blue
Hair Color	Brown/Grey
Height	6 Ft. 0 Inches
Weight	182 Lbs
First Appearance	Detective Comics #66 August 1942

Attributes
-Hideously scarred on half of his face
-Extremely skilled with his twin .45 semi-automatics
-Psychotic obsession with duality and the number two
-Defers to his half-scarred coin in choices of life or death

District Attorney Harvey Dent was one of Batman's strongest allies in Gotham City, until a criminal threw acid in Dent's face, hideously scarring him.

The wounds fractured his psyche, and he was reborn Two-Face, a schizoid criminal mastermind obsessed with duality. His former good-luck charm, a "two-headed" trick silver dollar, was damaged on one side in the attack, and Dent has seized on it as a reflection of his half-scarred visage. He flips it to decide the fates of his victims.

Two-Face is thriving in Arkham City, rallying inmates to join his gang using tried and true campaign tactics.

After the cutscene, it's time for Batman to take action. Walk to the end of the hallway and explore the area until you see an indication to use the Grapnel. This quickly pulls Batman up to the next floor.

Climb to the next ledge and slowly walk toward Two-Face's goon. He's packing heat, so it would be reckless to attack him straight on. Instead, knock the goon out by employing a Silent Takedown. Just get behind the enemy, press the appropriate button when it appears and follow the on-screen directions.

Remove the lookout with a Silent Takedown.

Enter the room using the wire suspended near the ceiling. Drop down on the other side and start attacking Dent's subordinates. It's a sudden and frantic engagement. Stay near the rear wall to avoid getting surrounded. Dent shoots into the fray periodically, but his shots are wild and inaccurate. Stay on the move to avoid any bullets, thrown objects, and most melee attacks.

Drop in on the proceedings.

CATWOMAN

REAL NAME Selina Kyle

Occupation	Professional Thief
Based In	Gotham City
Eye Color	Green
Hair Color	Black
Height	5 Ft. 7 Inches
Weight	125 Lbs
First Appearance	Batman #1 [Spring 1940]

Attributes
-Trained gymnast and athlete
-Expert hand-to-hand combatant
-Highly skilled with whips
-Unrivaled stealth capabilities
-Obsessed with stealing famous and well-protected items

An orphan who learned to survive on the mean streets of Gotham, Selina Kyle turned to thievery to survive. Determined to do it with style, she learned martial arts and trained in gymnastics to perfect her skills.

Her criminal activities are tempered by a reluctant altruism, making her an inconstant villain and occasional hero. She maintains a complicated, adversarial relationship with Batman that frequently turns flirtatious and occasionally romantic.

Since the opening of Arkham City, reports of Catwoman burglaries are down, though underworld rumors have her hunting down Two-Face for an unknown reason.

A SNIPER WITH A SMILE

■■ PRIMARY OBJECTIVE **Find Joker to learn about Protocol 10.**

Batman has every reason to be wary right now. Someone just shot their way through one of the windows and it would be dangerous to walk around without figuring out where the sniper was shooting from.

INVESTING IN NEW TECHNOLOGY

At this stage of the game, you will have probably gained enough experience to advance Batman's level. This means that it's possible to start adapting his technology and fighting techniques to suit the enemies at hand.

Access the WayneTech screen and cycle through the menus to find the specific WayneTech sub-screen that controls Batman's Batsuit and Combat functions. Whenever Batman gains a level, invest a point in one of the upgrades that shows up with the green arrows.

If survival is a big issue, choose an armor upgrade (try Combat Armor, as it comes into play more often than Ballistic Armor). For more advanced players, Critical Strikes is very effective because it focuses on getting Batman's combos up to speed right away. This makes a huge difference in late-game combat.

SCANNING FOR CLUES

▶ ▶▶ ▶ GOAL: **Use Batman's evidence scanner to find the remains of the bullet and track the sniper's location.**

Press the Detective Mode button to initiate Batman's evidence scan. This visual mode makes it possible to see many clues that would otherwise go undetected.

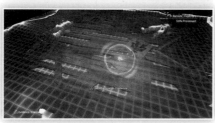

While in this mode, inspect the windows on the sides of the courtroom. One of them is broken! Move closer to that window and scan the bullet hole. Batman identifies the type of bullet that was used, but he needs to learn more. Turn around and observe the floor. There's another hole, so scan it as well.

Now it's possible to determine where the shot originated, so start looking for the shooter. Although there are exits at the front and back of the courthouse, go toward the rear exit. A side stairway leads down into some holding cells and Calendar Man is inside one of them.

CALENDAR MAN

REAL NAME Julian Day

Occupation	Professional Criminal
Based In	Gotham City
Eye Color	Blue
Hair Color	None [formerly brown]
Height	5 Ft. 9 Inches
Weight	215 Lbs
First Appearance	Detective Comics #259 [September 1958]

Attributes
-Obsessed with quirks of the calendar

Fixated on the calendar, Julian Day became Calendar Man, a villain who timed and tied his crimes thematically to certain holidays throughout the year, often leaving clues by which he could be caught.

Gotham City's hopes for a day off are often clouded by the knowledge that any holiday of note is likely to be shadowed by Calendar Man's presence.

SEARCH FOR THE JOKER

 Reach the church to the east.

Leave the courthouse via the upper front entrance and defeat the thugs in front of the building. They can't block the courthouse doors if they're all unconscious! If you

purchased something new when Batman leveled, now is the time to try it out during this straightforward engagement. Batman's next target is a building to the east (refer to the map for its location).

OFF THE BEATEN TRACK

There are plenty of side tasks to undertake at this time. Explore Arkham City to find a couple of extra fights. Also, there

are some political prisoners on the north side of the map (northeast from the courthouse).

This is also the first time that you have more control over where to travel. For those who enjoy puzzles and searching for treasure, take to

Each trophy is worth experience and possibly more.

the rooftops and the alleyways. The Riddler has scattered trophies for Batman to find all over Arkham City. Some of them are hard to find, while others are out in the open.

The appearance of green question marks is a sure sign that the Riddler has been nearby. Be curious! Every trophy found is worth experience, plus there may be greater rewards as well!

When you're ready, proceed to the church marked on the in-game map. There are several guards outside complaining about the weather. For a great start to this fight, zip above them and then drop down. This gives Batman a decisive advantage, plus it also looks rather intimidating.

Eliminate the threat outside of the church doors and listen to Alfred when he calls in. Word is that Harley Quinn is inside the church. Most people would take that as a sign to stay far away, but not Batman!

HARLEY QUINN

ARKHAM CITY

REAL NAME Dr. Harleen F. Quinzel

Occupation	Professional Criminal
Based In	Gotham City
Eye Color	Blue
Hair Color	Blonde
Height	5 Ft. 7 Inches
Weight	140 Lbs
First Appearance	Batman: Harley Quinn #1 [October 1999]

Attributes
- Surprising strength and stamina
- Superior gymnastic skills
- Total disregard for human life

An Arkham Asylum psychiatrist assigned to treat the Joker, Dr. Harleen Quinzel instead became obsessively fixated on her patient, believing herself to be in love with him.

She helped him escape and took on her own criminal identity as Harley Quinn. Quinn is a violent and unpredictable felon whose only motivation is achieving the Joker's approval.

Because of his cruel and mercurial nature, this in some ways makes her just another of his victims—albeit a very dangerous one.

Since the Joker's Titan overdose in Arkham Asylum, Harley's mind has further deteriorated. She is blindly determined to put a smile back on his face.

CHURCH/MEDICAL CENTER

>>> >> GOAL **Save the hostages.**

Batman doesn't make it too far into the church before Harley attacks. This would normally be a good time to fight, but there's bad news: Harley has hostages and they'll die if Batman makes the wrong move. Hit Harley once and then back off.

CHURCH

1	Entrance
2	Main Room (Medical Team Area)
3	Pipe Organ
4	Path up to Clock Tower

Harley leaves, but her armed goons stay behind. Drop a Smoke Pellet (follow the on-screen command) right away and grapple to safety. This causes the enemies below to lose sight of Batman, giving the initiative back to him. It's time to become a predator!

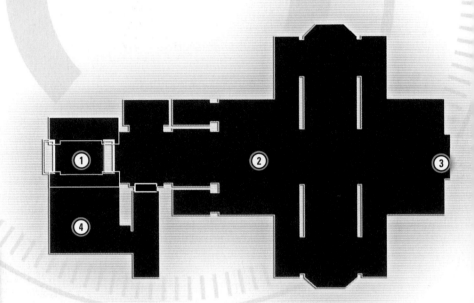

Use a Smoke Pellet to conceal your getaway.

THE POWER OF THE SHADOWS

Armed enemies are extremely dangerous. Batman's powers aren't magical; his gifts are those of intelligence, training and preparation. Even his suit won't stop many bullets, so the key is to fight with caution and decisiveness.

To defeat armed foes, stay in the darkness as often as possible. Hide in the upper reaches of a room to get an aerial view of your victims. The goal is to find enemies who are off on their own. When that opportunity arises, pick one off, flee to the shadows and repeat the process.

Be wary of making too much noise. Many Takedowns, although effective, may alert other guards to the situation. Flee quickly and remember that danger presents opportunities; mobile guards sometimes end up exposing themselves or leaving their buddies behind.

Enter Detective Mode once Batman is safe. This shows the room in a clear way, even when it's dark. Batman's scanners can see through walls, so tracking enemies is quite easy. There are four shooters down below watching the hostages and saving the innocents is Batman's primary responsibility.

HOSTAGE № 1: Observe the hostage taker on the right, glide over toward him and land on the platform above. Use a Silent Takedown and then knock him out before returning to the ceiling.

HOSTAGE № 2: Glide past the foe on the other side of the room. Land behind him and break through the weakened wood panel behind the unaware guard. This causes him to go down like a ton of bricks, releasing the second hostage in the process.

Watch out for opportunities to eliminate enemies with a quick takedown.

HOSTAGES № 3 & № 4: Zip to the end of the church and drop behind the last two guards. Walk toward them and utilize a Double Takedown. They're standing so close together that it's possible to knock them both out at the same time!

Talk to anyone who catches your interest. There are guards and medical personnel in this area. One doctor has a particularly interesting story, so visit him on the other side of the room. Aaron Cash takes his position by the front door. Talk to him to learn more about what happened inside the church.

BATS IN THE BELFRY

>>> >> **GOAL** **Access the top of the church.**

Use the door near the church's front entrance to reach the bell tower. Harley destroyed the stairs leading up to the top, but Batman can grapple his way up.

No stairs? No problem!

Climb the ladder at the top of the room. This is where the sniper must have made the shot. Go into the evidence scanner and examine the remote gun near the window. Listen to what Joker has to say, then leap through the large window behind the rifle to escape the building. Have Batman glide to safety once he's outside.

Make your escape when the opportunity arises.

TRACKING THE SIGNAL

PRIMARY OBJECTIVE: Continue tracking the Joker.

Now that Batman knows the Joker's signal frequency, it's possible to track the villain. A scanner reveals if Batman is getting closer or further away from Joker. Follow the signal through the city streets. It appears that the signal is coming from somewhere in the Industrial District.

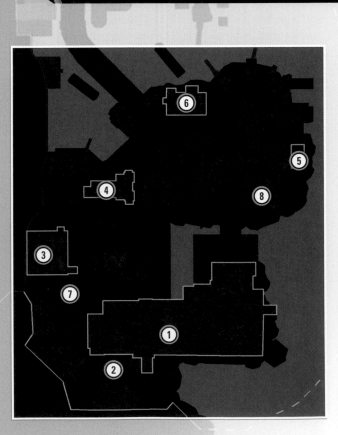

INDUSTRIAL DISTRICT

①	Steel Mill
②	Steel Mill Rear Entrance
③	Enigma Conundrum Building
④	Zsasz Hideout
⑤	Enigma Conundrum Building
⑥	Nora's Location
⑦	Sewer Entrance
⑧	Azrael Symbol Location

FRAGILE ALLIANCE & COLD CALL KILLER

At this point, a side mission appears on the right side of the Arkham City map. If you want, go inside the Krank Toy Factory in the southeast corner of the map to start "Fragile Alliance," which involves blowing up TITAN containers with Explosive Gel.

Another mission is triggered when Batman picks up a ringing phone underneath the broken section of overpass, just north of the church. "Cold Call Killer" begins once this happens. Ringing phones appear while in Detective Mode, so turn it on if you hear one.

Side Missions appear around the city throughout the game's main storyline.

Lead Batman to the top of the Steel Mill in the southeastern section of Arkham City. This large building has become the hotbed of the Joker's activity. The clues are in abundance—just look at the decorations in the area!

HAVING FUN IN THE INDUSTRIAL DISTRICT

There are many henchmen wandering around the lower parts of the Steel Mill. For extra fighting, descend and knock them all out. Solving Riddles results in extra experience here, too. Another way to have fun is to pop Joker's balloons using Batman's Batarangs.

Popping Joker's Balloons results in extra experience and contributes to Riddler's Riddles.

When Batman reaches the top of the radio tower (the second highest structure on the Steel Mill), he has a conversation with Alfred. The best way to enter the mill undetected is to drop down through the chimney.

Grapple to the top of the chimney; it's the highest point on the Steel Mill. After a short cutscene, Batman gets inside the mill to continue his investigation.

Grapple to the top of the chimney to gain access to the Steel Mill.

THE BATARANG

The Batarang is the ideal gadget for several tasks. This tool stuns enemies at range, triggers switches, and can be used to solve a number of Riddler puzzles. When used properly, they're quite effective in combat.

The Remote Control (RC) Batarang is used during more intense puzzles. This gadget can be thrown through small holes, around corners, and used to navigate a considerable distance. Use it to stun enemies who are just outside of Batman's line of sight.

THE STEEL MILL

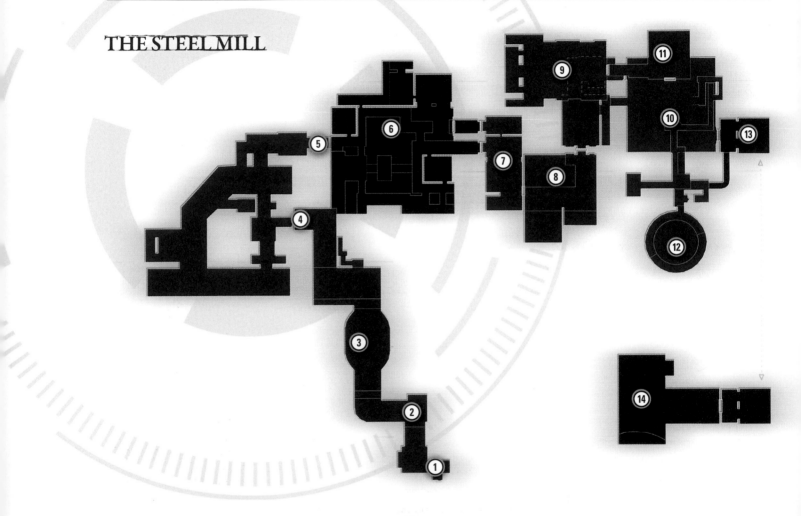

STEEL MILL		
1	Rear Entrance	
2	Boiling Water (Cooling Tunnel B)	
3	Large Series of Waterways	
4	Door (Access Cooling Tunnel B)	
5	Door Between Cooling Tunnels and Main Plant	
6	Smelting Chamber (Obtain REC Here)	
7	Office (Part of Assembly Line)	
8	Assembly Line (Used to Avoid a Sniper)	
9	The Joker's Fun House	
10	Loading Bay (Crane Puzzle, Manager's Office Access)	
11	Manager's Office	
12	Waste Exchange (Chimney Access Early in Game)	
13	Freight Elevator (Access to Boiler Room)	
14	Boiler Room ("Hot and Cold" Side Mission)	

>>> >> GOAL: Sneak into the building without getting torched.

Batman lands on a thin wire stretched precariously across the searing room. Jump and glide to the northern ledge, then slide underneath an outcropping. After a couple of hurdles, Batman arrives in front of the water valve control. Switch to the Batclaw and target the large ring on the control mechanism. Launch the Batclaw and pull the ring until the door swings open to cool down the room. Next, follow these steps

Glide down to the north ledge.

1. Drop to the ledge below.

2. Go to the other end of that ledge and hang down from it.

3. Shimmy to the side, climb back up, and get atop the damaged railing.

4. Walk to the end of the railing and turn to the right.

5. Jump from that location to another set of rails.

6. Proceed forward and switch to the Explosive Gel gadget.

7. Use Detective Mode to spot a damaged section in the floor.

8. Spray the Explosive Gel onto the weakened area and detonate it!

EXPLOSIVE GEL & THE BATCLAW

Explosive Gel, a tool that Batman has been using for quite some time, works well against damaged floors and walls. These vulnerable sections always appear in Detective Mode, so they're easy to spot from a distance.

During a fight, Batman can use the gel in a quickfire mode. This knocks enemies around, causing them to take damage and lose any weapons or defensive items in their possession.

The Batclaw opens vents and duct covers that are otherwise inaccessible. It's also a combative gadget that pulls items away from attackers, or pulls the attacker himself!

LOADING BAY

>>> >> GOAL: Sneak up on Joker's henchmen.

Drop through the new exit and get your bearings. Batman is now in the Steel Mill's loading bay. Another hatch isn't far from this location. Use the Batclaw to rip open a hatch, then use the claw again to pull a Riddler Trophy from its resting place.

Don't forget about the Riddler Trophy.

The small room ahead is filled with steam, but there's a control mechanism slightly above eye level. Use a Batarang to stop the steam from pouring into the room and climb into the crawlspace above. The sounds of the Joker's henchmen fill the corridors. Enter Detective Mode to see just how many enemies are nearby. To make matters worse, Harley's sing-song voice adds to the mix!

Before long, Batman reaches a steam blockade with three control mechanisms behind it. Use the fast tap version of the Batarangs to hit all three mechanisms within a few seconds. Doing so shuts off the steam and allows Batman to pass through the remainder of the tunnels. Backtrack, crouch underneath the low ceiling, and creep under the main floor. Pop out of the grating at the end and attack the henchmen in the room above.

Use the grate to surprise the henchmen.

ASSEMBLY LINE

>>> >> GOAL: Ambush the Joker's men and take them all down.

Crawl through the tunnels while listening to the people in the main room. There are spouts of flame on the right side of the tunnels; study the timing. Wait for the first one to go out, move past it, and do the same thing with the next jet.

Time your movements past the flames.

10 ON 1—ALMOST A FAIR FIGHT!

Even without guns, 10 foes can inflict quite a bit of damage. This crew can throw large objects. Counterattacks are quite effective here, but it's important to use more techniques to win this fight. Notice that enemies with thrown weapons have a "tell" before they strike, just like normal melee attackers. Use this opportunity to catch and return the thrown weapon by pressing the counterattack command button.

In addition, it's possible to accrue a massive combo very quickly in a battle with this many targets. Make the most of special attacks; the Special Combo Takedown is quite effective. If you've purchased other special moves, now is the perfect opportunity to test them out.

A NICE REMINDER

There are two Riddler Trophies in the adjoining room, although you can't get them right now. Batman needs the city's Municipal Codes to access the cell with the goodies and it's going to be a little while before those codes are available.

Scan the inaccessible Riddler's Trophies.

Since you can't snag the trophies, use the command that appears on-screen to save their location on your map. This is a great tool for reminding yourself of collectible objects that are currently inaccessible.

Take the door that leads out of that room and stop when you hear more henchmen talking. Someone seems to think it's sane to edge in on the Joker's relationship. Knocking that guy out might be doing *him* a favor! Since all three foes have guns. a frontal assault would be suicidal. Instead, throw a Batarang at the controls near the conveyor belt. Crouch and slip into the area beyond and grapple up to the top to gain a better vantage point.

Hop down and sneak behind the lone henchman on the other side of the room. Use a Silent Takedown to drop him without alerting the other guards. Next, jump behind both remaining guards to knock them out. No shots fired, nobody permanently hurt. That's the way to do it!

Take down the lone gunman first…

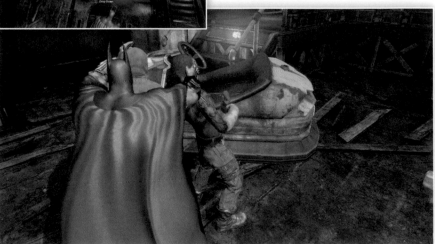

…and then eliminate the other two.

Someone got wise and locked the door between this room and the next one. Leap through the nearby window to reach the next chamber. This doesn't cause any damage or even slow Batman down, however, it produces quite a bit of noise. Grapple to the top of the room and blow through another

obstacle to obtain a Riddler Trophy. There are more enemies in the next room, so move slowly and be prepared.

SMELTING CHAMBER

>>> >> GOAL Save Dr. Stacy Baker; obtain the Remote Electrical Charge (REC).

There are two armed guards in front of the main doorway in the smelting chamber. Luckily, they like to talk to each other. Just be patient and eventually they'll stand close enough together to enable a Double Takedown.

It helps when the henchmen make things easier.

Next, crawl toward the southern side of the room. A wandering guard approaches that corner and Batman can ambush him quietly in a place where the other guards can't see or hear much.

That leaves only a few more targets. Two men are in the room with a hostage, while the other is on the main floor. Take him out next because he's effectively orphaned and won't get any support. Use a drop attack when descending from the upper levels, then pound the guy with a ground attack to leave him unconscious. Remember to grapple back to the upper tiers immediately afterward.

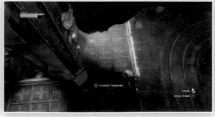

Take this guy down with an Inverted Takedown if possible.

If a guard hears his buddy getting pounded, he'll come outside to check on things. If this occurs, use Batman's Inverted Takedown to stop him.

ALTERNATE METHOD

If you miss the Inverted Takedown, hop onto the gargoyle hanging above the guard, drop down, and plunge near him when he turns in the wrong direction. A Silent Takedown is perfectly effective.

Crouch near the windows and wait for the last guard to get close to Batman's position. Break through the window with a final takedown to clear the room.

Take down the final guard by busting through the window.

Stacy Baker gives Batman an earful of information about Joker. Batman grabs a new toy as he finishes the conversation. The Remote Electrical Charge (REC) is a godsend for finding Riddler Trophies and getting through areas with power generators and electromagnets.

THE REMOTE ELECTRICAL CHARGE [REC]

The REC stuns enemies, opens electronically controlled doors and activates some types of machinery.

WHERE IS THE JOKER?

>>> >> GOAL: **Backtrack to the Joker's office and confront him.**

Use the REC to gain entry into the Joker's office, which is the room back by the loading bay. Be on the lookout for the Harley speakers littered throughout the building (see "Popping Heads" note).

POPPING HEADS

Harley's internal speaker system for the building is rather unique. She has deployed Harley Quinn statues all over the place. Interact with the statues to hear from her.

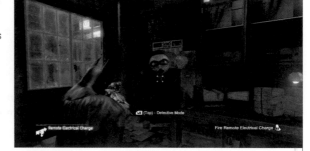

However, if you don't want to listen, use the REC to pop the heads off each statue. This gets you some experience and unlocks Riddler Secrets, too!

Return to the assembly line and use the REC to open the sealed doors. This route leads back to the assembly line via a higher path. Follow it and drop down behind several thugs who are trying to weld the main door shut.

ADVANCED FIGHTING

Practice fighting using a mix of gadgets and normal attacks. Using a combination of gadgets and attacks is a solid gameplan. In fact, the more variations that are used, the more experience you earn at the end of each battle. Learn how to mix in Batarang tosses and charged shots to disrupt enemies with weapons. Use various combo attacks to get even more experience.

Use gadgets during fights to earn more experience.

Return to the loading bay and use the REC on the large machine at the southern end of the room. The controls swing a large crane hook back and forth. Give it some distance and slam the hook into the Joker's office. Remove the hook from the door, then grapple to the top when it's safe to do so. After the boss fight, zip up to the Joker's office and confront the villain. Words are exchanged, plans are hatched and everyone learns a little about themselves.

THE JOKER

REAL NAME Unknown

Occupation	Professional Criminal
Based In	Gotham City
Eye Color	Green
Hair Color	Green
Height	6 Ft. 0 Inches
Weight	160 Lbs
First Appearance	Batman #1 [Spring 1940]

Attributes
- Unrepentant homicidal maniac
- Surprisingly strong hand-to-hand combatant
- Unknown past
- Employs various deadly weapons, often based on party-gag items
- Uses a fatal toxin that stretches victim's faces into Joker-like grins

The self-styled Clown Prince of Crime has no superpowers beyond a capacity for incredible violence and a skill at creating deadly mayhem.

Since his last encounter with the Dark Knight, the Joker has been transferred to Arkham City. Eye witnesses claim he is stricken with a serious disease, possible caused by his Titan overdose on Arkham Island.

He has been lying low, delivering orders through Harley Quinn, so no one can confirm if the Joker is actually in poor health or playing another sick joke.

Swing the hook into the office wall.

Some of Joker's deadliest henchmen drop from his office in pursuit of Batman. These guys aren't scared of anything. One of them is a one-armed slugger with a heavy sledge—it's no wonder they call him Mister Hammer!

Draw the majority of the enemies away from Mister Hammer and stay mobile to avoid his wide swings. Any time your combo starts to get high, use special attacks to thin the ranks of the goons.

Hitting Mister Hammer with the REC is a great way to ruin the bad guys' day. Hammer goes a bit crazy when he gets shocked and the thugs nearby suffer for it. Also, try to stun and leap over Mister Hammer. Pummel him from behind to unload some serious damage!

Mister Hammer is an easy target once his cronies are history. Run in, hit him once and roll away before he strikes. As soon as he tires from swinging, rush in and unload several attacks and repeat the technique as soon as he winds up a second time. Batman can make short work of the brute.

Alternately, double tap the Jump button to leap over Mr. Hammer to avoid his attacks, along with those of his cronies. This allows Batman to evade and jump over an enemy before he can attack. Plus, it enables you to sustain your flow on Mr. Hammer when done properly.

FIND THE COLDEST POINT IN GOTHAM

PRIMARY OBJECTIVE: Locate Mister Freeze.

Upon exiting the Steel Mill, Batman emerges on the northeast side of the building. Listen to a conversation between Batman and Alfred and then wander through Arkham City. Mister Freeze is somewhere out there and he's the next target.

AMUSEMENT MILE	
①	Poison Ivy's Hideout
②	Enigma Conundrum Building
③	Gotham City Police Department
④	Fragile Alliance (Bane Hideout)
⑤	Enigma Conundrum Building
⑥	Azrael Symbol Location

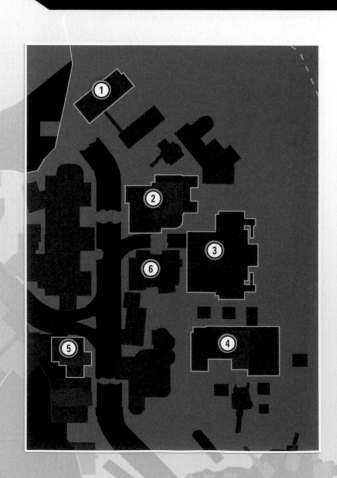

MISTER FREEZE

REAL NAME Dr. Victor Fries

Occupation	Professional Criminal
Based In	Gotham City
Eye Color	Blue
Hair Color	None
Height	6 Ft. 3 Inches
Weight	190 Lbs
First Appearance	Batman #121 [February 1959]

Attributes

- Scientific genius, with a specialty in cryonics
- Employs an extensive array of cryo-weaponry
- Permanently altered to survive in a sub-freezing state
- Wears protective, freezing armor
- Motivated by grief over the fate of his wife Nora

Victor Fries was a brilliant cryogenicist whose beloved wife Nora was stricken with a fatal degenerative disease.

He placed her in suspended animation while obsessively searching for a way to cure her; but the corporation that funded his research pulled the plug, triggering an accident that transformed Fries' body into a cold-blooded form that must always be kept below zero. At normal room temperature he will die.

Wielding a number of freezing weapons, he wears protective armor in his quest to somehow bring back his lovely wife and avenge her fate. Since the opening of Arkham City, Mr. Freeze has seemingly disappeared.

THE JOKER'S MESSAGE

While exploring, Batman gets a voice message from the Joker. To listen to it, access the Character Bios and look for a new tab in the Joker's subsection. You can always count on him to stay in touch!

The Joker left a message for Batman.

Use the temperature sensor to find the coldest spot in Arkham City.

Batman uses a temperature sensor to locate Mister Freeze, who is likely in the coldest spot in Gotham. Look at the temperature gauge while exploring. Follow the chilly air to the north.

The Gotham City Police Department (GCPD) building is on the north-eastern side of the city, which seems to be Mister Freeze's hideout at the moment. Don't approach the building casually, though, As there are armed guards all over the place. There are a couple of guards on the roof and they aren't supporting each other. Grapple over to them and silently take out both guards.

SILENT BUT DEADLY

Make any noise during this takedown attempt and it alerts the four guards below, as well as anyone left on the roof. It's a fun fight, but silence makes it more likely that Batman will win without taking any hits.

One proven tactic involves removing both roof guards and then splitting up the lower men by hitting them at range with a Batarang. Disappear into the night before the gunners make it to the upper level of the building. At this point, they split up to find Batman. Stalk a lone guard on patrol and perform a Silent Takedown. If two guards are close together, creep up behind them and grab the closest one. As long as the takedown is silent, the other foe is oblivious to the going on.

Try to get each guard when they split up.

When the area is clear, explore the south side of the GCPD building to find a garage, which is the ticket into the structure. Use the REC on the mechanism above the door. This opens the way somewhat, but Batman can't crawl through the opening. Have him back up, run up to the door, and then

slide underneath it. Inside are some downed thugs from the Penguin's gang. Take a card from one of them to intercept messages in the future. Then, go through the door.

Slide underneath the garage door.

INSIDE THE GCPD BUILDING

> >> >> GOAL: **Knock out the Penguin's men and interrogate the last man standing.**

Armed guards litter the old police precinct. The main group is stationed inside a large room near the entrance. There are openings on the left and right sides of the hallway. A direct approach is extraordinarily dangerous; even a fast ambush will result in a difficult fight. There must be a better way!

1. Walk along the right hallway and grapple to the top of the room.

2. Jump from ledge to ledge to reach the far wall.

3. Open the grate against the wall and crawl into the ductwork.

4. Drop into the main room without being seen and unleash a Silent Takedown on the closest guard.

5. Do the same thing on the second guard as quickly as possible.

6. Take cover when the Penguin alerts more guards.

7. Sneak up on the new forces and use a Double Takedown on the closest pair.

8. Approach the last of the Penguin's men and begin the interrogation.

GOTHAM CITY POLICE DEPARTMENT (GCPD)	
1	Entrance
2	Municipal Security Console (Door Control)
3	Rear Exit
4	Main Room
5	Dangerous Wiring

Interrogate the last of the Penguin's men.

TRY, TRY AGAIN!

If anything goes wrong, retreat to the entrance at high speed. The guards check out what happened to their buddies, but Batman can slip into the large room as guards leave. Roll up their group with Silent Takedowns. Anyone who sees Batman should catch a Batarang to the face and then be eliminated with a Ground Takedown. If that happens, leave quickly and come in from another angle.

After interrogating the last guard, Batman gets locked inside the building as he attempts to leave, but that won't be a problem for long. He downloads the Municipal Codes for all of Gotham. There are special locked areas throughout the city that are now accessible with Batman's Cryptographic Sequencer. You might remember one of the consoles from the Steel Mill (that place with two Riddler Trophies that couldn't be reached). It's time to get them!

To open the GCPD doors, crawl through the ducts below the floor. Locate the side room with a computer console. Use the Sequencer on it to hack the device and input the special code.

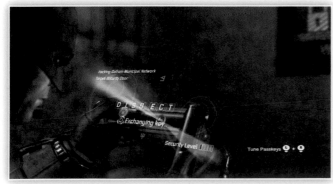

Use the Cryptographic Sequencer to hack into the Security Panel.

MANIPULATING THE SEQUENCER

To complete this mini-game, just rotate the two controls in a circular pattern. When each half of the code word unlocks, stop moving the controls for that side and work on the other one. When both pieces of the code unlock, you'll uncover the correct word to use.

Advanced codes may have multiple word fragments on each side. If the letters don't line up to form a real word, continue rotating the controls and try a different sequence.

Don't leave the GCPD building yet. Return to the front but look for another side room off the main hallway. Unlock that door using the Sequencer and blast through a weakened wall within to find a Riddler Trophy.

Snag a Riddler Trophy before exiting the building.

THE MUSEUM

>>> >> GOAL Attempt to investigate the Museum.

THE BOWERY	
1	Museum
2	Front Entrance to Museum
3	Iceberg Lounge Entrance
4	Subway Entrance
5	Processing Queue Entrance
6	Riddler Hideout
7	Azrael Symbol Location

Leave the GCPD building and explore the city's surroundings once again. There is a new side mission available ("Medical Team Missing"). Batman's new target for the main objective is the Museum, which is located in the south-west side of Arkham City.

ENIGMA CONUNDRUM

To take part in another side mission, return to the church. Batman talks to the Riddler inside and receives a riddle that isn't too difficult to decipher. Walk to the back of the area and use the environmental scanner on the organ. The mission proceeds from there.

There are several guards in the southwestern part of Arkham City, so don't go rushing into the situation without knowing what to expect. Stay on the rooftops to get a clear view of all the enemies to the southwest. Be especially wary of gunmen or large groups. Most of the larger groups

have a couple of people with melee weapons (including knives, which are more dangerous than baseball bats).

Eliminate as many enemies as possible.

Use the view from the rooftops to scout the enemies below.

It's conceivable to slip through to the Museum without fighting all of these groups, but there is considerable experience to gain by cleaning up the streets along the way.

The only required fight is in front of the Museum. Dispose of the guards, then use Batman's Sequencer to open the door. Afterward, go inside and be ready! The Penguin has two of his best men guarding the foyer. After the fight, jump through the side window to enter the main portion of the building.

DEADLY WEAPONS REQUIRE MORE CARE

It's not as easy to counter knives compared to basic melee weapons. In this scenario, you need to rely on Batman's Blade Counter ability. When there are groups of enemies, focus on the knife-wielding

foes first. Don't let them mix in with the rest of the fodder, because they'll have a higher chance of landing attacks that Batman won't see coming.

Pressing and holding the Counter button and the movement button away from the thug for the duration of the attack allows Batman to Blade Dodge knife attacks, but timing is very important. The move must be timed properly. Note that these foes normally stab in sets of three.

The side room has a security panel, so use Batman's Sequencer to unlock the system. Unfortunately, something is wrong. Penguin must have known that Batman would use his Sequencer. There must be a jammer somewhere outside. Destroy the penguin figurine in the side room, then exit the building.

BREAKING THE PENGUIN

The penguin figurines located throughout the Museum are worth experience, so destroy any that you find. A simple Batarang does the trick at almost any range.

THE FIRST TWO TRANSMITTERS

GOAL: Seek and destroy two of the Penguin's transmitters.

One transmitter is on top of the Museum, on the northeastern side of the roof. Knock out the guards and keep them away from the gun crate located against the wall. Punch anyone who tries to mess with it!

WEAPON CACHES

Those green crates are filled with assault rifles, which explains why the thugs are so keen to open them. Punch anyone near the crates to prevent them from unlocking the containers. If they succeed, it introduces a heavy weapon to the fight. Knock the newly armed guard down as soon as possible. Don't let anyone pick up and use the gun afterward.

Another transmitter is located on top of a building to the north of the Bowery. There are four gunmen guarding it, so be very cautious. Look for the foe standing near the edge of the rooftop. Take him out quietly and then make some noise to draw the others closer. Hop off the roof and hang until they turn around and perform Silent Takedowns. Destroy the transmitter after all four men are knocked out.

Fully disable the transmitter before moving on.

Disable the transmitter after the fight and go off in search of the other two. Note that Batman must smash several pieces of the transmitter to disable it. Don't leave the area until the signal is dead.

BENEATH GOTHAM'S STREETS

▶ ▶▶ ▶▶ GOAL: Find a way to get underneath Arkham City.

SUBWAY	
1	Subway Station (Bowery Entrance)
2	TITAN Container
3	Subway Terminal
4	Route to Wonder City
5	Sewers (Industrial District Entrance)
6	Line Launcher Required to Progress
7	Entrance to Subway from the Sewers

Now it's time to venture all the way south again. the Penguin's men are setting up a third transmitter underground. Two armed guards patrol the entrance to the subway, but they wander away from each other and don't turn around often. Silence them both and enter the tunnel.

Dispose of the two thugs when they wander away from one other.

Two more men are below, both armed. They're close together, so a Double Takedown is optimal. Go into a small office on the far side of the building and crawl through some ductwork. Blast through the floor on the other end to get a Riddler Trophy.

Backtrack and then walk past the gate where the two guards were standing. Descend through the tunnels and get another Riddler Trophy from a grate near the bottom of the area. The tunnels empty into a defunct subway station; follow the tracks and climb onto an old train. Maneuver along the train, sliding underneath pipes and other obstacles.

Maneuver over and under the pipes.

THROUGH THE TUNNELS

Ambush a few thugs on the other side of the trains, but be on the lookout for a variety of goodies in this area. Riddler Trophies, a TITAN tank and other treasures are hidden inside the old station and its tunnels.

Take care of the thugs and destroy the TITAN tank!

RIDDLER PUZZLES

There are hidden questions marks throughout Gotham City. Placed by the Riddler, Batman must take pictures of them to get Riddler Trophies. However, this won't be available until the start of the "Enigma Conundrum" side mission.

Line up the question mark and scan it.

The transmitter isn't very far away. Proceed through the hallway with the TITAN container, then open a door using Batman's REC and slide underneath it. Guards are standing in the next open room. For a stealthy approach, open the vent and slip inside. Listen to Penguin's thugs while they speculate on the future. Take some time to thoroughly examine the room. There's only one free knockout here, so it must count! Penguin alerts everyone about 10 seconds after the first guard gets knocked out.

It's best to focus on two armed guards patrolling the walkways above. Since they have a great vantage point of the area, life will be easier without them. Grapple behind the first one, perform a Silent Takedown, then rush the second guard on the upper level before the Penguin sends out the warning. Once both are down, grapple onto the upper statues and wait for the next victim to appear.

Take out the guards on the upper level first.

Once the guards spread out, find one without any backup and take him down. Dispose of the last two and interrogate the final thug in the room. Search the ground floor and destroy the transmitter before leaving. Get any trophies or goodies in the area, then backtrack through the entire subway system. Climb back to the surface streets of Arkham City.

THE PENGUIN CAN'T HIDE NOW

> **GOAL** Siege the Museum.

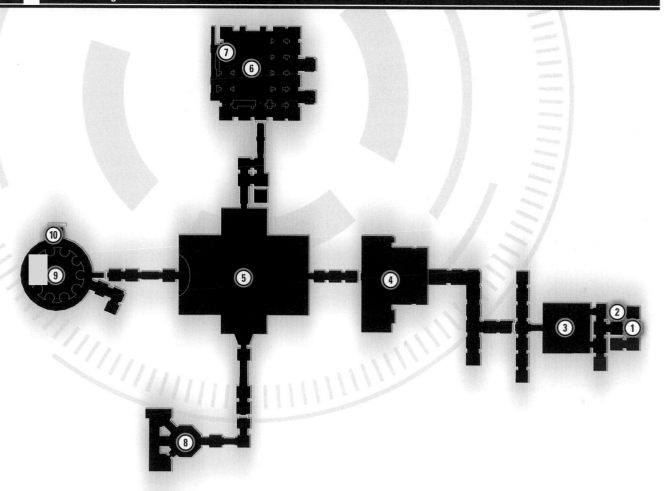

MUSEUM	
1	Main Entrance
2	Security Console
3	Trophy Room
4	Gladiator Pit
5	Torture Chamber
6	The Armory
7	Victor Fries' Suit
8	War Room
9	Iceberg Lounge
10	Rear Exit

There are new guards stationed at the Museum entrance. Pummel these foes with your favorite moves before entering the Museum. Once inside, use the Sequencer on the console that was previously scrambled. Now the main portion of the building is unlocked.

Without the jammers, the Security Panel can be hacked.

Follow the main hallway to proceed. The Museum is beautiful, but there are more thugs dirtying up the place. There is a trio of guards down in the next room. One has a knife, while the other is sporting body armor. That's something new, so Batman needs to use different tricks to finish off that fiend. Once the threat is stifled, talk to GCPD Officer Elvis Jones. It seems that there are a number of officers inside the Museum. Who knows how many of them need assistance. Gordon is going to want his men back alive and Batman can surely help.

Rescue the GCPD Officers .

Take the lone doorway that leads deeper into the Museum. The door to the west leads to yet another hall. Its southern side has an electric mechanism that controls a door. Open it using the REC to obtain a Riddler Trophy. The other direction, as an arrow ominously points, leads north toward larger rooms.

Use the REC to find another Riddler Trophy.

Use a Remote Batarang to open this route.

Send the Batarang over the gate and keep it moving slowly for maximum control. Once the gadget reaches the other side of the gate, descend and maneuver the Batarang so that it hits a red control box. This opens two sets of gates. Follow the corridor until Batman reaches the Gladiator Pit.

THEIR NUMBERS ARE IRRELEVANT

> **>>> >> GOAL: Survive the fight in the arena.**

Batman must fight a horde of opponents in the Gladiator Pit. It's a tremendous melee. Don't fight defensively; instead, cover as much ground as possible to deal damage while staying mobile. The longer Batman stays in any single position, the more likely that enemies will surround him making it easier to break his combo. When the last thug falls, Penguin deploys a new threat.

BODY ARMOR BEATDOWN

Batman can lay a wicked Beatdown on foes and this high-hit tactic is especially effective against opponents wearing body armor. The only downside of a Beatdown is that the long series of blows leaves Batman exposed to counterattacks. Try to eliminate, or temporarily stun, everyone else in the room before performing a Beatdown on a foe wearing body armor.

Stay mobile while fighting each enemy.

Use the Ultra Stun to start a Beat Down on a Titan infected thug

(B) (B) (B) Ultra Stun

One of the Penguin's men has been infected with TITAN. Although this monstrous thug lacks much intelligence, he's extremely dangerous.

Stay near the walls and wait for the big guy to charge. Dodge to the side to avoid damage, then quickly close in. Use the on-screen commands to stun the thug three times. Once he's fully disoriented, continue to attack to get the thug on his back.

Batman holds on for dear life and can partially control what the infected man does during this time. More enemies deploy, but they don't pose much of a threat. Charge the TITAN-infected thug into them.

When Batman gets thrown to the ground, wade into the weaker enemies right away. Don't pursue the TITAN-infected thug again until the arena is otherwise clear. Evade to avoid the boss's attacks and use the Super Stun/Ultra Stun sequence to end this fight.

BOSS FIGHT TITAN-INFECTED THUG

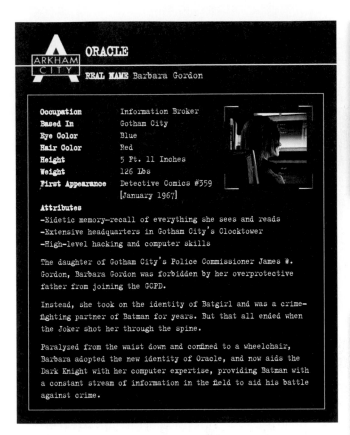

ORACLE

REAL NAME Barbara Gordon

Occupation	Information Broker
Based In	Gotham City
Eye Color	Blue
Hair Color	Red
Height	5 Ft. 11 Inches
Weight	126 Lbs
First Appearance	Detective Comics #359 [January 1967]

Attributes
-Eidetic memory-recall of everything she sees and reads
-Extensive headquarters in Gotham City's Clocktower
-High-level hacking and computer skills

The daughter of Gotham City's Police Commissioner James W. Gordon, Barbara Gordon was forbidden by her overprotective father from joining the GCPD.

Instead, she took on the identity of Batgirl and was a crime-fighting partner of Batman for years. But that all ended when the Joker shot her through the spine.

Paralyzed from the waist down and confined to a wheelchair, Barbara adopted the new identity of Oracle, and now aids the Dark Knight with her computer expertise, providing Batman with a constant stream of information in the field to aid his battle against crime.

After the fight and a brief cutscene with Alfred and Oracle, Batman has to find a way to leave the arena. Explore along the southern side of the room. An electrified fence prevents Batman from reaching an emergency override. Use a Remote Control Batarang to hit it; guide the gadget over the fence and back down to the red override button.

Use the Remote Control Batarang to hit the button on the other side of the fence.

Proceed through the southwestern gate when it opens and hack into a console in the next hallway. This opens a door leading into a small elevator room. Hop into the elevator and use the REC on the machinery to reach the top of the room. Set Explosive Gel on the ceiling and blow through it.

Use the REC to control the elevator.

The hallway above is relatively empty. Use the Batclaw to pull a hatch off the wall and find the Riddler Trophy, then blast through another weakened wall. Turn left at the junction and continue until Batman reaches the Torture Chamber.

FROM BAD TO WORSE

GOAL: Cross the frozen floor with caution; get Batman to the Armory.

The Penguin has gotten his hands on a very effective weapon. There are three police officers in the torture chamber, but saving them won't be simple. The men are on thin ice—literally! Batman must slowly walk across the ice to avoid falling into the water underneath.

WHAT'S MOVING UNDER THERE?

Batman is an expert swimmer and his suit protects him from a number of environmental elements, including the cold. However, it would be lethal to fall through the ice in this chamber. Something is moving in the water underneath the ice and it doesn't seem friendly.

While walking, crouch to move at a decent clip without risking falling through the ice. It's still foolish to go at full speed, but you have more control this way.

1. Slowly walk toward the first cop to free him.

Venture out onto the ice to rescue the first officer.

2. Walk toward the northern part of the room.

3. Use the Batarang to knock down the platform suspended over the water.

4. Use the Batclaw and latch onto the platform's rings.

5. Pull the makeshift boat toward Batman.

6. Get on the platform and use the Batclaw to grab a ring near the next prisoner.

7. Pull Batman toward that part of the room, then exit the platform. Save the officer.

8. Repeat this tactic for the next one.

9. Leave the Torture Chamber using the exit on the northern side of the room.

Search the next hallway. An electrically sealed door results in another trophy after finishing an easy Batarang puzzle. There's also a penguin figurine in a display to the side of the hall.

THE ARMORY

> **>>> >> GOAL** **Save the hostages by knocking out all the armed guards.**

Enter the northern doorway to find a room with several more hostages. The thugs are wearing thermal imaging goggles, so sneaking up on them will be harder than usual. Even hiding along the ceiling isn't safe, so speed and care are the best tools.

There are six gunmen and many of them stay up high to utilize a good vantage point over the rest of the chamber. In this rare situation, it's better off to start on the ground floor and work your way up. The two patrolmen on the ground are the most vulnerable targets at the outset. Sneak up behind them and score Silent Takedowns before Penguin can alert the other men.

Eliminate the guards on the lower floor first.

Find cover right away so that Batman isn't spotted when the other guards come to investigate. At least one guard will split off from the main pack. Dispose of him and the next goon who makes the same mistake. The grates in the room provide good places to hide. Also, destroying weakened walls causes a great deal of noise, so avoid using that method if your goal is a silent victory.

Without their allies to support them, there are myriad ways to eliminate the last two guards. Finish them off and then save the three hostages at the top of the area. Talk to Tom Miller, search for trophies in the room, and then leave.

If one of the guards grabs a hostage, take him out using a stealth approach.

SEARCH THE WAR ROOM

>>> >> GOAL: Turn south and search the war room for Victor Fries.

Although there are no police officers in the room south of the torture chamber, it's wise to fully explore the Museum. Pass through the torture chamber and grapple to the southern ledge to reach the south hall.

Use the Sequencer to bring down the security system in the hallway, then fight three thugs. Enter the next room and take a look around. Try to blast through the weakened wall of the war room and see what happens.

Use Explosive Gel on the weakened wall.

Several of Penguin's men attack, led by a Penguin Lieutenant armed with a wicked scythe. Pull the weaker thugs away from their leader and slap them around. Once Batman has thinned the herd, leap toward the Lieutenant and unleash a number of fast attacks. Roll away to evade his sword swings.

Thin out the weaker thugs before focusing on the Lieutenant.

Once the thugs are down, visit the back of the war room. Use a console to open the cage that the Penguin has built for Fries. Talk to Victor and "convince" him to assist the Dark Knight.

CONFRONT THE PENGUIN

>>> >> GOAL: Get the Override from Mister Freeze's suit; confront the Penguin.

Use the Batclaw to pull the platform across the torture chamber. Most of the ice is already gone, so the platform provides the only means to

accomplish this. Get back to the Armory and look for Victor's suit on the upper floor inside a display case. This nets Batman the Disruptor: Freeze Override.

Find Mister Freeze's suit in a display case on the upper floor.

DISRUPTOR

The basic Disruptor is only useful for stopping Mister Freeze's gun from firing. This is used in the upcoming fight with the Penguin and again during a boss fight later in the game. However, there are ways to upgrade the Disruptor and those cases are discussed later in this walkthrough.

Return to the torture chamber and cross to the western part of the room. While traveling through the chamber, there is a sudden attack that comes from the depths. Batman's raft is grabbed by the Penguin's "Tiny" friend. Follow the on-screen commands to finish the fight and continue toward the western exit. Get onto the ledge above the waterline and head toward the

Iceberg Lounge, where the Penguin is patiently waiting. He has Fries's gun, but the Freeze Override can even the odds.

Rush into the lounge and take cover. Located in the center of the chamber, the Penguin shoots the Freeze Gun at regular intervals. Dash from one wall to the next between his shots until Batman can approach the Penguin from the walkway on which he's standing.

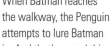

When Batman reaches the walkway, the Penguin attempts to lure Batman

in. And that's a good thing! Approach slowly and use the Override every few steps. As soon as the white crosshairs start to line up, the Override is within range. When the icon turns green, you'll know that the gun has gone offline.

Penguin's new toy is broken and he doesn't even know it! Charge him and beat that smug expression off his face. After an impressive cutscene, Batman is faced against another powerful enemy.

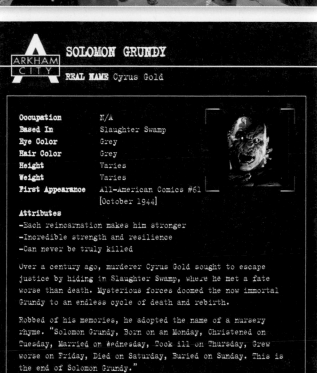

SOLOMON GRUNDY

REAL NAME Cyrus Gold

Occupation	N/A
Based In	Slaughter Swamp
Eye Color	Grey
Hair Color	Grey
Height	Varies
Weight	Varies
First Appearance	All-American Comics #61 [October 1944]

Attributes
- Each reincarnation makes him stronger
- Incredible strength and resilience
- Can never be truly killed

Over a century ago, murderer Cyrus Gold sought to escape justice by hiding in Slaughter Swamp, where he met a fate worse than death. Mysterious forces doomed the now immortal Grundy to an endless cycle of death and rebirth.

Robbed of his memories, he adopted the name of a nursery rhyme. "Solomon Grundy, Born on an Monday, Christened on Tuesday, Married on Wednesday, Took ill on Thursday, Grew worse on Friday, Died on Saturday, Buried on Sunday. This is the end of Solomon Grundy."

Solomon Grundy is large and strong and, as such, he's quite slow. Batman can't hurt him with regular attacks right now, so an alternate method is needed. Look for three generators on the ground. They're blazing with energy and periodically they spark with electricity. These are the keys to victory!

Stand in each generator when it's not sparking and use quickfire for the Explosive Gel to deploy it on the ground. Detonate the gel to destroy each generator.

Stay focused on Grundy at all times. His sweeping attacks cover a massive amount of ground. Use evasive rolls to back away when he swings the balls around the room. Don't get close until Grundy stops moving, otherwise he'll catch Batman on the next turn. After all three generators are destroyed, Solomon Grundy collapses. Have Batman charge in to pound on him, again and again.

During the second phase of the fight, the generators must be destroyed again. This time, though, each generator has a protective cover that closes periodically. Batman can deploy the Explosive Gel at any time, but the gel must be detonated when the protective cover is pulled back; if not, it protects the generator. If you can't see the orange glow around the generators, don't trigger the explosion!

Solomon Grundy continues his brutal attacks and deploys creepy maggots to crawl after Batman. Use quick Batarang throws to eliminate the maggots in short time. It's also possible to outrun them. Once all three generators are damaged, Grundy falls again. Attack him without remorse.

It appears that Grundy has more fight left in him in this fight's next phase. Solomon Grundy grabs the Dark Knight and pulls him alongside. As Grundy restores himself, Batman must struggle to break free of the monster's grasp.

Get some distance from Grundy once Batman escapes. As you might expect, a final set of generators form on the ground and all three must be destroyed. The areas alternate between arcs of electricity, a protected state and full exposure. When the generators open, race onto one, deploy the Explosive Gel and detonate it.

The beast throws his globes onto various points in the room. When they hit the floor, an electrical surge radiates in all directions. Batman must evade at the right moment, otherwise he'll incur damage. Rush in to stop Grundy as soon as he's vulnerable. This ends the main portion of the encounter.

During the fight's last phase, the Penguin attacks as Solomon Grundy falls. The waddling bird launches a series of grenades at Batman. Roll to the side to avoid each volley, then hurry forward in between attacks. Batman only needs to get close once; he'll throw enough attacks to give the Penguin a long nap. Afterward, Batman and Victor share a consultation. The next target soon becomes clear.

TRACK THE ASSASSIN

PRIMARY OBJECTIVE: Find Rā's al Ghūl and get a sample of his blood.

An enemy overheard Batman talking to Victor Fries and has fled the museum. She injured herself in the process, leaving Batman a trail of blood to track. When all of the plans are set in motion, enter Crime Scene Mode and scan the assassin's blood.

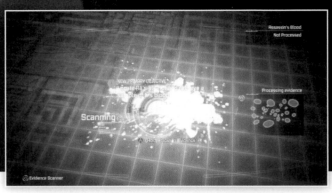

Scan the blood to pick up a trail.

 TALIA AL GHŪL

REAL NAME Talia al Ghūl

Occupation	Assassin
Based In	Mobile
Eye Color	Green
Hair Color	Brown
Height	5 Ft. 7 Inches
Weight	141 lbs
First Appearance	Detective Comics #411 [May 1971]

Attributes
-Trained in stealth and combat by the League of Assassins
-Ruthless and brilliant tactician
-Runs legitimate business empires for the League

The headstrong daughter of Rā's al Ghūl and on-again/off-again lover of Bruce Wayne, Talia al Ghūl is second in command of the League of Assassins.

A master of hand-to-hand combat and swordplay, Talia has dueled with Batman on several occasions and considers him an honorable opponent.

Despite Batman's elusiveness, her attraction to him has only increased—an attraction that her father encourages in his made quest for a male heir.

Talia knows that one day she may be forced to choose between her father and her beloved.

RĀ'S AL GHŪL

REAL NAME Unknown

Occupation	International Terrorist
Based In	Mobile
Eye Color	Green
Hair Color	Grey with white streaks
Height	6 Ft. 0 Inches
Weight	210 lbs
First Appearance	Batman #232 [June 1971]

Attributes
-Genius intellect and strategist
-Superior strength and stamina
-Superb hand-to-hand combatant
-Nearly immortal thanks to his Lazarus Pits
-Commands the League of Assassins

Little is known about the early years of the nearly immortal Rā's al Ghūl, leader of the League of Assassins, whose name means "the Demon's Head."

He has lived for many centuries due to the Lazarus Pits, mystical and alchemical brews that restore his youth. A brilliant master of strategy and organization, Rā's goal is to save the Earth from eventual ecological devastation by destroying most of its population.

He recognizes Batman as both a worthy foe and a possible ally—except that Batman cannot accept Rā's dystopic worldview.

To bring Batman to his side, Ra's has even orchestrated a relationship between Batman and his beautiful daughter, Talia al Ghūl.

If Batman is correct, the assassin will lead him directly to Rā's al Ghūl. After the blood has been scanned, Batman can track the assassin's trail. Leave the building and turn left to follow the blood splatters.

THE PENGUIN'S GOONS

There are more goons nearby. It's possible to avoid them, but the experience from this fighting is substantial.

Fight the pack of goons to gain additional extra experience.

There's a stopping point just below the Park Row title on the map. Batman loses the blood trail and is forced to scan the assassin's bandages to learn more. After learning of the location, an ambush comes out of nowhere!

Scan the bandages when the trail goes cold.

IN HOT PURSUIT

>>> >> GOAL: Chase the assassin across Arkham City's rooftops.

The assassin knocks Batman around, but she isn't looking to start a prolonged fight. Watch as she leaps away, across the rooftops. Follow her once Batman recovers.

A STEADY PURSUIT

Avoid using the Grapnel unless it's absolutely necessary. Although it's slower to run and jump, it's easier to mimic the assassin's movements when Batman is performing the same acrobatics. When using the Grapnel, there is a chance of losing her trail.

Stay calm and follow the assassin around the rooftops. She'll occasionally stop if Batman gets too far behind. That's worrisome…It's almost like she wants him to catch up.

During a cutscene that takes place on a rooftop, Batman lands near the assassin and is forced to counter an attack from her. In the process, he plants a tracking beacon on the woman. She and her ninja friends flee, then Batman meets Robin. Robin introduces the Line Launcher, a device that allows Batman to move horizontally across areas.

ROBIN

REAL NAME Tim Drake

Occupation	Student
Based In	Gotham City
Eye Color	Blue
Hair Color	Black
Height	5 Ft. 10 Inches
Weight	170 lbs
First Appearance	Batman #436 August 1989

Attributes
-Keen detective skills
-Trained to fight crime by Batman
-Arsenal of gadgets and advanced technology

Young Tim Drake was in the audience the night the Flying Graysons were murdered, where he witnessed Batman leap to the scene. Inspired by Batman's heroics, Tim closely followed the chronicles of Batman and Robin.

Eventually deducing their secret identities using his self-taught detective skills, Tim convinced Bruce Wayne and Dick Grayson—now Nightwing—that a new Robin was needed in the never-ending battle for justice.

Tested by the Dark Knight himself with a grueling training regimen, Tim earned the right to become Robin, and has since lived up to the name.

THE LINE LAUNCHER

This newest gadget shoots a line across an area and anchors it to a wall. It can be used to cross large gaps, ambush guards, or even get around corners by shooting additional lines while crossing on the first one!

FOLLOW THE ASSASSIN

>>> >> **GOAL:** Chase the target down into the subway tunnels.

The tracking device leads to the Industrial District. At first, it's a curious signal because the assassin would have to be below ground for it to make sense. Then, Batman finds the Subway Maintenance Access.

SEARCH FOR GOODIES!

There are lots of goodies to corral in this area, like the Joker teeth in the main corridor. Expect to see more of them in the tunnels ahead. Also, there are several trophies in the sewers, so stop to hunt for treasure whenever the opportunity arises.

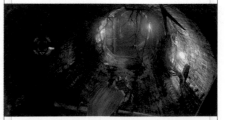

Look for Joker teeth in the Subway.

There are plenty of trophies to find down here.

Jump down the hole, run down the main corridor, leap over a gap in the floor, and take the left turn at the junction. The left tunnel leads to a lower area. Drop in for a fight against some of the Joker's minions. One of them is wearing body armor, so isolate him before focusing on the others.

Finish off the armored enemy last with a Beatdown.

Take the only open tunnel and follow it. The assassin must have gone down the southern passage. A break in the path prevents Batman from following her any further without using the Line Launcher.

Stop at the broken floor and select the new gadget. Shoot it at the far side of the tunnel, but don't relax. While zipping down the line, release the appropriate button and press it again. This allows Batman to set up the Line Launcher for a second shot even while he's still on the line from the first one! Shoot any target down the left path of the tunnel to proceed.

Use the Line Launcher to follow the assassin.

FAILING THAT

Batman climbs back to his original position if he falls into the water. If you get stuck on the other side of the tunnel, turn around and return to the starting point to try again. It's possible to attempt a second Line Launcher shot during the return trip.

The western tunnel doesn't go far before it dead ends. There are thugs below, but Batman needs to find a way to reach them. Look at the terminal points of the tunnels for a weakened section of flooring. Use Explosive Gel on a weak point to break through the floor to take down several men standing in the lower room. This triggers an epic fight.

Break through the floor to topple an enemy below.

The thugs have a few things going in their favor, like their melee weapons. More importantly, any thug who isn't directly engaged by Batman will attempt to open one of the two security containers in the room. These boxes hold assault rifles.

Try to prevent the guards from opening the containers. Ranged attacks, like thrown Batarangs or REC shots, work well. Or, cross distances quickly and make sure that Batman keeps as many men engaged in fisticuffs as possible.

Don't let the guards access the gun crates.

DISARM & DESTROY!

If you have the Special Combo Disarm and Destroy, use it to stop any armed thugs. That way, you won't need to worry about other foes picking up any dropped weapons.

After the fight, hack the security console on the wall. Batman opens the large doors that lead into the subway station. This is the same station from earlier, so it should be mostly clear of trouble. Be on the lookout for random Joker teeth, though! Use the door in the northeastern part of the room to continue. This leads to a water-filled chamber that was previously blocked. But now that Batman has the Line Launcher, it's quite easy to traverse the gap. Grapple to the door above and leave the subway behind.

Span the chamber using Batman's new toy.

THE COLLAPSED STREETS

>>> >> GOAL: Get to Wonder Tower.

FEELING KIND OF STRANGE

Batman is hot on the trail of his quarry, but things aren't going as planned. In this section, Batman doesn't have access to his full health bar. Therefore, it's going to take more caution and skill than usual during the upcoming fights. When you spend points from levels here, consider investing in Batman's Combat Armor upgrades.

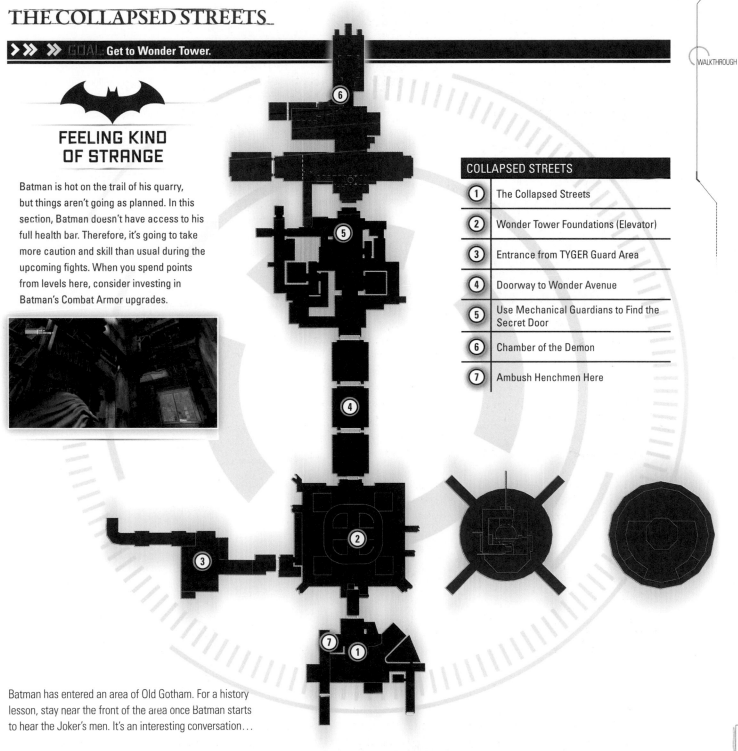

	COLLAPSED STREETS
1	The Collapsed Streets
2	Wonder Tower Foundations (Elevator)
3	Entrance from TYGER Guard Area
4	Doorway to Wonder Avenue
5	Use Mechanical Guardians to Find the Secret Door
6	Chamber of the Demon
7	Ambush Henchmen Here

Batman has entered an area of Old Gotham. For a history lesson, stay near the front of the area once Batman starts to hear the Joker's men. It's an interesting conversation…

Use the Line Launcher to start across the gap at the end of the corridor. Don't go too far, though, as Batman may cross in front of the Joker's men. Instead, use a double Line Launcher shot to reach the right side of the area. From here, snag the Riddler Trophy using the Batclaw and grapple above the Joker's group. For an easy victory, detonate the ceiling above the goons and throw the last two into the water. Afterward, use the door to the north.

WONDER TOWER FOUNDATIONS

▶ ▶▶ ▶▶ GOAL: Save Fiona Wilson; find a way into Wonder Avenue.

The room to the north of the ambushed thugs is guarded by several men and one of them has a signal jammer. These clever devices are so effective that even Batman's Detective Mode won't function until the device is turned off.

Stay near the front of the room and use Detective Mode. The location of the signal jammer is one of the only things that Batman can see. Periodically, more information will leak through, so he can still get a vague notion for what's nearby.

The signal jammer makes Detective Mode very ineffective.

Quietly drop from the balcony onto a gargoyle, then hang and slip onto the floor below. Circle the edges of the room on that tier; it's one of the few sections that currently isn't heavily watched. Mirror the signal jammer's movements until he's at the back of the room. Grapple behind the unsuspecting lout, climb over the railing and thrash him. Or, simply use the REC to temporarily disable him.

Eliminate the signal jammer so Batman can use Detective Mode.

Detective Mode is back! There are five more armed guards in the room, but it won't be an easy fight. Make haste to remove the guy in the corner. He's close to where Batman ambushed the signal jammer thug and the Joker won't send out a warning for a few more seconds. Take that guy unaware to bring the number of enemies down to four.

The guards on the ground floor will rush to the top to respond to the Joker's warning. Ambush the rearmost thug, then proceed after the other one. Use Silent Takedowns against both.

With only two enemies left, any group of techniques should work well. Clear the room to save Fiona Wilson. Grapnel to the top to save her.

Save Fiona Wilson and take her to safety.

Jump to the ground floor of the main room and use the door at the northern end. Don't leave, though, without first scanning the globe. This takes Batman into Wonder Avenue.

WONDER AVENUE

>>> >> GOAL Make contact with Rā's al Ghūl.

Batman's health further deteriorates, but there's nothing he can do about it. Prepare the REC and use it on the device in front of the northern doors. A dying thug falls at Batman's feet, but his assailant remains unseen. For an even more disquieting sight, look up while crossing the second set of doors. Use the REC again to open the next chamber.

Three ninja attack before Batman can open the third set of doors. These women are fast and tough. It's quite difficult to hit them with gadgets and countering their sword swipes is dangerous. So, try to evade whenever the women get too close. Plant Explosive Gel on the ground and detonate it when the ninja pass over it and duck in for short combos of melee attacks against individual ninja. Also, utilize the REC or perform Cape Stuns to disable enemies.

COUNTERATTACKING THE NINJA

Try to switch between counterattacks and Blade Dodges. Normal ninja attacks have a blue aura, just like attacks that can be countered from any other enemy. When the opportunity arises, counter them.

Try to evade yellow-colored attacks, or treat them like a knife stab. In that case, pull away and counter to trigger a Blade Dodge.

Take out the ninja with some quick combos.

Once the assassins are knocked out, use more gel to detonate the flooring above another machine. After it's exposed, use the machine to open the last set of doors. Batman is now in the main portion of Wonder Avenue.

To proceed, walk to the northern end of the room. Batman realizes that he can't open the next doorway without knowing how the ninja use it. To do this, he must reconstruct a video from the Mechanical Guardians that are lying on the ground. Scan each Mechanical Guardian in the area.

RIDDLER TROPHIES

Riddler Trophies abound in this section of Wonder Avenue. Take some time to thoroughly search the area to obtain plenty of rewards!

MECHANICAL GUARDIAN LOCATIONS

GUARDIAN № 1: Next to the secret door at the northern end of the room.

GUARDIAN № 2: South of the first guardian.

GUARDIAN № 3: Inside a display case, directly south from guardian #2.

GUARDIAN № 4: Directly across from guardian #3's location.

GUARDIAN № 5: Inside a small room above the northern door.

GUARDIAN № 6: Inside an upper room on the western edge of the chamber.

GUARDIAN № 7: High up on a ledge on the southeastern side of the chamber

ATTACK!

Scanning three of the guardians triggers an attack by two ninja. In addition, prepare for another attack after Batman finds guardian #6.

Be ready for more ambushes from ninja.

After scanning all of the Mechanical Guardians, return to the northern side of the room. Batman watches the video and learns the location of the secret passage. Approach the brick wall on the left (to the west of the first guardian) and use the secret entrance, as seen in the video footage. One of the ninja tries to help.

Take the passage to its conclusion, stopping for either of the Riddler Trophies that you want to collect, and climb to the top when Batman reaches the ladder.

Although nearly crippled with pain, Batman must walk to the northern side of the Chamber of the Demon. After meeting an old friend, descend to the lower tier of the room. This begins the trial.

THE FIRST TRIAL

>>> >> GOAL: **Traverse the dreamscape and glide into a hole on the other side.**

Batman is whisked away to another world at the mercy of Rā's al Ghūl. Throughout the new series of trials, the goal is to complete entire sections without bumping into anything. It's a great deal like augmented reality training, except the consequences of failure are severe.

Drink from the goblet when Batman arrives. The blood of Lazarus restores Batman's health. Afterward, Rā's explains the nature of this test. When he's done, approach the edge of the first platform. Use the following sequence to safely reach the next pillar.

1. Leap off the platform and alternate between short dives and quick glide climbs.

2. Use these moves to maintain Batman's height as best as possible while moving quickly.

3. Don't swing to either side.

4. Grapple to the edge of the next pillar as soon as possible.

Dive to get extra distance while gliding.

Grapple to the pillar right away.

Walk to the edge of the platform and prepare for a more challenging flight. There is an object that magically weaves through the air in the path that leads to the next platform. Follow it!

1. Start with a dive, a steady climb, followed by another dive.

2. Tap the Grapnel button as Batman nears the pillar of ice and use it to escape to safety.

ANOTHER TRY

Although Batman is doomed if he touches the ground or lands anywhere, you don't have to make another pass through the trial to get to your previous location. Batman is sent back to the last platform he safely landed on.

Two clones made of sand are summoned on the platform and they attack Batman without thought or hesitation. Defeat them both! Leap from the pillar and glide toward a hole in the sands below. Dive to follow the path, then glide to keep an even speed as Batman descends into the next stage of the test.

Glide and dive to the second trial.

THE SECOND TRIAL

>>> >> **GOAL:** Complete Rā's al Ghūl's test and fight the assassin.

The second trial is trickier because Batman must maneuver more to get from one pillar to the next. Wait for Rā's al Ghūl to banter a bit more, then leap off the starting point.

1. Wait to dive until Batman is directly over the descending line.

2. Pull out of the dive late to ensure that Batman goes between two girders without hitting either one.

3. Glide for a long time to avoid further problems.

4. Grapple to safety as soon as possible.

The next flight is long and Batman loses too much speed if you don't dive multiple times. Instead of taking the line of colored air all the way to the target, use it only as a vague guideline.

1. Run and leap off the starting pillar.

2. Only do enough of a dive to pick up speed.

3. Pull out of the dive to continue forward.

4. Dive again when Batman's speed ebbs.

5. Maintain enough speed to grapple to the next pillar before it descends.

Four foes attack when Batman reaches the platform, But their numbers aren't significant enough to overwhelm the Dark Knight. Use counterattacks to keep them off balance and fight conservatively.

When the encounter is over, Rā's al Ghūl invites Batman to face him directly. Run off the end of the pillar and use dives to pick up speed. Another hole in the sand isn't too far away and it's well within reach. Dive through the hole and prepare to face Rā's al Ghūl!

Batman appears back in the Chamber of the Demon. Walk through the door and climb the staircase beyond. Ignore the ninja, as they aren't interested in attacking. Talk to Talia at the top and let her escort Batman to Rā's al Ghūl.

Ascend the stairs to face Rā's al Ghūl.

Run forward and look around until Rā's al Ghūl descends from the sky. The master assassin splits into an army of mirror images that attack independently. Regular counterattacks only work against their blue moves; evade or use Blade Dodge if any orange attacks are inbound. Also, try to evade every time there is a charging whine. This noise precedes Rā's al Ghūl's sword strike, an attack that cannot be countered! Defeat all the mirror images to isolate Rā's al Ghūl, then pound him down as well. This ends the first phase of the fight.

The quickfired version of Batman's REC is essential for victory in this phase of the fight. Rā's al Ghūl hides behind a wall of clones and a large manifestation of the killer throws blades at Batman from the center of the mirror images.

Fire the charge between the gaps in the clone wall. The quickfire version of the gadget works well because there's no time to set up complex shots. It's imperative to evade the long-range blade attacks.

It's safer to quickfire the REC just after each evasive roll. Focus on Rā's al Ghūl's attacks and spend the remainder of the time avoiding them. Although many of Batman's shots may miss, the ones that get through still inflict plenty of damage.

Rā's al Ghūl uses two types of attacks here. His clones launch volleys of slow-moving shurikens, while the larger manifestation unleashes faster shurikens. Evade left and right at regular intervals to avoid slow-moving blades. Use sudden evasive rolls to dodge the faster attacks. Once enough charges hit Rā's al Ghūl, this phase of the fight ends.

During the next phase, be ready to counter as soon as Rā's al Ghūl emerges from the sand. Continue to counter as the assassin swings his weapon at Batman. When Rā's al Ghūl grows tired, unleash several attacks in succession.

A legion of Rā's al Ghūl clones leaps from the sand and attacks as one. Use the counterattack command as quickly as possible to stop the entire group before they land.

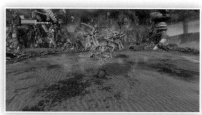

The remainder of this phase closely resembles the first phase of the fight (although Batman has many more targets to eliminate). Avoiding attacks is much more important than scoring hits.

When Rā's al Ghūl is the only target that remains, Batman can easily defeat him. Roll away from his attack, then evade back toward the assassin to beat him once more.

During this phase, Rā's al Ghūl takes more hits from the REC plus he uses a new attack. Instead of throwing the fast spinning blade, he uses his manifestation to clobber Batman with a massive sword. Failure to avoid this attack spells instant doom! Stay near the back of the area so that it's easier to see when the blades are approaching. Evade them while firing the REC repeatedly so that an occasional hit gets through the wall of mirror images. As before, it's better to dodge aggressively and fire often than to go for that one perfect shot!

Rā's al Ghūl descends into the sands once more. Counter his attacks when he rises, then launch a flurry of Batman's fists to stop him.

After another scene, Batman must knock Rā's al Ghūl away with a surprise attack. As such, Batman reprograms the Batarang so that it can be used as a Reverse Batarang. When it's ready, target Rā's al Ghūl and use the on-screen directions to lock onto the fiend. As soon as the lock-on is complete, release the Reverse Batarang and let the weapon do its job.

TIME TO MANUFACTURE A CURE

▪▪ PRIMARY OBJECTIVE: Force Mister Freeze to manufacture a cure made from Rā's al Ghūl's blood.

Batman has a sample of blood that he needs to deliver to Mister Freeze. It's time to get back to the GCPD building in the northeastern section of town.

LEAVING THE UNDERGROUND

⟫⟫ ⟫ GOAL: Return to the streets of Arkham City.

Reverse Batman's steps to leave the Chamber of the Demon. Use the old sewer entrance to revisit Wonder Avenue followed by a long run through the Wonder Tower Foundations. Meanwhile, Batman gives Oracle an update. The situation outside of Arkham City isn't that much better than it is inside, but people are doing everything they can to help.

Grapple from the southern side of the Wonder Tower Foundations up to the collapsed streets. Walk back to the room where Batman defeated all the thugs earlier and use the Line Launcher to get back across the gap nearby. Take the door that leads into the Subway Terminal to escape.

Use the Line Launcher to get back across the gap.

Thugs have retaken the subway tunnels, but they don't know Batman is in the area. There is a signal jammer within this group, so taking him out is a top priority. Hide in the subway cars until the wandering foe gets too close. Knock him out quietly and scan the rest of the station. There are five other targets, all armed!

116

OVER THE TOP

Defeat the guard with the backpack jammer device first.

Batman can defeat shielded enemies by utilizing aerial attacks. Set up the combos by employing a Cape Stun. This stunning move delays the thug from attacking, thus leaving him vulnerable. Next, double tap the Evade button to leap over the shield and knock down the target.

Also, the quickfire Explosive Gel works very well against shielded foes. Evade the enemies while dropping explosives nearby. Detonate the bombs afterward to knock down the thugs to make them drop their shields, making it much easier to knock them around.

Climb onto the side of a subway car and wait for some of the Penguin's thugs to investigate their downed comrade. At least one target will wander close to Batman. Dispose of him with stealth to make it much easier to grab anyone else in the area. Now it's time to take out the others. Start up to gain the advantage and lure an enemy away from his allies. Or, use aggressive techniques to plow through the enemies if battling armed guards isn't a problem. When the room is clear, leave via the western exit.

There are three enemies standing in the next hall and two of them are carrying heavy shields. Being that this is a new form of defense, some fresh tactics are needed during this encounter.

Some guards are carrying shields.

Continue west through the tunnels and over the subway cars. While crawling through the next section, Batman overhears even more thugs who are preparing for a shipment of weapons.

Approach from underneath the men's leader. He's the one wearing body armor, so getting a Takedown on him starts the fight off well. That leaves a mere dozen foes to beat up.

Surprise the leader of the group with a Takedown.

DIRTY DOZEN

There are a few foes wearing shields here, so focus on them first. Dodge through the throng, using explosives to

Try explosives to separate the guards from their shields.

knock their shields away before starting a major brawl. Once that happens, use attacks that make Batman move between targets. This builds his combo meter and makes it harder for enemies to connect with their own attacks.

Special Combo Takedowns are excellent for knocking out shield users. If Batman grabs the wrong target, so be it. Back off, start deploying explosives again and repeat the process.

Special Combo Takedowns work wonders on the shield users.

Use the Sequencer to unlock the doors on the northern side of the station. Once they're open, climb toward the surface and leave the subway. This happens just in the nick of time, because Hugo Strange has an announcement for everyone.

MAYOR QUINCY SHARP

REAL NAME Quincy Sharp

Occupation	Mayor of Gotham City
Based In	Gotham City
Eye Color	Blue
Hair Color	Gray
Height	5 Ft. 8 Inches
Weight	190 Lbs
First Appearance	Batman: Arkham Asylum [August 2009]

Attributes
-Intense dedication to "clean up" Gotham
-Pompous and old-fashioned in demeanor
-Focused on his own political aspirations

Quincy Sharp was the warden of Arkham Asylum on the night that the Joker broke free 18 months ago. Unknown to most, but discovered by Batman, Sharp suffered from a split personality disorder and had been committing atrocities in the asylum, believing himself to be possessed by the Spirit of Amadeus Arkham.

In reality, he was being influenced by Hugo Strange, who had provided Sharp with powerful mind control drugs that allowed him to manipulate Sharp's behavior, enabling him to plant the seed that led to the creation of Arkham City.

Hugo Strange used the evidence of the atrocities committed by Sharp as collateral to make sure that, whatever happened, Sharp must remain loyal to him.

TALK WITH MAYOR QUINCY

> >> >> **GOAL: Rescue the Mayor.**

Quincy Sharp isn't far from the subway station. Come topside but remain quiet. Many of the lone guards in the area are packing heat now, so stealth is of the utmost importance. Clear the ground of these enemies before exploring. There are larger melee fights to be had to the north, so that's a good place to go to gain experience. Otherwise, grapple higher and turn east to locate the Mayor.

Take this opportunity to earn some more experience.

Quincy is on the ground, being interrogated by a squad of armed goons. These guys are well deployed and will see Batman if he tries to get too close. Take cover during the approach and use the REC on a magnetic engine near the interrogators. This rips their weapons away, making the upcoming fight much safer. After the fight, take Mayor Quincy to safety and listen to a rather illuminating conversation.

Use the REC on the magnetic engine.

NO TIME LEFT: BACK TO THE GCPD!

>>> >> GOAL: Take the blood to Mister Freeze.

Run across town to the GCPD building (the one in the northeast corner). More of the Joker's men are guarding the structure, but only one is armed. Grapple to the rooftop and drop onto the armed guard to knock him out before anyone else can react. Afterward, it's a slugfest against shielded enemies and guys who are eager to toss propane tanks. Counter any of the thrown objects for a flashy way to deal damage and drop down to the ground if Batman needs time to set up an ambush.

There is still only one entrance to the old GCPD precinct. Use the REC to open the garage doors on the ground floor and slide underneath them. Ice has formed around the doors. Freeze must have made it here safely.

Once inside, enter the main room where Victor is working. Hand over the sample and see if there is anything that Mister Freeze can do with it. The scene continues, but the discussion doesn't go as well as it might. Before long, a fight breaks out.

REMOTE HIDEAWAY

The undercover cops in the Museum have an upgrade for Batman. Go to the door in the northwestern part of the building on the outside. Knock on the door; the people inside unlock it once they realize who it is.

Batman is allowed to enter the Iceberg Lounge without moving through the rest of the building. Talk to the cops inside to receive the Disruptor: Mine Detonator.

Mister Freeze has one weapon that is more powerful than his gun, suit or any of his other technology: it's his mind! This is a villain who understands tactics. He can adapt to Batman's techniques, so the key here is to stay one step ahead at all times. Ambush him again and again, but use different tricks each time.

There are several ways to stun Mister Freeze:

 Use the Disruptor on his suit and gun, then close in and attack.

 Walk away from Mister Freeze, let him follow, scamper to circle around behind the villain and attack with a Silent Takedown.

 Lure Victor over to one of the industrial electromagnets along the wall and hit the machine with the REC.

 Glide Kick the villain after luring him to the lower level of the room.

Walk over to the grates in the middle of the room and hide inside. When Mister Freeze approaches, use a Vent Takedown.

 Walk underneath a ledge and then rush up to the level above it. Use a Takedown when Victor comes to investigate.

 Explosive Gel won't work when it's used on the ground, but detonating the gel on a wall near Mister Freeze will stun him.

 Line Launcher attacks work just as they would against a common thug.

 Look for the exposed wires laying in a pool of water at the bottom of the room. Lure Freeze into the water and use the activation switch inside the room to make the wires hot and disable Victor's suit.

Note that in New Game Plus, you must perform 10 Takedowns against Mister Freeze. Here are two more:

 If Batman is crouched on one side of a window and Freeze passes close by it, Batman can dive through the window and perform a Takedown.

 Batman can perform a Drop Down Takedown by dropping on top of Mister Freeze from high above.

Be careful when using Detective Mode in the fight. If this is your second time through the game, Mister Freeze will start to jam Detective Mode when it's used for too long. Use each setup once and only once, then pound Mister Freeze every time that he is disabled. When his suit runs out of juice, the fight ends and Batman gets a projectile weapon called the Freeze Blast.

Now it's time to return to the Industrial District again. Nora Fries is there and, hopefully, Joker is still there, too.

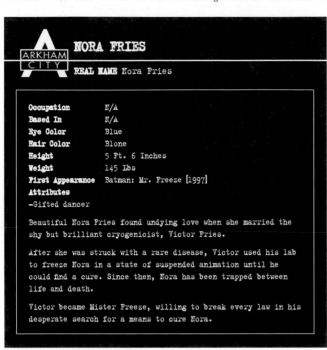

ⓐ NORA FRIES

REAL NAME Nora Fries

Occupation	N/A
Based In	N/A
Eye Color	Blue
Hair Color	Blone
Height	5 Ft. 6 Inches
Weight	145 Lbs
First Appearance	Batman: Mr. Freeze [1997]

Attributes
-Gifted dancer

Beautiful Nora Fries found undying love when she married the shy but brilliant cryogenicist, Victor Fries.

After she was struck with a rare disease, Victor used his lab to freeze Nora in a state of suspended animation until he could find a cure. Since then, Nora has been trapped between life and death.

Victor became Mister Freeze, willing to break every law in his desperate search for a means to cure Nora.

FREEZE BLASTS

If you've noticed areas with steam that Batman cannot bypass, then these sections require the Freeze Blast! This device stops the steam from hurting Batman for a short period of time, thus allowing him to get Riddler Trophies and access new areas.

RETRIEVE THE CURE

⠿ PRIMARY OBJECTIVE **Find Joker and take the cure back from him!**

Harley is exiting the GCPD building as fast as her legs can carry her. Lead Batman into the side hallway and use the Freeze Blast on both steam vents that block his way to the eastern exit. Make sure to throw the gadget into the vents instead of merely tossing them into the steam.

Duck underneath the gate beyond the vents, search the small office in back for a trophy, and then leave the building. A helicopter gets its spotlight on Batman, but fortunately it's a news chopper instead of a TYGER helicopter. Vicki Vale is onboard, but she's forced to leave the scene in a hurry. Pursuing Harley must wait; Vicki Vale is in trouble!

SAVING THE DAMSEL IN DISTRESS

>>> >> GOAL **Save Vicki Vale.**

Vale's helicopter is west of the GCPD building. Get to the rooftops and start pushing in that direction. It won't be long before armed thugs start to appear. These fiends are using sniper rifles to track the helicopter. If anything moves, they'll shoot. Vicki Vale is pinned down and she doesn't have any hope of making it out on her own.

There are two pairs of snipers to the east of the crash site. Both are safe to approach from the east. Grapple above these goons, sneak up to them, and use Silent Takedowns to avoid trouble.

Use Silent Takedowns on the snipers.

Once all four of the snipers are down, glide to the ground and look for Vicki Vale. Grapple her out of the area and speak to her.

PROCEED SOUTH ONCE AGAIN

>>> >> GOAL **Travel to the Steel Mill.**

Now that Vicki is safe, head toward the Steel Mill. Harley is already there, so there's no hope of catching her out in the open. To make matters worse, there are more snipers in the Industrial District. Avoid taking to the streets, as it's easier for snipers to spot Batman when he's out in the open. Instead, stay high and dive into the sharpshooters to start fights.

Be alert for snipers perched on the rooftops.

It isn't necessary to bring down every sniper in the Industrial District. Make a clear path for Batman, but aim for the top of the Steel Mill, where Batman accessed the building earlier in the night. Sadly, the smoke stack isn't available to anyone. As such, change directions and use the door on the south side of the Steel Mill.

There are several snipers above that doorway and more armed guards are down on the ground. Dispose of the snipers first, since they are higher up and will thwart all of Batman's efforts until they're eliminated. Start from the highest sniper and work down to the ones below. Afterward, look down on the large team of gunmen protecting the door.

Clear out the upper threats before dropping in on the guards below.

HASTE MAKES WASTE

Don't try to rush the door to the south-west. Batman can't slip through when there are still armed targets in the area. Play it slow and steady.

It's difficult to make a perfect predator run against so many foes. Most of the guards are located so close together that they'll notice if someone takes out one of their members. The safe and slow way is to use glide attacks, eliminate one gunmen right away, drop a Smoke Pellet, and then grapple back to the rooftops. Use Remote Batarangs prior to this to disable any guards who may be watching your intended victim. When the coast is clear, finish the door guards and enter the Steel Mill.

Drop in on the gunmen and quickly grapple away.

There are easier fights in the area if things get hairy.

LOW ON HEALTH?

If Batman gets low on health, then back off and attack any unarmed groups in the area. There are a couple of thugs in the western corner. It's also possible to go camera/balloon hunting. Destroying these items triggers a game save and helps Batman's health as well.

Take out a security camera or balloons to help Batman's health.

SNEAKING IN

>>> >> GOAL: **Use a combination of gadgets to find a back door to the Steel Mill.**

Several thugs are waiting inside the Steel Mill's cooling tunnels. A prompt explains how Batman can use the Freeze Blast as an in-battle gadget. Ambush the guards and try out the Freeze Blast once the fighting starts.

THE STEEL MILL

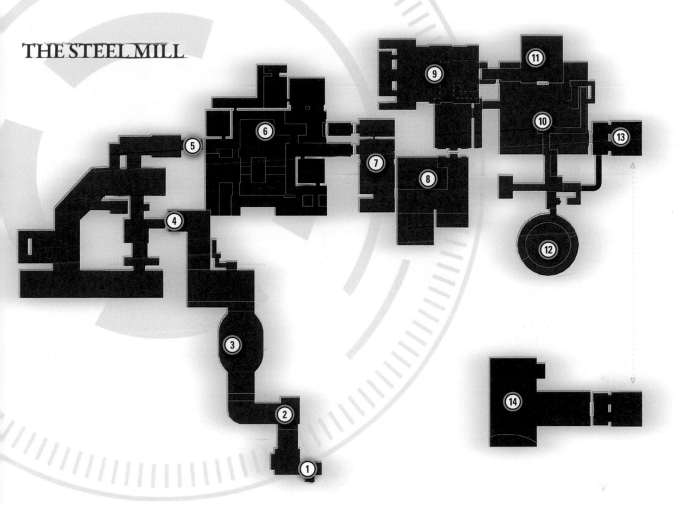

STEEL MILL	
1	Rear Entrance
2	Boiling Water (Cooling Tunnel B)
3	Large Series of Waterways
4	Door (Access Cooling Tunnel D)
5	Door Between Cooling Tunnels and Main Plant
6	Smelting Chamber (Obtain REC Here)
7	Office (Part of Assembly Line)
8	Assembly Line (Used to Avoid a Sniper)
9	The Joker's Fun House
10	Loading Bay (Crane Puzzle, Manager's Office Access)
11	Manager's Office
12	Waste Exchange (Chimney Access Early in Game)
13	Freight Elevator (Access to Boiler Room)
14	Boiler Room ("Hot and Cold" Side Mission)

FREE POINTS!

At this point in the game, Batman has access to a large number of gadgets to use in fights. If you have trouble incorporating multiple weapons into a skirmish, try using all of the gadgets at least once when the fight begins (before you try to accrue a combo and use special moves).

This way you won't have to break a combo or lose your combat flow just to work in a gadget that isn't essential to your tactics.

Advance along Cooling Tunnel B until Batman reaches a flow of steaming-hot water. To get underneath the barricade along the west wall, Batman needs some type of platform. Use the Freeze Blast to create a block of ice for Batman to float on. Hop onto it and then quickfire the Batclaw at the ring above the barrier. Pull the block along to get the ice moving, but stop using the Batclaw to make Batman duck. Momentum and the current carry the ice back underneath the barrier.

Fire the Batclaw again to make Batman pull his makeshift boat toward the northern wall in the next chamber. Climb to the top of the wall as soon as possible. Note that Batman can't create two ice blocks at the same time using the Freeze Blast.

Climb up the northern wall as soon as possible.

The next section of water is a bit more complex, as a large drill is operating in the middle of the flow. Slamming a vulnerable block of ice into that obstruction isn't a good idea.

Create a block of ice, drop onto it and use the Batclaw to drag the ice toward the side of the room. Shift from one ring to the next using the Batclaw to stay away from the drill until Batman passes by it. Then, grapple to the far wall and climb up.

Maneuver the ice around the big drill.

Open the vent up top and crawl through the small duct. Locate the walkway on the other side; stand over the water and look across the gap to find several hardy goons. They're only protected by a fragile pain of glass, so it's time to make a glorious entrance.

Glide through the room and smash the window while Batman kicks the first thug. Use gadgets to prevent anyone from activating the weapon container along the far wall. If a thug gets an assault rifle from the box, hit him with the Freeze Blast to buy some time to defeat more enemies.

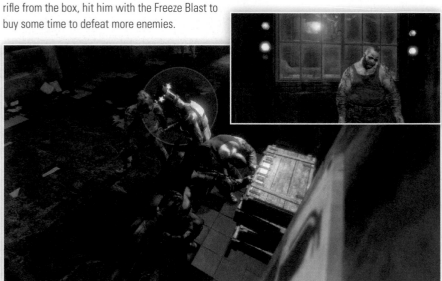

Keep the goons away from the gun racks.

MORE HARLEY TO LOVE

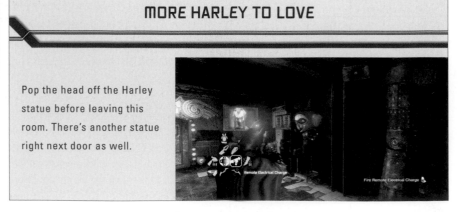

Pop the head off the Harley statue before leaving this room. There's another statue right next door as well.

A door leads Batman away from the previous encounter. There are two men in the adjoining chamber. Ambush them for a quick victory and consider saving the other goon they were interrogating. Use the button on the console to lower the hapless criminal.

Enter Detective Mode and examine the surroundings. Destroy a weak section of wall using Explosive Gel and walk up to the edge afterward. It's time to traverse another water section.

- Form an ice raft and drop onto it.
- Use the Batclaw to pull Batman toward the side wall.
- Switch to a ring and pull the ice block to the low ceiling.
- Release the Batclaw and duck underneath the barricade.

Blast the steam vent with ice.

- Use a quick Freeze Blast and drag Batman across the water.
- Climb onto the nearby ledge and peer through the gateway.
- Throw a Remote Batarang through the gate.

- Use the ring to the right to yank the ice block into a small side passage of water.
- Hop off the ice block and step onto a tiny ledge.
- Use the Line Launcher to shoot at the other side of the waterway.

- Maneuver the Batarang through an electrical current in the next room, turn it around and use the other gate on the right to reach a small chamber.

- Use the Remote Batarang to hit the electrical panel in that room while it's charged with electricity.

Once on safe ground, use the Freeze Blast to stop a steam vent and do it again around the next corner. Jump a series of pipes, and launch the Dark Knight into another puzzle. This time, there's more than water to contend with.

- The gates open and allow access to the next waterway.
- Create an ice block, drop onto it and pull Batman forward.
- Grapple up the right side of the room.

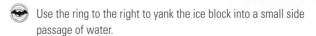

THE RETURN TRIP

There aren't many puzzles left, because Batman is almost back into the main portion of the Steel Mill. Use the Sequencer to open a gate in this area to move freely between the two sections of Cooling Tunnel D. This makes it easier to backtrack when you decide to hunt for Riddler Trophies.

LOOK OVER THERE!

Mines can be detonated remotely if you have completed the side mission "Remote Hideaway," which involves the undercover cops in the Museum.

Try to distract the three men at the bottom by detonating the mine next to them. All three start to look in the same direction, making them easy pickings when Batman drops behind them.

A DEADLY TRAP

>>> >> GOAL: Defeat Joker's men in the next room.

Cross the steel platform to the north. The last time Batman saw Joker he was in his office above the Loading Bay; it's worth trying to find him there again. While leaving Cooling Tunnel D, Batman runs into Dr. Stacy Baker. The doctor gives Batman more information, letting him know that the next area is mined.

Talk to Dr. Stacy Baker for some good intel.

Start by quickly taking out the leftmost guard.

Go through the doors and sneak along the catwalks in the smelting chamber. The guards here are armed, so a fair fight won't be in Batman's favor. Sneak up to the first man on the left walkway and dispose of him before he patrols within visual range of his ally. Take out the roving guard and use corner cover to hide. When his buddy arrives to investigate, silence him too. Make as much noise as possible with the guards so that their friends from above join the fray. Ambush them in the same manner to clear the upper part of the room.

Because the guards are facing each other on the bottom floor, it's somewhat difficult to ambush them. If detonating the mine next to the men isn't an option, use a combo of Batarang attacks to knock them all down. This provides a great opening to drop down and start fighting. Use the eastern door to leave the Smelting Chamber. The REC opens the two locked gates. From there, crawl through ducts to arrive at the Assembly Line.

A WELL PREPARED SNIPER

>>> >> **GOAL** Hide inside boxes to get behind a vigilant sniper.

A lone sniper has gone above and beyond the call of duty. He's deployed enough mines to make the Assembly Line impossible to safely traverse. On top of that, he has a great view of the office. Batman can't detonate the mines from there or do much of anything else.

Drop into the office and stay low for a moment. Use the Grapnel on the upper tier of the room when the sniper isn't looking, then drop past the fence into the side of the room. A conveyor belt is sending boxes around the perimeter of the area. Crawl into a box and wait for the conveyor to take Batman behind the sniper. Creep out, dispatch the goon, and continue forward.

The Assembly Line has been well mined.

Hide inside a box and let the conveyor belt deliver Batman to the sniper.

Creep through the remainder of the Assembly Line and enter the Loading Bay where several more of the Joker's men are waiting. Locate the two snipers standing side by side on a ledge above. Crawl into the room and get an angle to grapple beneath them. Hang beneath the window and employ a Double Takedown!

Perform a Double Takedown on the snipers.

OH, HARLEY!

Somebody went to a lot of effort and tied up Harley. She's attempting to escape her bonds in the upper part of the room. Why not ungag her and hear what she has to say? This opens a side mission called "Hot and Cold."

Drop immediately afterward to stop the three lower goons from arming themselves. Work with haste to dispose of them and fire the REC at the electro magnet if anyone grabs a gun. The magnet is in the center of the room, so you can't miss it. This disarms the group even if anyone finds a way to snag a weapon. After the fight, grapple up to Joker's office.

Use the electro magnet to disarm the guards.

ANOTHER HEAD FOR YOUR COLLECTION

Zap another Harley statue before exploring the Joker's office.

VISITING YOUR BEST OF FRIENDS

>> >> GOAL: Don't let the Joker get away!

The only door in the Joker's office leads into a large room with, you guessed it, the Joker. After a brief dialogue, the Dark Knight and his old nemesis decide to take it man to man.

BOSS FIGHT — THE JOKER & HIS MEN

During the first part of this fight, the Joker charges Batman and practically asks to be smacked around. Use any attacks in Batman's arsenal. After a couple of rounds, the Joker pleads for mercy.

Little trains of thugs arrive, bolstering the Joker's

spirits, and he attacks with renewed vigor. His minions aren't armored, but some of them have bladed weapons. Take out the armed foes first.

Eventually, Mister Hammer comes out to play. He makes everything more difficult because of his long range and high damage. You should decide immediately whether or not to focus all of Batman's attacks on Mister Hammer to eliminate him right away, or whether to avoid him. The middle ground is a worthless option.

It's easier to avoid Mister Hammer and work on thinning the guards, but there is a downside. A TITAN thug joins the Joker's men as well. Fighting Mister Hammer and the TITAN thug simultaneously is quite tricky.

Use the big guy to your advantage if you get the chance.

When using special combo attacks, target regular enemies instead of just throwing out the maneuvers on a whim. Hitting the Joker with a special move is a waste because he'll counter it and break Batman's combos. Make the most of each special attack by disabling groups of enemies or by automatically knocking out one of the thugs.

Avoid the train tracks when the signal bells start to chime. The Joker's trains scream through the station, knocking aside everything in their path. In fact, try to lure enemies onto the tracks to thin the enemy herd!

All of these enemies fight using similar tactics from previous encounters. The challenge is that there are multiple foes attacking simultaneously. Batman can't afford to take hits, so err on the side of defense. Evade away from Mister Hammer when he starts swinging and stay far away from the TITAN thug until it's time to finish the job. Even in victory there are several complexities. After an important scene, the next chapter begins and Batman must turn his attention to Protocol 10!

SAVE THE PEOPLE OF ARKHAM CITY

PRIMARY OBJECTIVE: Stop Hugo Strange from completing Protocol 10.

As Batman leaves the wreckage from his battle, helicopters throughout the area begin a full-on assault of Arkham City. They're launching missile strikes all over the place. Batman needs to find the TYGER Master Control Program. It's the only way to get inside Wonder Tower and stop these attacks!

FIND THE CODE

>>> >> **GOAL:** Scan the TYGER helicopters to locate the Master Control Program.

Bring Batman back into the city and explore the districts while scanning TYGER choppers. Batman must get fairly close to make an accurate scan, but try to avoid a helicopter's spotlights. If a pilot sees Batman, he'll use the chopper's guns to attack. Drop a Smoke Pellet and flee if this happens. Batman must scan a number of vehicles to find the correct code. Make sure to stay still while scanning and move onward if the code isn't detected.

Drop a Smoke Pellet and flee if a chopper spots Batman.

When the scanner turns green, that means the primary helicopter has been found and the code is present. Grapple up to the chopper and download the code.

GAIN ACCESS TO THE RESTRICTED AREA

>>>> >> GOAL: **Break into the Security Yard on the western side of Wonder Tower.**

Drop from the chopper and glide toward the western side of the restricted area. Using the code, Batman can get through the main gate there. Stay high and bring down the snipers surveying the area by the gate. It's possible to drop behind the snipers and knock them out using stealth. Hack the console behind the gunmen and enter the door.

STUN STICKS ARE DANGEROUS WEAPONS

A stun stick is capable of blocking Batman's attacks. They're great tools for attacking because Batman can't counter their blows as easily. Aerial attacks are extremely effective against stun stick guards. Batman can attack normally when he's behind these men.

The route through the corridors is damaged, so Batman must switch levels soon. Walk down the first corridor and open the next door using the REC. Drop to the lower level from there and use the REC on another door. This leads to the processing area, which is where Bruce Wayne was taken early in the game by TYGER guards.

Explosive Gel is also an option when fighting enemies with stun sticks. When quickfired, the gel knocks down the guards down and makes them release their stun sticks.

There are three guards here that must be disabled before anything else can be done. One man has an assault rifle, while the other two sport stun sticks.

Hit the armed guard from behind and wade into the two stun stick users. Blast them away from each other using Explosive Gel, then knock the guys out before they can recover.

Strange sends in another wave of his security forces into the yard. After Strange explains his actions, a larger fight begins with about a dozen guards. Some have shields, while others have stun sticks or lighter melee weapons. When the reinforcements arrive, one foe comes to battle wearing body armor.

Evade over Stun Stick thugs and strike them from behind to avoid being shocked

Ⓐ Ⓐ Ⓧ Evade and Strike Backwards

There are two crates of rifles in the yard as well, so make sure no one slips over to get them. Fight near one of the crates so that at least that weapon isn't easily accessible.

USE WEAKNESS TO DEFEAT STRENGTH

The easiest way to beat this powerful group is to exploit their weakest members. Instead of attacking the guards with shields, armor, or stun sticks directly, focus on the more vulnerable TYGER guards. Use them to score combo points, then unleash Special Combo Takedowns against the units with better equipment.

Any guards who secure assault rifles are best eliminated in this manner, although it's also worthwhile to use the Disarm and Destroy technique if possible. This prevents future enemies from picking up the downed enemy's gun.

After the fight, search the area to find a couple of hidden Riddler secrets. When done, crouch and use the manhole in the yard to reach the Collapsed Streets.

START AT THE BOTTOM

> >> >> GOAL: **Gain Access to Wonder Tower.**

Head down the main tunnel upon entering the Collapsed Streets. Drop to the bottom of a damaged floor and examine the eastern chamber. The room is large and mostly destroyed by age and water damage, meaning there aren't many good floors or ledges to stand on.

Use the Line Launcher to slide south across the gap and fire it again midway to reach a ledge on the northeastern corner.

Jump and cling to the red ledge above. Shimmy hand over hand to the right and leap into another room at the end of the route. Use a Batarang on the question mark on the ceiling, then destroy the floor below using Explosive Gel.

Toss a Batarang at the question mark above.

Batman falls into a lower chamber with another Riddler Trophy. Grab the trophy and exit the room. The door leads back into the Wonder Tower Foundations, where Fiona is still hiding. Talk to her before entering the main room.

Eight armed guards arc protecting the tower's foundation. They have the best weapons possible: shotguns, assault rifles and sniper rifles. The patrols can spot almost anything in the room, so no place is safe. These guys can see the gargoyles, the floor, and most of the corners. You can run through this place any way that you like, but here is a reliable method.

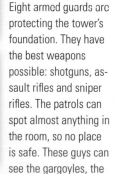

⚫ Wait by the entrance and use Detective Mode to watch the gunmen.

⚫ One man walks to the western side of the foundations. After this lone patroller turns south, drop behind him and knock the guard out silently.

⚫ Use stealth to reach the northern end of the room and grapple/glide behind the sniper.

⚫ Once Hugo alerts his men, use hit-and-run tactics against individuals.

WATCH THE MINES

Use Detective Mode to locate any mines. Walking over one will cause damage and alert the guards to Batman's presence. Try to use the Disruptor on them and let the mines become a distraction. Have guards look the wrong way to expose their backs.

When the security force is disabled, approach the main elevator. The TYGER console has wicked encryption, so keep searching for a viable combination if the first word doesn't work. The password is "Obsessions." Get into the elevator and use a second console to send it up toward Wonder Tower.

The encryption on the Security Panels is much improved.

ALL THE WAY UP

▶▶▶ ▶▶ GOAL: **Breach the Wonder Tower observation deck.**

Ride the elevator to the top, but grapple onto the roof of the machine when it stops. TYGER guards blast everything when the elevator doors open and Batman is much safer up above.

Immediately grapple to the roof when Batman reaches the top.

Creep over the guards and look down on their position. These foes bring a mix of stun sticks, assault rifles, and regular troops. Ambush the squad and immediately start building a combo against the lighter troops. Use a Special Combo Takedown against the leader or one of the stun stick wielders. Repeat this technique and finish off any stragglers.

USE BEATDOWNS FOR EASY COMBO POINTS

If the enemies back away from the guard wearing body armor, use him to rack up some combo points. Start a Beatdown with a stun followed by regular attacks. This builds up so many points that it's possible to use a Special Combo Takedown on anyone who approaches. You don't even have to finish off the armored guard to make this happen.

Hack the console on the platform and input "Safeguarding" as the password. Due to the high security, it's essential to hold the controls for a few extra seconds while the Sequencer cracks the final letter of the code. Don't let go until the password is fully entered.

Make sure the password is accepted before releasing.

A narrow ledge leads past the security gate. Climb down and grab it, then hang and traverse the ledge until Batman is on the north side of the tower. Drop onto a small platform below and walk onto a rod with transformers on its terminus. Grapple to another ledge high above. A thin railing is suspended beside the ledge, so jump to it.

Walk onto the rod to get a better angle.

NOT TOO FAST, NOT TOO SLOW

That railing is hard to land on. Without some momentum, Batman will fall just short of the goal. However, it's possible to jump twice as long as you push forward when Batman lands on the railing. To avoid this, stop moving just as Batman is about to touch down.

Walk along the railing until Batman gets to the end. Grapple up and then again to another rail. Take this ledge to a ladder and climb it to the summit

DON'T JUMP!

Do not jump down the elevator shaft at the top of the ladder. The bottom of the shaft is where Batman entered the tower, so falling all the way down is a massive waste of time.

Now glide across the shaft and use railings and wires to maneuver around the tower's outer perimeter. One more use of the Grapnel gets Batman into a private elevator room. Hack its console and enter "Maintenance" as the password. A hatch opens at the top of the room.

Take the hatch and move through the ductwork, another outdoor area, and a second duct. After climbing into the last duct, Batman bumps into a damaged wall. Blow through it to enter another room.

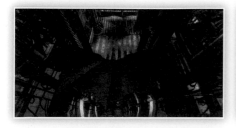

Use the ductwork to reach the Observation deck.

THE OBSERVATION DECK

>> >> >> GOAL: **Defeat the security forces; find Hugo Strange.**

Armed security forces are patrolling the Observation Deck. These guys are moderately spread out. Getting a perfect grouping of stealthy knockouts is very difficult, but disposing of all them isn't a tough task.

Use the room's crates for cover and let the first guard patrol near Batman, then knock that gunman out. Hugo notices after a time and alerts his men; make sure to be elsewhere before that happens. Circle around and hit mobile guards from the rear when they go to examine the first downed man.

When all the guards are gone, hack into the console outside of Hugo Strange's quarters and enter the password.

NOT A GREAT BOSS TO HAVE

Stay out of Strange's line of sight at all costs. He's in an internal room at the top of the tower. If he sees Batman, he'll alert his troops.

THE CONCLUSION

PRIMARY OBJECTIVE: **Race to the theater and stop the Joker.**

The Joker has the potential to learn very powerful secrets. Stopping him is important for Gotham and—perhaps—for the entire world. What's more, the Joker has a hostage, which makes everything more difficult.

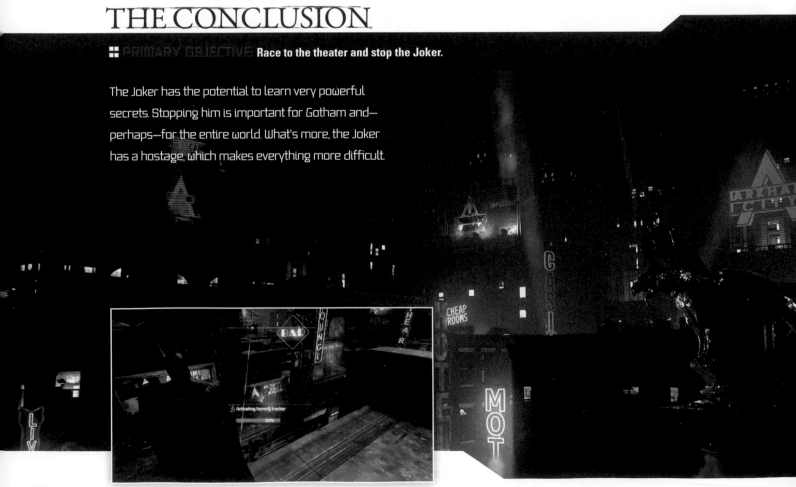

WHERE IS JOKER HIDING NOW?

>>> >> GOAL Knock out the snipers near the theater.

Fortunately, Talia activated a tracker back at the Steel Mill. The Joker has moved to the theater, northeast from the Ace Chemicals building. But don't approach the area on foot. There are so many snipers scouring the street that an army couldn't make it through the front doors.

Start west of Ace Chemicals. The snipers are more spread out over there and they won't notice a southern approach as long as the timing is good. Sneak up on the snipers when they're not looking and start knocking people out.

Sneak up behind the snipers when their aim is away from Batman.

ALTERNATE STRATEGY

The Remote Batarang is an ideal gadget for this whole affair. There are often multiple snipers who can see one another's positions. When one spots Batman, even more snipers will turn to fire on that position. Speed and Smoke Pellets might not be enough.

Instead, look for the laser beams that crisscross the area. Find a sniper and see if there are beams pointing in that man's direction. Now determine which sniper is watching his buddy. Hit that foe with a Remote Batarang, take out the nearby sniper nearby and flee before the stunned sniper can get his weapon back.

Leave the two snipers by the theater entrance for last. When they're isolated, leap down on them and use gadgets to stun them.

INSIDE THE THEATER

>>> >> GOAL Defeat Clayface and get the cure.

Enter the theater and watch the next cutscene. Batman gets a glimpse of the cure, but it's soon grabbed by a powerful enemy. To retrieve it, Batman must defeat Clayface!

During his double axe sweep, Clayface forms a crude weapon out of his arms and sweeps them across the room from one side to the other.

CLAYFACE

REAL NAME Basil Karlo

Occupation	Professional Criminal
Based In	Gotham City
Eye Color	Black
Hair Color	None
Height	8 Ft. 2 Inches
Weight	410 Lbs
First Appearance	Detective Comics #40 [June 1940]

Attributes
- Can mimic anything and anyone
- Extremely difficult to injure or contain

Horror film icon Basil Karlo went mad when he uncovered plans for his most classic film to be remade with a different actor in the lead role. He took on the mark of the film's villain, Clayface, and killed several of the remake's cast and crew before being stopped by Batman and Robin.

Later, Karlo stole and injected himself with experimental compounds that transformed him into a mass of living clay who can alter his composition to mimic anything...or anyone.

Less often, Clayface leaps forward in an attempt to slam into Batman directly. Like the others, use evade to avoid taking damage. In this case, it's better to evade backward instead of dodging side to side.

Stay at medium range during the first phase of the fight. Clayface has four types of attacks, and none are easy to counter at close range. His most basic attack is a combination of punches. These are telegraphed by a blue indicator above the boss, meaning they can be countered. Either evade or counter the attacks to avoid taking damage.

Finally, Clayface will roll into a ball and spin around the room. Evade while standing somewhat close to a wall to stop the ball. Luring Clayface into a corner causes him to take massive damage because there are explosives at all four edges of the room.

In between these attacks, have Batman quickfire Freeze Blasts into the boss. These don't do much damage by themselves, but over time they add up. When Clayface is badly wounded, he slows down. Charge into him and beat the foe until Batman rips the sword from his back. Then, have Batman slash the brute down.

This stage is similar to the first one, but this time Clayface brings his best moves to the fight. The setup to his hammer swing resembles the axe swing, but don't make the mistake of trying to evade. This will only get Batman nailed in the head. Instead, crouch and crawl underneath the hammers.

The boss also spins around on occasion and tosses clay bits at everything in sight. Crouch if the clay is flying high, but evade if it's low. The other trick is to wait until the spin starts, because Clayface takes a moment to get going and evading prematurely is worthless.

His rolling attack is slightly more dangerous during this stage because Clayface can bounce off walls and make a second attempt to hit Batman. Use this against him by lining up a path toward explosives if Clayface avoids them the first time.

During the next phase of the fight, Batman falls onto a lower stage of the theater. Clayface is so badly squashed that he can't reform right away. Blobs of animated clay rise instead, attacking Batman with slow movements that can be countered.

Slash through the clay men. Clayface won't appear until Batman destroys a number of his offspring. As soon as he reforms, prepare to evade. Clayface spits a large ball at Batman. After dodging aside, quickfire a Freeze Blast into the boss to knock him back down. Hit Clayface as soon as his mouth opens.

This sequence repeats several times, but there are more blobs each time around. In his second manifestation, he spits at Batman twice. In his third, he spits three times.

Keep hurling Freeze Blasts into Clayface when he rises, then approach the boss when he fully freezes over again. Rip the cure from Clayface and watch the scenes afterward.

Completing the game unlocks New Game +, so you can go back through the story with all of your gadgets and upgrades. The enemies get harder during the second playthrough, though, so the challenge is still quite engaging!

Note that after this fight, you can continue to play the game as Batman and collect all remaining Riddler Trophies and complete all outstanding Side Missions.

A GIRL'S GOTTA HAVE FUN

Catwoman's episodes are part of *Batman: Arkham City* DLC that covers four episodes that take place from Catwoman's perspective in the game's main story. The DLC occurs during and after Batman's trials in Arkham City. Once purchased, the episodes are available at the game's Main Menu.

EPISODE #1

■■ PRIMARY OBJECTIVE: Break into Two-Face's home and crack his safe.

BREAKING IN

>>> >> >>>>>> GOAL: Knock out six thugs and crack the safe.

In this episode, which takes place before the main story begins, Catwoman is breaking into a house. The safe in this house has something that Catwoman needs. Six thugs are milling about, ready to fight. It's time for Catwoman to show these baddies who's the boss! A standard complement of strikes and counters will suffice in this instance. Drop all of the goons and crack the safe to end Episode #1.

The Special Combo Takedown is still extremely effective.

Crack the safe and watch the scene that follows.

CATWOMAN EPISODE 2

:: PRIMARY OBJECTIVE: Get Poison Ivy's help to break into the confiscated goods vault.

This episode takes place early in the game around the time when Batman is starting his investigation into Arkham City.

GETTING CATWOMAN'S EQUIPMENT

> **>> >> GOAL:** Go to Catwoman's safehouse and find the stash of equipment.

Catwoman starts this episode in Park Row, southwest of the courthouse. Swing from building to building using her whip and climb to the top of each. Move northeast, past the courthouse and look for her safehouse (it gets marked on the in-game map).

Refer to the in-game map to find Catwoman's safehouse.

Several thugs are standing in the alley beneath the safehouse. Dispose of them, if you want, and climb to the roof. Catwoman can slip through hatches in certain areas and, fortunately, the roof has a cage with hatches. Simply follow the on-screen instructions and watch as Catwoman clings to the ceiling underneath. Ambush the guards below to take them out.

The safehouse is nearby. Use Thief Vision (the equivalent of Batman's Detective Mode) to spot the blue cat claw marks on the side of the building. Approach these and enter the safehouse.

Catwoman gears up with her Caltrops and Bolas.

NEW GEAR!

Try out this new gear before going any further. Catwoman's toys are a little different from Batman's. The  Bolas seem like they should function similar to Batarangs, but they're actually heavier and, as such, a bit trickier to use. When Quickfired, they can tie up a target for a short period of time and take them out of a fight.

The Caltrops are ground traps that hamper movement for anyone who walks over them. They're perfect for leading groups  into an ambush. Catwoman is unaffected by them; she can deploy up to three groups of them before or during a fight!

There is a modest group of enemies to the east, which is on the way to Ivy's place. Try out Catwoman's new equipment on them to get a feel for their usability.

FOLLOW THE SCENT OF HENCHMEN

> >> >> **GOAL:** Enter Ivy's lair.

Continue toward Ivy's home, which is marked on the in-game map. Three gunmen guard the outer entrance. Latch onto the edge of the roof and use  a Ledge Takedown to eliminate the first enemy. Stay around the corner and use Catwoman's whip (it's similar to the Batclaw) to bring him closer. Knock him out with a Ground Takedown, then do the same thing for the final guard.

Get onto the walkway that leads to Ivy's front door. When prompted, follow the commands to go underneath the walkway. By following this approach, Catwoman skirts the locked gate ahead. Crawl underneath the gate and pop back up through a hatch. Enter through the front door to continue.

Climb up here to gain access to Ivy's lair.

FIGHT TO REACH IVY

> >> >> **GOAL:** Get to the top of Ivy's lair.

Ivy isn't terribly happy to see Catwoman. After a short cutscene, Catwoman ends up at the bottom of Ivy's lair surrounded by hormone-addled  thugs. Dispose of them, quickly get to the ceiling and climb to the next level.

There are four guards on the first floor, five more on the second, and even more thugs on the third floor. These men don't pose much of a problem, but there is a larger threat up top. Poison Ivy has trained her plants to fire spores! This happens even when thugs are attacking, so stay mobile at all times. This episode ends after defeating the final goon.

Defeat all the thugs to end this episode.

EPISODE #3

:: PRIMARY OBJECTIVE: Break into the confiscated goods vault and steal a fortune

This episode takes place when Batman assaults the
Steel Mill for the second time.

GET TO THE VAULT

>>> >> GOAL: Travel west to reach the confiscated goods vault.

Crawl out the vent
and start leaping
between buildings.
The confiscated
goods vault is in Park
Row. Three guards
are guarding a man-
hole cover, so try to
ambush them from the
rooftops and leap down into their midst.

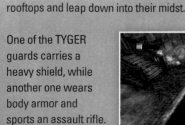

Exit Ivy's lair via this hatch.

One of the TYGER
guards carries a
heavy shield, while
another one wears
body armor and
sports an assault rifle.
The third foe is not
as prepared. Disrupt
the armored goon with

After the fight, enter the manhole to continue.

a Bola, then smack the shield user with an Aerial Attack. Eliminate the
empty-handed thug and perform a Beatdown on the armored attacker.

STEAL INTO THE VAULT

>>> >> GOAL: Sneak into the vault.

Follow the sewer
tunnels to find the
broken vault wall. Use
the door to enter the
computer console
room. After Catwoman
examines the monitors,
she devises a plan.

Quietly steal three security cards from the TYGER guards near the vault.

STAY OUT OF SIGHT

This isn't an easy task! The men in the vault area can lock down the
security system almost instantly. If anyone spots Catwoman before
she pickpockets the cards, the game is up!

Use the ceilings in the next room to explore while watching the guards. Use Thief Vision to learn the routes of the patrolling trio.

Openings in the walls allow Catwoman to proceed without being exposed.

SMART PURSUIT

Never pursue a guard when he's near the main vault door. There are two stationary guards here and they can see everything that moves!

Each guard carries one key card. To steal the cards, approach each man from behind and perform what would otherwise be a Silent Takedown. Catwoman won't knock out the guards, as that would trigger an alert.

The green glow signifies the presence of a key card.

Use the holes in the ductwork to get around the area and avoid detection by the guards. Always watch the guards in other areas before dropping to the ground and make sure

Stay on the ceiling whenever possible.

no one in the distance can see Catwoman before she creeps up on a guard.

Take all three cards back to the computer console and use them to open the vault. Unfortunately, this alerts the guards so stay on the ceiling while making stealthy attacks on the patrollers. Don't go after anyone in the main hallway, as the two vault guards will likely spot Catwoman.

Instead, pick off targets on the periphery. When it's time to hit the guy in the middle of the hall, use Catwoman's whip to pull him over out of the guards' visual range. When the patrollers are down, the final two men will split up. Silently take them down and open the vault door.

Enter the vault and take the briefcases, but watch out for an ambush. After the fight, pick up the briefcases again and leave the vault. Note that there is a choice to make along the way.

There are a variety of thugs inside the vault, some shielded and some unarmed.

EPISODE #4

∷ PRIMARY OBJECTIVE: Get Catwoman's loot!

This episode takes place after the end of the normal game.

BACK TO THE SAFEHOUSE

>>> >> GOAL: Retrieve Catwoman's loot from her safehouse.

After a short cutscene, proceed to the northeast of the courthouse to reach Catwoman's safehouse. After another short scene, it's time to fight several of Two-Face's thugs. They're a fairly tough group, despite having somewhat weak weapons. Be very aggressive with counters to avoid taking too much damage. Catwoman interrogates the last conscious enemy. Now it's time to visit the Museum to get her things.

TAKE IN SOME CULTURE

>>> >> GOAL: Keep following the loot.

Travel southwest to the Museum. Beware of several men outside the entrance; dispose of them and go inside. More enemies await near the first room, too. Wade through those thugs and try to attain a nice combo in the process.

Run through the Museum until Catwoman reaches the arena. There are over a dozen thugs prepared to stop her progress. Some have bladed weapons, while others come with heavy shields. Build up

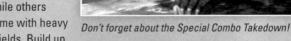

Don't forget about the Special Combo Takedown!

combos, like the Special Combo Takedown, and stay on the move to make short work of these foes.

Use all the non-shielded enemies to build up combos.

Slide underneath another gate to leave the arena and climb to the highest floor in the hallway. Continue to the torture chamber (the flooded room). Although it may seem like there's nowhere to go, there is definitely a way through.

1. Crawl underneath the ledge at the front of the room.

2. Use the hatch on the right to get back onto the ledge.

3. Jump to the ceiling.

4. Crawl along the grating on the ceiling.

5. Drop back down at the northern end of the chamber.

Use Takedowns against the gunmen above to lure them away from Two-Face. Note that even if you defeat all of his thugs, Two-Face will call in reinforcements. Once he's isolated, pound him with melee attacks. It takes five attacks (either Takedowns or full Beatdowns) to smash Two-Face to the ground and end the episode.

When Two-Face's allies return, flee to the shadows and lose the gunmen as soon as possible.

The last room is filled with gunmen. Three are down at the bottom of the chamber, while the others are closer to Harvey Dent. Get low to eliminate the three stragglers; they're not close to one another, making it easier to take them down without alerting their buddies.

THE HERO GOTHAM NEEDS

This chapter reveals the 12 side missions that are available in *Batman: Arkham City*. These incidental stories don't affect how the main game is played out, but you do get to help quite a few people in the process. Completing these missions also unlocks many Trophies/Achievements, plus the missions are just plain fun! A number of major characters featured in these side missions don't otherwise appear in the game. Lastly, this is also a great way to obtain a couple of gadget upgrades like the Freeze Grenades and the Mine Disruptor!

SPOILER ALERT!

Some of the information in this chapter could be considered "spoilers," so you have been warned! An attempt has been made to avoid revealing too much, but it's impossible to conceal some of the characters involved in these activities.

FRAGILE ALLIANCE

AVAILABILITY: After suiting up as Batman   **GOAL:** Destroy six TITAN containers.   **REWARD:** Bane Trophy

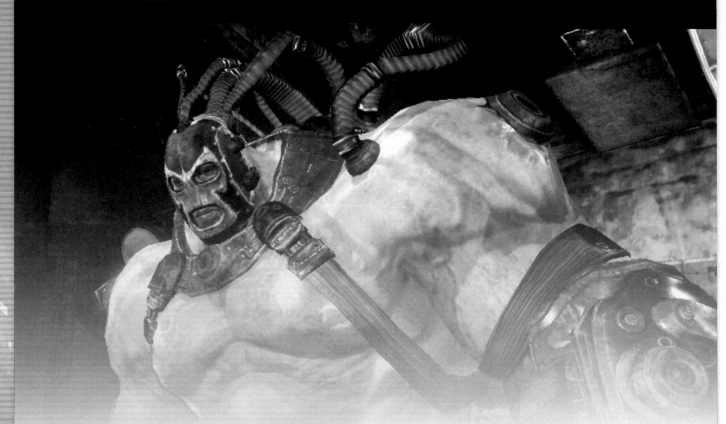

SOMEONE'S IN TROUBLE

A distress flare appears when Batman enters the streets of Arkham City after completing the events in the courthouse. Grapple from one building to the next to reach the other side of the city. Look for the small structure with the giant toy bear and the neon Krank Co. Toys sign on the roof. Once inside, talk to the person to initiate the mission "Fragile Alliance." Batman is tasked with destroying all hidden containers of TITAN in Arkham City. Note that the in-game map is updated to reveal their locations.

FINDING THE TANKS

The locations of all the TITAN tanks are listed here for easy reference. Note that in some cases there may be enemy presence nearby, so take that into consideration when destroying the tanks.

TITAN tank #1 is out in the open near the Museum. Expect armed guards to protect it.

TITAN tank #2 is beneath Gotham in an old subway tunnel. Blow it up shortly after leaving the subway station; it's in a side tunnel accessible after climbing over some trains.

TITAN tank #3 is found by exploring the Museum; search the War Room for it.

TITAN tank #4 is inside the ground floor door of the Steel Mill. It's positioned near one of the Harley statues.

TITAN tank #5 is outside the Steel Mill. Look in a recessed yard at the southwestern part of the Industrial District. Be on the lookout for a few guards.

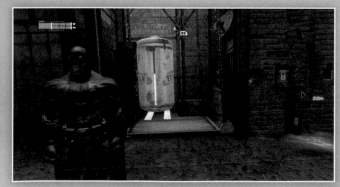

TITAN tank #6 is in Wonder Tower Foundation. Look for it on the second floor and blow it to pieces.

NEXT STEPS

After destroying all the containers, return to the hideout and talk to Bane. Enemies interrupt the conversation, so it's time to fight! Bane isn't the most graceful fighter; in fact, his attacks can inflict damage to Batman. Stay far away from Bane while fighting.

When the fight becomes more manageable, switch to the Batclaw and pull guards away from the fray and knock them out. After the fight, talk to Bane and destroy the TITAN containers in the side room before leaving the area. This completes the side mission and unlocks a Bane Trophy.

THROUGH THE LOOKING GLASS

JOIN THE PARTY, BATMAN

After rescuing Vicki Vale, look on the map. Alfred has set up a beacon where a cure has been deployed. A Bat-Vault is in that location, so grapple across the city to access the pod. There are gunmen on the roof. Knock them out before doing anything with the pod. Unleash a flying attack to bring down one of the enemies before the others can react. Deploy a Smoke Pellet and use cover to lure the others toward Batman. Stun them with Batarangs and finish them off.

Approach the pod and use it to "take the cure." Batman is soon placed under an enemy's control. After a cutscene, tap the controller quickly to break free.

Soon after, a fight ensues with men who are poorly armed. Use standard counters to dispose of them. Each time the Mad Hatter appears, focus all attacks on him. Eventually, he collapses and the remaining thugs disappear. Hit the Mad Hatter once again to escape from this nightmare.

IDENTITY THEFT

AVAILABILITY: After the events at the Museum.

GOAL: Scan evidence around three bodies and confront a killer.

REWARD: Hush Trophy

VICTIM №1

After Batman leaves the Subway for the first time, he learns about a murder victim in the southwestern portion of the city. Tucked away in an alley is a man with his face removed and his head wrapped in bandages.

Inmate: Wonder Tower? Who cares about that old crap. It's an eyesore.

Scan this body and the blood next to the corpse to learn more about the crime.

Follow the blood trail to a political prisoner, on the other side of the building. The man is a witness. Talk to him and learn more about the killer.

VICTIM №2

The second corpse is located north of the Ace Chemicals building in a narrow alleyway. Go there and scan the dropped knife to find a fingerprint. Don't forget to scan the victim, too!

Refer to the in-game map for the location of victim #2.

VICTIM №3

The third victim is located south of the Ace Chemicals building. Search the area around this body. Scan the man's head and examine the chemical sample near the victim's foot. It turns out the chemical is bleach, so follow that trail. Take the path to the western edge of Park Row, but stay in Detective Mode to remain on the path.

The trail eventually leads to a goon. Interrogate him and head toward the courthouse. A small building northeast of there is the Identity Thief's hideout. Find the door enter it.

Batman: You killed that man and dumped his body back there. Why did you take his face?

Listen to a recorded journal inside the hideout to shed some light on the situation. Watch what happens next and use the Sequencer on a console inside the room. Input "**Mockingbird**" to leave the building.

Doctor Thomas Elliot: I couldn't have put it better myself. I take it you're here to stop me?

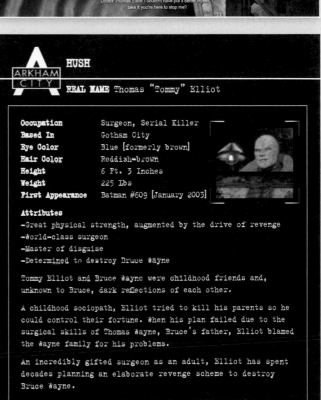

HUSH

REAL NAME Thomas "Tommy" Elliot

Occupation	Surgeon, Serial Killer
Based In	Gotham City
Eye Color	Blue [formerly brown]
Hair Color	Reddish-brown
Height	6 Ft. 3 Inches
Weight	225 Lbs
First Appearance	Batman #609 [January 2003]

Attributes
-Great physical strength, augmented by the drive of revenge
-World-class surgeon
-Master of disguise
-Determined to destroy Bruce Wayne

Tommy Elliot and Bruce Wayne were childhood friends and, unknown to Bruce, dark reflections of each other.

A childhood sociopath, Elliot tried to kill his parents so he could control their fortune. When his plan failed due to the surgical skills of Thomas Wayne, Bruce's father, Elliot blamed the Wayne family for his problems.

An incredibly gifted surgeon as an adult, Elliot has spent decades planning an elaborate revenge scheme to destroy Bruce Wayne.

HEART OF ICE

WHERE IS NORA?

Mister Freeze needs to find his wife and he thinks she's somewhere in the Industrial District. To get things started, refer to the text on the map where it reads Industrial District. Go north from the middle of "Industrial" and head for the waterline. Use the Freeze Blast to make an ice block and jump onto it. Locate the ring and pull the block toward the wall.

Refer to the map for the exact location.

Use Explosive Gel to blast through a weakened section of the wall. Inside the new area is a doorway; go ahead and enter that door.

MAKE SURE SHE'S SAFE

Nora is guarded by a handful of goons, some sporting body armor and others with heavy shields or blades. Sneak underground via a duct system and perform a Takedown on one of them to start the fight. Also, use Disarm and Destroy on shield thugs right away and employ the REC to blow away armored thugs to gain some breathing room.

Use special moves to bring down the body armor/shield enemies without resorting to slower moves like aerial attacks!

After the fight, it's time to return to Mister Freeze in the GCPD building and let him know that Nora is safe. Use the eastern entrance back into the GCPD building. Jump off the roof and glide around to the hole in the structure. Freeze Blast to get by the steam vents to return to Mr. Freeze's lab and tell Victor where he can find his wife.

NORA FRIES

ARKHAM CITY

REAL NAME Nora Fries

Occupation	N/A
Based In	N/A
Eye Color	Blue
Hair Color	Blone
Height	5 Ft. 6 Inches
Weight	145 Lbs
First Appearance	Batman: Mr. Freeze [1997]

Attributes
-Gifted dancer

Beautiful Nora Fries found undying love when she married the shy but brilliant cryogenicist, Victor Fries.

After she was struck with a rare disease, Victor used his lab to freeze Nora in a state of suspended animation until he could find a cure. Since then, Nora has been trapped between life and death.

Victor became Mister Freeze, willing to break every law in his desperate search for a means to cure Nora.

FAST TRAVEL

Unlock the console on the wall using the password **Frozenbait** to enter and leave the building without taking the watery way around.

WATCHER IN THE WINGS

AVAILABILITY: Any time except for late in the game.

GOAL: Find Azrael several times in Arkham City.

REWARD: Azrael Trophy

OMINOUS PORTENT

Once Batman is free to explore Arkham City, look for a fierce man on top of various buildings. Each time you find Azrael, he scratches a symbol onto the ground and then leaves. Scan the symbol before leaving and proceed to the next symbol area. Allow several minutes for Azrael to reach his next target. After scanning all four symbols, it's time to complete a short puzzle.

Symbol #4 is west of the GCPD building on a smaller roof. Available after rescuing Vicki Vale.

Enlarge the symbol on the map and rotate it so that the four smaller circles are aligned in the same way as the markings on your map. Then position the large symbol so that each circle rests on the spots where the symbols were originally scanned.

Symbol #1 is on a rooftop in Park Row, south of the courthouse. Available after exiting the courthouse after saving Catwoman.

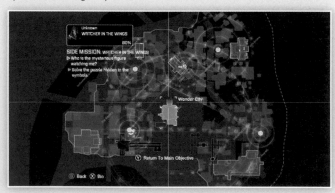

Symbol #2 is in the Industrial District on top of the Ferris wheel. Available after exiting the Steel Mill.

Finishing this task correctly reveals the location of a fifth symbol. Go to the northeastern side of the church and scan the symbol that is scratched on the wall.

Symbol #3 is northeast of the subway entrance in the Bowery on a roof. Available after interrogating Major Sharp.

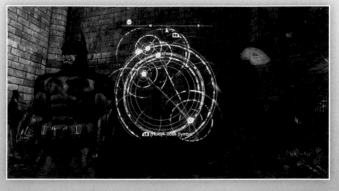

SHOT IN THE DARK

AVAILABILITY: After beating the Steel Mill for the first time.

GOAL: Find a deadly sniper.

REWARD: Deadshot Trophy

WHO'S SENDING THAT SIGNAL?

After completing the initial run through the Steel Mill, Batman intercepts a radio signal. A man is hiding on top of the radio building just outside of the Industrial District. Talk to him to trigger this side mission.

CASE №1

Scan the entire area after speaking with the man. Follow the bullet trajectory back into the Industrial District and scan a shell casing located in the caged area. The information isn't enough for Batman to finish the case yet; instead, the assassin must strike again.

Proceed with the main story after scanning the shell casing.

CASE №2

Eventually, another body surfaces on the northern side of town. The crack of a sniper rifle precedes the discovery. Go to the church, glide north, and land on the elevated section of highway to find the victim. Enter Detective Mode to see the corpse and stand near it to activate a crime scene.

Scan the area to find another impact site and track it to the east. A tripod was left at the corner of a roof; grapple to that location and scan the tripod.

Scan this tripod to conclude Case #2.

CASE №3

To find the body, walk to the church and start searching on the west side. Proceed west down the road that leads away form the church and look on the north side of the street at the first bend. Scan the area and listen to Oracle.

Follow the bullet's trajectory while in Detective Mode and scan a roof to the west. This is only a temporary stopping point! The real crime scene is further west at the edge of the zone. Scan the evidence on that roof to get more information about Deadshot's location.

THE HIT LIST

There are three potential sites where Deadshot could be stashing his materials. Reference the map and compare it with the screenshot shown here, which indicates the correct location to search. Once there, scan the maintenance hatch. Open it and hack the console, then scan the PDA to find Deadshot's hit list.

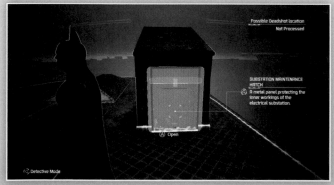

Search this area on the northeastern edge of the city.

There isn't much time! Jack Ryder is the next target and Deadshot is ready to pull the trigger. Immediately head to the southwestern side of town before it's too late!

Get to Jack Ryder in a timely manner, or his time will be up!

Run up to Jack Ryder and tackle him. After a short cutscene, it's time to face off against Deadshot. Wait until the killer's back is turned, then slip into cover. Stay crouched and repeat this until Batman gets into the crawlspace underneath Deadshot. Take him down from there to end this case!

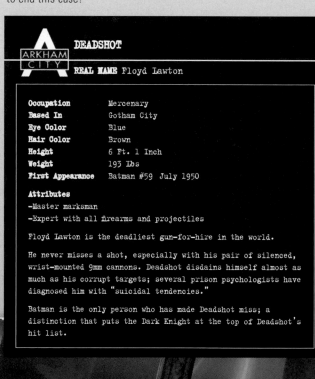

DEADSHOT

ARKHAM CITY

REAL NAME Floyd Lawton

Occupation	Mercenary
Based In	Gotham City
Eye Color	Blue
Hair Color	Brown
Height	6 Ft. 1 Inch
Weight	193 Lbs
First Appearance	Batman #59 July 1950

Attributes
-Master marksman
-Expert with all firearms and projectiles

Floyd Lawton is the deadliest gun-for-hire in the world.

He never misses a shot, especially with his pair of silenced, wrist-mounted 9mm cannons. Deadshot disdains himself almost as much as his corrupt targets; several prison psychologists have diagnosed him with "suicidal tendencies."

Batman is the only person who has made Deadshot miss; a distinction that puts the Dark Knight at the top of Deadshot's hit list.

COLD CALL KILLER

■ AVAILABILITY: As soon as Batman can freely explore Arkham City.　　**■ GOAL:** Catch Zsasz.　　**■ REWARD:** Zsasz Trophy

RING, RING

There are a number of working public telephones in Arkham City. Batman can detect the ringing phones and track them using Detective Mode. Zsasz is on the other end of the line, but he hangs up right away.

WHO'S THERE?

Listen for another ringing phone and answer it. When this happens, the mission formally begins. Batman brings up the Casefile Feed for Victor Zsasz. Access the information on the righthand side of the screen to learn more about the call. Read each piece of information to trace the call.

Zsasz threatens to kill a hostage if Batman doesn't switch to another phone, so get moving! Use the Grapnel to maximum effect to find the next ringing phone with time to spare. Once that happens, the Batcomputer attempts to trace Victor's call. Use the movement controls to track Victor's signal. The signal switches between phones periodically, stopping for a few moments at each new phone. Just stay on it for as long as Zsasz keeps talking.

Repeat this process several more times to obtain all the necessary information. Afterward, Batman finally receives the location of Zsasz's hideout—it's in the Industrial District on the western side of that zone.

Track the calls to triangulate Zsasz's hideout.

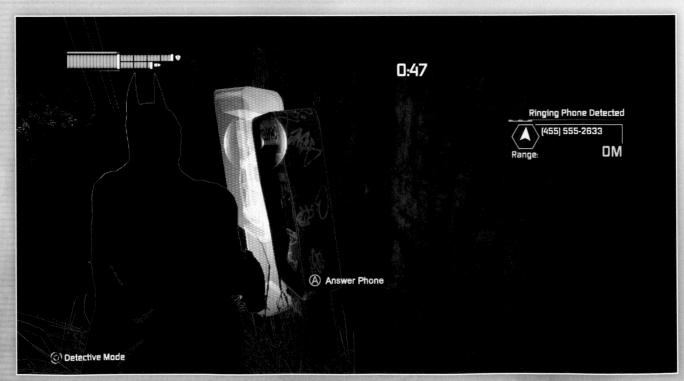

Quickly find a new phone before Zsasz kills a hostage.

THE HUNT

Enter the hideout and descend the stairs. The main door is locked, but a vent on the right provides access. Use the Batclaw to tear off the cover and enter the vent. Creep through it and drop down into Zsasz's room.

The water level in the room rises and falls at equal intervals, so Batman must move through the area without falling into the water. Follow these steps:

1. Drop onto a floating walkway; hop onto the next ledge.

2. When the water level drops, jump to the third platform and pull up before the water rises.

3. When the water goes down again, run and slide underneath the low pipes around the bend.

4. Grab the ledge behind Batman when he slides off the edge.

5. Traverse the hanging section and pull up at the far side.

6. Leap across another gap.

7. Use a Freeze Blast to make a bridge; grapple to the next wall.

8. Use the Batclaw to reach a higher ring near the upper walkway.

9. Climb onto the walkway and approach the nearby glass. Knock out Zsasz through the glass to save the hostages.

ZSASZ

ARKHAM CITY

REAL NAME Victor Zsasz

Occupation	Professional Criminal
Based In	Gotham City
Eye Color	Blue
Hair Color	None [formerly blonde]
Height	5 Ft. 8 Inches
Weight	150 Lbs
First Appearance	Batman: Shadow of the Bat #1 [June 1992]

Attributes

- Sociopath with no regard for human life
- No pattern of killing, making him difficult to track
- Compulsive need to kill others

A true sociopath, Zsasz grew up in a life of ease, but nonetheless became a serial killer. Indiscriminate in his prey, body count is the only thing that matters to Zsasz.

He carves a mark for each of his victims into his own body, and is saving a special spot for the Batman.

Since being thrown into Arkham City, his whereabouts are unknown, though reports of rising body counts fit his modus operandi.

ENIGMA CONUNDRUM

AVAILABILITY: After getting a distress call from the medical team. **GOAL:** Save the hostages from the Riddler. **REWARD:** Riddler Trophy

CHECK OUT THE MEDICAL TEAM

After going to the GCPD, Batman loses contact with the medical team. Return to the church to see what has transpired. Once there, Batman must answer questions for The Riddler.

Question #1: *"I am an instrument that always comes from the heart. What am I?"*

Answer: *Go to the other side of the church and use Environmental Analysis while looking at the church organ.*

GO TO THE COURTHOUSE

Leave the church and fight a few thugs. Only one of them is important; just defeat the ones not highlighted in green. Avoid hitting the "special" goon by countering whenever he tries to attack.

INFORMANTS!

When you encounter other informants in the city, repeat this process to receive hints for nearby Riddler Secrets.

Rush to the courthouse and save M.P.T. Eddie Burlow. Several foes are guarding him in the main room. Eddie was given the code **2-7-5**, **3-2-5**. Use the sequencer and adjust the frequency to **275x**, **325y**. Decode the signal and retrieve the Enigma Machine from Eddie. Adjust the Enigma Machine until Sec and Ret are facing each other to form a single word.

Question #2: *"If you know me, you'll want to share me, but if you share me, I'll be gone. What am I?"*

Answer: *Secret.*

RIDDLER'S FIRST HIDEOUT

The reward is the location of another hostage. This time, it's someone located south of the church. Travel to that location and search a wall with a large question mark on it. Batman breaks through the loose bricks and enters the building.

Medic Adam Hamasaki is in an electrified room. To save him, Batman must navigate through narrow squares of safe flooring. At first, there are no safe routes in the room, so use the Batarang to hit the question mark across the way. Run through the only safe section of floor that isn't electrified. Once at a safe spot on the left, stop!

Look for additional question marks.

Look for additional questions marks across from this new position (and one to the right, as well). Hit them to advance to another section. The tricky part comes in making sure to activate the electric floor switches to complete the safe path to the elevator and then reaching the elevator before time runs out. Once on the elevator, Batarang the remaining switches to make it rise. Once it's high enough, glide down to get the hostage.

Get to the lift before the timer runs out. When the lift reaches the top of the room, glide off it and rescue Adam. He provides another frequency to scan, this time it's **6-2-5**, **9-2-5**. Note that you must have obtained 80 secrets to unlock the Riddle for the next room.

Question #3: *"The more there is, the less you see. What could I be?"*

Answer: *Darkness.*

THE SECOND HIDEOUT

Southeast from the church is a hidden entrance where the next hostage is being held. Get to that area and look for the entrance. Go inside the building and look around.

Locate the pressure plate below the entrance. Drop down and stop on it to start the next challenge. A Gotham City police officer is tied down across the way. To save him, turn on Detective Mode to discover where he's being hidden. Throw a Batarang at the question mark nearest to the officer, then jump over to untie him after the Riddler accepts defeat. The police officer reveals the code **860**, **120**. Scan that frequency with the Sequencer. Note that you must have obtained 160 secrets to unlock the Riddle for the next room.

WHAT'S NEXT?

Continue through the story until Batman gets the Line Launcher. These two gadgets are required before you can rescue the hostage at the third hideout.

THE THIRD HIDEOUT

The next area is on the eastern edge of the city, to the northeast of the Steel Mill. Travel there and find your way into the secret area. Enter the first door to start the puzzle. After the Riddler finishes his speech, a screen retracts that reveals the waterway that dominates the room. Throw a Freeze Blast into the water and use the Batclaw to cross the water, or Line Launch across it. Grapple to the far ledge when the time is right.

The next part of the puzzle involves two electromagnets above the Riddler's screen. Use the REC on the upper-left one to pull a generator to the left. Once it's there, throw a Remote Batarang under the fencing and hit the question mark on the left. Use the REC on the upper-right magnet, then hit the question mark on the right. This brings down the defenses in the adjoining hallway.

Use the Line Launcher to slip between the rotating blades along the hall. Double Line Launch down the right side of the passage to reach the last room of the challenge. There are three electromagnets in this room. There are two along the left wall and another one near the entrance. Use Detective Mode to spot all three before proceeding.

Pass by the spinning blades.

Use Detective Mode to find the electromagnets.

1. Use the REC to pull a box to the rightmost magnet (the higher one).

2. While the box is lifted, use the magnet on the far left to pull the box over the fence.

3. Use the REC's repulsing function on the left magnet to push the box toward the middle magnet.

4. As the box passes the middle magnet, use the REC repulse on that one to push the box closer to a pressure plate.

5. Continue repulsing until the box ends up on the pressure plate.

Follow these steps to set the hostage free, then approach and untie her. She provides the code **606, 120**. At this point, 240 secrets are required to unlock the next Riddle.

THE FOURTH HIDEOUT

The next goal is northwest of the Steel Mill in the Industrial District. Locate the entrance on the south side of the building and go inside. Let the Riddler gloat and enter the first door. Inside the larger room ahead, a massive blade rolls across the floor. Ignore it for now and turn around. Hack the console on the wall to reveal a walkway across the electrified floor. Run to the far end when it's safe to do so.

The next route is unveiled by using a Batarang on a question mark against a side wall. Throw the device after the blades pass to get plenty of time to reach safety.

1. Climb onto a ledge.

2. Continue to the top and get onto the closer of two safe panels.

3. Let the timer run out and avoid the blades.

4. Renew the safe route by using the Batarang against the safe question mark.

5. Jump to the far side of the walkway and step on another safe panel.

6. Avoid the blades once again.

7. Line Launch to an alcove at the rear of the chamber.

8. Look for a weakened wall in that alcove and blow it up using Explosive Gel.

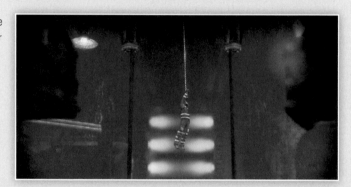

Use the REC on the magnet above Batman's position to pull a box away from the far wall. This creates room to throw a Remote Batarang above the fence ahead; maneuver the Batarang down and slip it underneath the next fence. Hit the button on the wall to make a force field drop.

Walk through the opening and take a deep breath. The next move requires a steady hand. Line Launch at the wall across from the next pressure plate and then do a Double Line Launch past the hanging hostage to save him. He relinquishes the next code: **115, 780**. Note that you must have obtained 320 secrets to unlock the Riddle for the next room.

THE FIFTH HIDEOUT

After getting enough Riddler secrets, proceed to the fifth hideout in Amusement Mile, which is located in the northeastern side of town. Once inside, take the first doorway. Run under another block and slide under the other gate. Note the electromagnet above. Use the REC on the electromagnet to lift a gigantic block and clear the way. Run and slide underneath two more gates; stay on the move to reach the corner of the room.

Step on the red panels near the corner to trigger the next puzzle and a series of question marks. Use the Batarang on the lit question marks to disable the electricity on the floor ahead.

Walk across the floor once it's safe, then use the REC on an electromagnet in the next hallway. This repulses a set of boxes through the wall, exposing additional question marks. A force field prevents further passage. Follow these steps to proceed:

1. Throw a Remote Batarang over a force field and slam it into the question mark on the left.

2. Jump across the gap and climb the ladder.

3. At the top of the ladder, stop and look forward.

4. Double Line Launch to cross the next area.

5. Shoot the first line over the electrified floor.

6. Aim right and shoot the next line through a bladed tunnel.

7. Hack the console in the small chamber beyond.

8. Return to the beginning of the Line Launcher section.

PRECISE AIMING

Knowing where to start aiming ahead of time makes it easier to strike all the question marks within the allotted time. Don't throw without aiming, as Batman takes damage when he misses.

Grapple to the top of the electrified room and examine the next panels. There are two magnets (one above, another on a slope in front of Batman); use the REC to repulse the top magnet. After several boxes fall, repulse the lower magnet. Grapple to a higher ledge and look to the left. The final obstacle involves guiding Batman through a triple Line Launch!

First, shoot the first line at the area ahead. Launch a second line around the next corner to stay on the move. Next, look left while moving down the line, then shoot the third line through the opening in the hallway. Finally, drop off the line while passing above the hostage's platform. Save the hostage and listen to what she has to say. Leave the building afterward.

SOLVING THE PUZZLE

Collect 400 secrets and Oracle eventually marks the Riddler's location on the in-game map. Go to that area in the Bowery. The building is in the southwestern part of the city, just north of the Museum. The entrance is near the border wall between Arkham City and the rest of Gotham (west side). Glide and dive to fly underneath the covered area. Sail over the electrified fence to reach the sectioned-off area. Land and open the door to enter the hideout.

The door to the main portion of the hideout is strapped with dynamite, so another entry point is needed. Grapple to the chamber's upper floor, rip a vent off the wall, and crawl through some ductwork. Drop down at the end of the vent and look around There are hostages moving through the building's lower level. Note the specific patrol pattern; when they stop, the charges on the hostages detonate. Slip behind each person as they move past and navigate along the route.

Carefully walk to the first corner followed by the next. Now continue across to where the Riddler is controlling the hostages. (Use Detective mode to spot the Riddler if need be.) Position Batman underneath the Riddler and use a Takedown to put an end to his evil plans!

AUGMENTED REALITY TRAINING

AVAILABILITY: Before reaching the Steel Mill for the first time and again later in the main story.   **GOAL:** Complete two groups of gliding exercises.   **REWARD:** Grapnel Boost Upgrade, Batwing Trophy

TEST №1

This side mission involves a series of Augmented Reality training modes in the Industrial District. Look high up on the northern side of the district to locate it. As soon as Batman approaches the AR module, the training begins. Glide off the building and pass through five bat symbols on the way down.

GLIDING TIPS

The first four symbols are easy to hit. Adjust left or right, but keep the same speed and pressure throughout the glide. The last icon is a bit lower, so get close to it and drop through the symbol to get credit.

Completing four AR modes unlocks the Grapnel Boost!

TEST №2

Climb back to the beginning of the AR challenge to start the next test. This one requires jumping and gliding to the first symbol. Continue in a normal fashion to the second symbol, but immediately stop gliding and plummet through the third and forth symbols. This one is much trickier! Also, make sure Batman has a mobile start when jumping off the AR platform. Failing this, he won't have enough height to hit the first target!

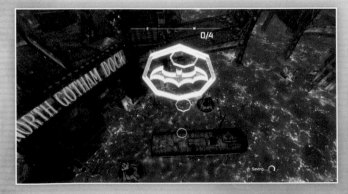

TEST №3

The third set of targets is nearly impossible to complete without learning a new technique. Dive quickly and then pull out of it to gain speed and restore height. Jump off the AR platform, glide to the first target, and then dive steeply downward to slice through the next two targets. Pull up and start flying to the fourth one. Glide through that target and resume gliding to reach the final target.

ALTERNATE METHOD

It's possible to complete Test #3 using Grapnel pulls that you cancel before reaching the far end. This approach is a bit trickier, but is not essential.

TEST №4

The final AR module involves a bit of dive-bombing. Get onto the smokestack, then jump and glide to the first symbol. Next, use the dive-bomb option to push through the second one. Release after passing through the second symbol and glide upward using the momentum of the dive. Continue in this manner to the next symbol and repeat the process. Dive to the fourth target and glide to the finish.

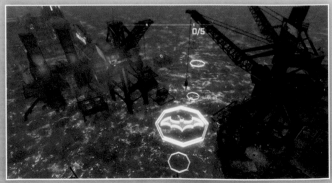

The reward for completing the AR side missions is the Grapnel Boost Upgrade!

After collecting the Grapnel Boost upgrade, new Augmented Reality modes become available. These training modes aren't linear; all four are accessible at the same time. The Advanced AR modules are in the following locations:

MODULE	LOCATION
Advanced AR Training 1	North of the Steel Mill
Advanced AR Training 2	Bowery
Advanced AR Training 3	North of the Industrial District
Advanced AR Training 4	Park Row

ADVANCED MODULE №1

This test is north of the Steel Mill, on top of an orange neon sign. Grapple to the top and take a position that lines up with the first symbol. Jump off the sign and glide to the initial target.

Jump off this neon sign to trigger the first advanced AR Module.

Dive down through the second and third symbols, but stay in the dive longer than normal. When breaking out of the dive, do not pull up immediately. Instead, let the momentum carry Batman close to

the tunnel before trying to capitalize on it for extra height. This lets Batman slip underneath the mouth at the tunnel entrance. Fly as horizontal as possible through the tunnel to avoid touching the ground or the roof. This creates the speed needed to reach the end of the area and hit the last symbol.

ADVANCED MODULE №2

Go to the Bowery to access the next test, which starts on a gargoyle. This one is an exercise in alternating between gliding and diving. Jump off the gargoyle, fly to the nearby symbol, and dive down toward the second symbol.

Emerge from the dive a little early to get above a fence while entering the tunnel ahead. Immediately do a quick second dive (briefly tap the appropriate button) to collect speed and pass underneath an overhang.

Fail to line up properly and you won't complete the final turn in time.

Next, swing to the right and start a left-hand turn to pass through the next symbol and fly toward the end of the course. Swing wide on the third symbol to line up for the finish.

ADVANCED MODULE №3

Search south of the GCPD building on the roof of a crane to start this module. Jump off the crane and glide to the first symbol. Dive and turn in place to get aligned toward the second symbol, then break out close to the

Jump from here to start this module.

bottom. Pass through the symbol and glide to the third symbol before hitting the water.

ADVANCED MODULE №4

To complete the fourth module, get atop the gargoyles in Park Row. Look for the first symbol and get a good jump to glide over to it; dive just after hitting the symbol. While diving, turn to the right

but do *not* continue pressing forward. The dive command is enough to make Batman plummet, but pressing down throws everything off course.

Near the bottom of the dive at the third symbol, emerge from the maneuver and glide through the opening in the bridge. Stay as close to the center as possible to avoid hitting the sides and failing the run. After completing all the modules, a **Batwing Trophy** is unlocked.

REMOTE HIDEAWAY

AVAILABILITY: After interrogating Mayor Sharp.

GOAL: Talk to the police officers in the Museum's Iceberg Lounge.

REWARD: Mine Detonator gadget upgrade

BACK TO THE MUSEUM

After talking to Mayor Quincy, Batman receives a message from the undercover cops in the Museum. Return to the Museum, but do not go to the main door. Instead, fight around to the Museum's north side and knock on the door to gain entry.

Talk to the men inside and accept the Mine Detonator. To get some extra experience while in this area, take some time to clear the Museum again. Return to the front entrance and eliminate the unarmed thugs.

Mine Detonator

Knock on the side door to gain entry to the Museum.

HOT & COLD

AVAILABILITY: During a second trip through the Steel Mill.

GOAL: Search the boiler room for new technology.

REWARD: Freeze Blast Grenades

NON-LETHAL GRENADES: SOUNDS INTERESTING!

This mission is unlocked when Batman ungags Harley Quinn inside the Steel Mill during a second visit. Instead of heading toward Joker's office to finish things off, use the REC to open a gate on the east side of the Loading Bay.

Use the "Password" command on the console in the next room. Hop down the elevator door and ambush several grunts stuck inside the elevator. Shift to the other elevator and use the REC to raise the car that the thugs were using. Duck underneath the rising car and grapple to the side of the shaft. Attack the gunman and thug in the next room, then enter the Boiler Room.

Remove the gag from Harley Quinn to start this side mission.

To clear the final room, Batman must defeat three gunmen and four unarmed thugs. The guard is wearing body armor, so stealth won't work. Instead, ambush the goon with a quick REC to blast him into the armed thugs.

ARKHAM ASSAULT

■ **AVAILABILITY:** Throughout most of the game.

■ **GOAL:** Save the political prisoners in Arkham City.

■ **REWARD:** Trophy or an Achievement

SIDE MISSIONS

PROTECT THE INNOCENT

Look for random citizens getting pushed around or pairs of people standing close together while exploring the city. The first and most obvious assault is found by heading west from the Ace Chemicals building after suiting up as Batman. This is when Batman encounters Jack Ryder, who is getting beaten up by several inmates.

IN-GAME MAP HELP

When Batman overhears someone threatening a prisoner, the location of the event is marked on the in-game map. This makes it much easier to pinpoint the assault later on.

When a prisoner is getting pushed around, beat up the attacker to get credit for protecting the innocent.

THE HERO GOTHAM NEEDS

RIDDLER'S REVENGE: MIND & BODY, HONED TO PERFECTION

The Riddler has created rooms to challenge Batman's fighting and stealth skills. The rooms are unlocked by collecting certain Riddler's Trophies in the Story Mode part of the game. Select Riddler's Revenge from the main menu to access these challenges.

There are two different types of challenges: Combat and Predator. Combat challenges test Batman's fighting skills, while the Predator challenges provide an opportunity to show off stealth techniques. Each room has a set of objectives to complete to earn three medals and these objectives are score-based (as in the Combat Challenges) or action-based (as in the Predator Challenges).

There are three modes from which to choose: Ranked, Campaign and Custom Challenges. Medals are earned from each room by completing the objectives and are counted separately for each character. There are 213 total medals for each in *Batman: Arkham City*. Note that Predator objectives differ between characters.

RANKED CHALLENGES

AVAILABLE MEDALS: 72 Ranked (93 with DLC)

The Ranked Challenges allow you to compare your skills with your friends and other players from around the world. Also, medals and times for each Challenge Room are posted on the online leaderboard. There are 12 Combat rooms and 12 Predator rooms to complete. Each one has three available medals to earn. Look for more information on each challenge near the end of this chapter.

CAMPAIGNS

AVAILABLE MEDALS: 108 Campaign (120 with DLC)

Are you tough enough to take on the Riddler's Campaigns? Fight through a brutal gauntlet of challenges, while tactically choosing which modifiers to use on each map. The only requirement is that you must use every modifier by the end of the Campaign.

There are 12 Campaign levels, each with three challenge rooms. These rooms are the same rooms from Ranked Challenges, except now there are modifiers that must all be used before the end of the Campaign. You must decide which modifiers to use in each room. You have three opportunities to complete it just in case the henchmen win in one of the rooms. There is no leaderboard for this mode.

The following lists the eight campaigns and the associated Challenges and the Modifiers from which to choose. Each modifier has a suggested room in which to use it; basically, this suggestion is what worked for our playthrough. How you use them is up to you, though. If you have more confidence in Combat than Predator, then make the Predator rooms easier with the Modifiers and vice versa.

SEARCH & DESTROY

Challenge Rooms: Meltdown Mayhem: Predator; Blind Justice: Combat; Police Brutality: Predator

	MODIFIER	SUGGESTED ROOM
	Time Limit	Meltdown Mayhem
	Protective Aura	Police Brutality
	Replenishing Health	Blind Justice

STREET JUSTICE

Challenge Rooms: Rooftop Rumble: Combat; Natural Selection: Predator; Survival of the Fittest: Combat

	MODIFIER	SUGGESTED ROOM
	Decreased Health	Survival of the Fittest
	One Hand Tied	Rooftop Rumble
	Takedown Projectiles	Natural Selection

CITY INVADER

Challenge Rooms: Top of the World: Predator; Prison Riot: Combat; Lost City: Predator

	MODIFIER	SUGGESTED ROOM
	Gadget Malfunction	Prison Riot
	Increased Aggression	Lost City
	Decreased Health	Prison Riot
	Super Powered	Prison Riot

OFFENSIVE MANEUVERS

Challenge Rooms: Funhouse Brawl: Combat; End of the Line: Predator; Hell's Gate: Combat

	MODIFIER	SUGGESTED ROOM
	Danger Zones	Hell's Gate
	Scattered Weapons	Funhouse Brawl
	Replenishing Health	Hell's Gate
	Free Medal	End of the Line

MIDNIGHT ASSAULT

Challenge Rooms: Natural Selection (Extreme): Predator; Hell's Gate (Extreme): Combat; Meltdown Mayhem (Extreme): Predator

	MODIFIER	SUGGESTED ROOM
	Increased Aggression	Natural Selection (Extreme)
	Scattered Weapons	Hell's Gate (Extreme)
	Danger Zones	Hell's Gate (Extreme)
	Free Medal	Natural Selection (Extreme)
	Replenishing Health	Hell's Gate (Extreme)

HOSTILE TAKEOVER

Challenge Rooms: Prison Riot (Extreme): Combat; Police Brutality (Extreme): Predator; Funhouse Brawl (Extreme): Combat

	MODIFIER	SUGGESTED ROOM
	Time Limit	Funhouse Brawl (Extreme)
	Decreased Health	Prison Riot (Extreme)
	Protective Aura	Police Brutality (Extreme)
	One Hand Tied	Prison Riot (Extreme)
	Super Powered	Prison Riot (Extreme)

RUTHLESS VENGEANCE

Challenge Rooms: Survival of the Fittest (Extreme): Combat; Top of the World (Extreme): Predator; Blind Justice (Extreme): Combat

	MODIFIER	SUGGESTED ROOM
	Gadget Malfunction	Survival of the Fittest (Extreme)
	Time Limit	Blind Justice (Extreme)
	Decreased Health	Survival of the Fittest (Extreme)
	Danger Zones	Blind Justice (Extreme)
	One Hand Tied	Blind Justice (Extreme)
	Super Powered	Survival of the Fittest (Extreme)

DOUBLE JEOPARDY

Challenge Rooms: Lost City (Extreme): Predator; Rooftop Rumble (Extreme): Combat; End of the Line (Extreme): Predator

	MODIFIER	SUGGESTED ROOM
	Gadget Malfunction	Rooftop Rumble (Extreme)
	Increased Aggression	Lost City (Extreme)
	Protective Aura	End of the Line (Extreme)
	Scattered Weapons	Rooftop Rumble (Extreme)
	Takedown Projectiles	Lost City (Extreme)
	Free Medal	End of the Line (Extreme)

COMBAT EXPERT

Challenge Rooms: Survival of the Fittest: Combat; Funhouse Brawl: Combat; Prison Riot: Combat

	MODIFIER	SUGGESTED ROOM
	Time Limit	Funhouse Brawl
	Increased Aggression	Prison Riot
	Danger Zones	Survival of the Fittest
	Replenishing Health	Survival of the Fittest

PREDATOR EXPERT

Challenge Rooms: Meltdown Mayhem: Predator; Lost City: Predator; Top of the World: Predator

	MODIFIER	SUGGESTED ROOM
	Gadget Malfunction	Meltdown Mayhem
	Scattered Weapons	Top of the World
	One Hand Tied	Lost City
	Takedown Projectiles	Lost City

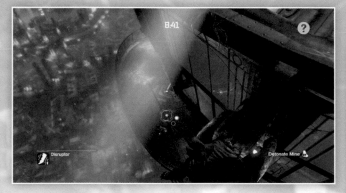

COMBAT MASTER

Challenge Rooms: Blind Justice (Extreme): Combat; Rooftop Rumble (Extreme): Combat; Hell's Gate (Extreme): Combat

	MODIFIER	SUGGESTED ROOM
	Decreased Health	Blind Justice (Extreme)
	Scattered Weapons	Hell's Gate (Extreme)
	One Hand Tied	Blind Justice (Extreme)
	Gadget Malfunction	Blind Justice (Extreme)
	Protective Aura	Rooftop Rumble (Extreme)
	Super Powered	Hell's Gate (Extreme)

PREDATOR MASTER

Challenge Rooms: Police Brutality (Extreme): Predator; Natural Selection (Extreme): Predator; End of the Line (Extreme): Predator

	MODIFIER	SUGGESTED ROOM
	Time Limit	Natural Selection (Extreme)
	Increased Aggression	Police Brutality (Extreme)
	Danger Zones	End of the Line (Extreme)
	Protective Aura	Police Brutality (Extreme)
	Scattered Weapons	Police Brutality (Extreme)
	Free Medal	End of the Line (Extreme)

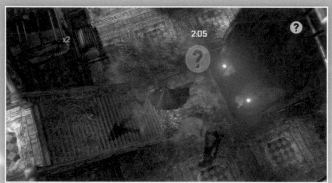

DLC CONTENT!

BLACK MASK CAMPAIGN

Challenge Rooms: Black Mask: Predator; Freight Train: Combat

	MODIFIER	SUGGESTED ROOM
	Decreased Health	Freight Train
	One Hand Tied	Freight Train
	Gadget Malfunction	Freight Train
	Super Powered	Black Mask

WAYNE MANOR CAMPAIGN

Challenge Rooms: Wayne Manor Armory: Combat; Wayne Manor Main Hall: Predator

	MODIFIER	SUGGESTED ROOM
	Protective Aura	Wayne Manor Armory
	Danger Zones	Wayne Manor Armory
	Scattered Weapons	Wayne Manor Main Hall
	Takedown Projectiles	Wayne Manor Main Hall

END DLC CONTENT!

CUSTOM CHALLENGES

AVAILABLE MEDALS: Medals don't count toward Achievements/Trophies or progression stats

In Custom Challenges, you choose from the same rooms as in Ranked Challenges, but you get to select the modifiers to use. There isn't a leaderboard for this mode and no medals to earn, but there are thousands of possibilities to try out!

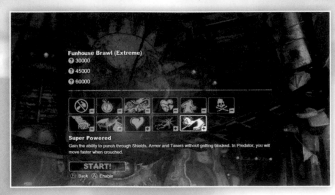

CHALLENGE ROOM MODIFIERS

There are several "modifiers" that are used throughout the challenge rooms to either increase or decrease the difficulty. You get to choose a select few modifiers in Campaigns, and it's a free-for-all in Custom Challenges. Most modifiers have a different effect in Combat rooms and Predator rooms.

INCREASE DIFFICULTY

The following modifiers tend to make a challenge more difficult to complete.

GADGET MALFUNCTION

Combat Challenge: Gadgets are disabled, so you must rely on regular fighting skills to survive.

Predator Challenge: Detective Mode is scrambled for the entire challenge. This makes the challenge difficult when the location of the thugs is unknown. As such, use the environment to sneak up on enemies.

TIME LIMIT

Combat & Predator Challenges: The challenge must be completed within a set amount of time. To get additional time, simply defeat enemies.

INCREASED AGGRESSION

Combat & Predator Challenges: Enemies are stronger, faster and tougher. They attack more often, inflict more damage and it's tougher to perform a Counter.

DECREASED HEALTH

Combat Challenge: The player starts with half health.

Predator Challenge: The player starts with one-hit health, which essentially means you can't take any damage!

PROTECTIVE AURA

Combat & Predator Challenges: This modifier surrounds one enemy with a protective aura that makes him invulnerable. Enemies with this modifier appear with a red glow. It stays on a particular foe for a few seconds before moving to another. When this modifier is present, only attack when an enemy doesn't have it.

DANGER ZONES

Combat Challenge: Gun racks are activated during a challenge so that enemies can obtain firearms. Once open, any foe can retrieve a gun from a gun rack. Try to keep thugs from opening them to make fights more manageable.

Predator Challenge: Explosives are placed on Vantage Points that trigger a delayed explosion when the player grapples or climbs onto them. The Vantage Point is lost once it blows up.

ONE HAND TIED

Combat Challenge: Enemies don't display Counter prompts, similar to New Game Plus. Rely on gadgets and big combos to earn the medals.

Predator Challenge: The player cannot perform Silent Takedowns from behind.

SCATTERED WEAPONS

Combat Challenge: Enemies pick up objects in a room and throw them at the player. Watch out for thugs holding items above their head; when this occurs, attack quickly or counter the throw.

Predator Challenge: The environment starts pre-mined with proximity-activated explosives. Watch for mines on the floor!

REDUCE DIFFICULTY

The following Modifiers make a challenge a little easier.

REPLENISHING HEALTH

Combat & Predator Challenges: The player slowly regenerates health over time.

TAKEDOWN PROJECTILES

Combat & Predator Challenges: Upgrades the primary Quickfire projectile weapon (Batarangs/Bolas) so that a single hit knocks out an enemy. This is great for Predator mode when you need to clear out a couple of enemies or finish off stragglers after achieving the medals. In Combat, use projectile weapons only when necessary, as it doesn't help build a combo much.

SUPER POWERED

Combat Challenge: Gain the ability to punch through shields, armor and tasers without getting blocked. Great for Combat rooms such as Prison Riot (Extreme) where guys with this gear are very prevalent.

Predator Challenge: Player moves faster when crouched and will not set off proximity-activated explosives.

FREE MEDAL

Combat & Predator Challenges: The player receives a medal even if he doesn't complete all three objectives. Note that the player won't receive a fourth medal if he completes all objectives. This medal only appears in Campaign Challenges!

THE COMBAT CHALLENGES

The time to show off your fighting techniques occurs in Combat rooms. Each room is split into four rounds of enemies and medals are awarded when your score reaches three preset limits.

At the end of each round, a scoreboard lists the points and bonuses gained for the current round and the total for previous rounds completed. You can also select Statistics to view the number of specific attacks, abilities and gadgets used throughout a round. After the fourth round, as long as you are signed into the network, the score and medals earned are uploaded to the leaderboards.

In Combat Challenges, your medal is totally dependent upon the score. Each time an attack or another move lands, the score for that move is multiplied by the combo number. At the end of a round, these are all tallied to make your Base Score. The following table shows the score earned for each of Batman and Catwoman's moves:

MOVE	SCORE
Strike	10
Counter	10
Projectile Counter	20
Critical Strike	20
Combo Batarang	10
Aerial Attack	25
Batclaw Slam	25
Beat Down Finisher	50
Special Combo Takedown	50
Special Combo Bat Swarm	10 x #enemies stunned
Special Combo Whiplash	5 x #enemies hit
Special Combo Disarm & Destroy	25
Special Combo Multiple Takedown	20 x #enemies stunned
Special Combo Whip Trip	5 x #enemies stunned
Ground Pound	75
Blade Dodge Takedown	100
Lieutenant Takedown	50
Rodeo Strike	10 (while riding Titan)
Rodeo Shock Wave	10 x #enemies hit (riding Titan)
Titan Takedown	100
Collateral Damage	10 x #enemies hit by attacking enemy

BONUSES

The bonuses that you may be familiar with from the combat in Story Mode also result in bonus points in the challenges. These bonuses can boost your score, although the best scores come with big combos.

VARIATION BONUS:

The more moves you combine into a single combo, the greater the variation bonus.

GADGET VARIATION BONUS:

Earn a bonus for using different types of gadgets during the round.

# MOVES	SCORE
3	100
4	250
5	500
6	1000
7	2000
8	3000
9	4000
10	5000
11	6000
12	7000

# GADGETS	SCORE
1	100
2	250
3	500
4	1000
5	2000

PERFECT ROUND BONUS: Complete a round without taking a single hit (Score: 500).

FLAWLESS FREEFLOW BONUS: Defeat an entire round in one flowing combo (Score: 1000).

COMBAT CHALLENGE STRATEGIES

Achieving the medal scores is all about obtaining a big combo. Work the combo up by bouncing between thugs and countering when necessary. As the number gets larger, perform a special move or takedown.

Ground Pounds are worth 75 points, but you are vulnerable while performing it. However, it can result in several thousand points with one score.

Some enemies cause more trouble than others, such as the guys with tasers, knives, shields and armor. If you are having trouble attacking the stun stick guys, use Special Combo Takedowns on them to get them out of the way.

Aim attacks at enemies who attempt to throw projectiles.

There are items scattered around the rooms that enemies toss at Batman, including explosive barrels and fire extinguishers. Toss a Batarang their way to knock the item out of their hands, counter the move and toss the item back, or simply hit the enemy before the item gets thrown. Enemies also grab guns out of weapon crates, so be alert!

Use Lieutenants and their scythes to your advantage to gain points.

Lieutenants join in on Funhouse Brawl and some of the Extreme challenges. These guys give points for Collateral Damage when they swing their scythes, although not a lot. When fighting near one, use a Redirect to get behind and start a Beatdown. If someone interferes, counter or redirect on them. You can hit these guys with the REC and cause them to spin around with the scythe, decking anyone caught within range.

Titans can be difficult if not handled properly. Try to lure one away from the crowd, then perform an Ultra Stun followed by a Beatdown. While riding these guys, you can rack up a massive combo! It will eventually toss Batman off, but with a third stun and Beatdown, you can perform a Takedown that is worth 100 points times the combo score!

BLIND JUSTICE
LOCATION: Park Row: Solomon Courthouse

Combat Objectives: 6000, 12000, 24000

Extreme Objectives: 8000, 16000, 32000

This is the most basic of the combat challenge rooms. There aren't a lot of enemies and the armored thug is the fiercest foe in Extreme. Just build up a combo between the enemies and eliminate them with Special Combo Takedowns or Ground Pounds whenever possible. Armored and knife-wielding enemies appear in the Extreme room.

SURVIVAL OF THE FITTEST
LOCATION: Museum Gladiator Pit

Combat Objectives: 8000, 16000, 32000

Extreme Objectives: 15000, 30000, 60000

In the appropriately named Gladiator Pit, Riddler sends a large number of thugs at Batman. Build up a big combo between them and finish each one off with a Takedown. In Extreme rounds 2 and 4, a Titan enters the fray. Get out of its way when it charges! Hit it with an Ultra Stun without breaking a combo, then follow that up with a Beatdown to mount the beast. Now increase the combo by using Rodeo Strikes. Lastly, watch out for enemies with knives and armor.

ROOFTOP RUMBLE
LOCATION: Rooftop across the street from the Courthouse

Combat Objectives: 8000, 16000, 32000

Extreme Objectives: 10000, 20000, 40000

Armored henchmen and Knives are the worst that you see in the regular version of Rooftop Rumble. Work up a good combo and these medals are well within reach. The Extreme version adds shielded thugs in the first round and Ninjas in the second. Besides attacking four times with their sword, treat the Ninjas just like any normal henchman. Watch out in the fourth round when a Lieutenant drops in. Be ready to do a Reversal when he begins to attack and take him down with a Beatdown.

HELL'S GATE
LOCATION: Wonder City

Combat Objectives: 8000, 16000, 32000

Extreme Objectives: 12000, 24000, 48000

The first go-round in Wonder City includes several ninja and some armored thugs. Be quick to counter against the ninja while building up a combo. Hell's Gate Extreme throws everything at Batman, including enemies with knives, tasers, shields and armor, plus plenty of ninja! Evade away from the group if things get too hectic. Use Special Combo Takedowns on the henchmen with tasers to avoid fighting them straight on.

FUNHOUSE BRAWL

LOCATION: Steel Mill, Joker's Funhouse

Combat Objectives: 15000, 30000, 60000

Extreme Objectives: 15000, 30000, 60000

Funhouse Brawl contains a large number of thugs, some sporting knives, shields and armor! If that wasn't bad enough, a Lieutenant joins the fray in the final round. Stay clear while thinning out the crowd, then perform a redirect to get behind the Lieutenant and get in as many hits as possible until he turns around or someone else attacks. Next, counter their attacks or evade back over the big guy. The Extreme version mixes it up more with tasers, so watch out while building a combo. Not only does a Lieutenant enter in the second round, but a Titan gets involved, too! Try to perform an Ultra Stun on the Titan and try to mount him to clear out the room a bit using his Rodeo Strikes. The fourth round steps it up even more with a Lieutenant and two Titans.

PRISON RIOT

LOCATION: Arkham City Processing Center

Combat Objectives: 8000, 16000, 32000

Extreme Objectives: 12000, 24000, 48000

The TYGER Guards are joined by the usual armored henchmen and enemies with knives and shields. Be mindful of the Tasers while moving between enemies. When the opportunity arises, perform a Special Combo Takedown on these men. The Extreme room provides more of the same, plus a few ninja. Take advantage of special moves with every opportunity and perform Takedowns on the taser guards to reduce their numbers.

DLC CONTENT!

THE JOKER'S CARNIVAL

LOCATION: Joker's Carnival

Combat Objectives: 100000, 500000, 1000000

Fill the meter by fighting enemies, then bank at any time to collect those points and increase your score. As the meter rises higher the rewards are greater, but so are the risks.

This downloadable challenge room adds an interesting twist to the usual combat rooms. The fight starts with a 3-minute timer. As your combo gets bigger, the meter on the right is filled. When the arrow reaches the top of the Level 0 bar, Level 1 is reached. At this point, press the proper button to get 10,000 points and add five seconds to the timer. You can also let it keep growing before "banking" it, but the meter is reset to Level 0 is the combo is lost. The following table shows the bonus earned at each combo level.

LEVEL	BONUS SCORE	ADDED TIME (SECONDS)
1	1000	0
2	5000	15
3	10000	30
4	50000	40
5	100000	60
6	500000	75
Clear	1000000	150

ICEBERG LOUNGE VIP ROOM

LOCATION: Iceberg Lounge VIP Room

Combat Objectives: 10000, 50000, 100000

The goal here is to survive as long as possible against an endless wave of enemies. It starts out with basic thugs, followed by a weapons drop, and then tasers and shields. Armored henchmen join the fray as the difficulty ramps up. Keep a combo going from the start, though, and it's possible to get all three medals before many of these guys join.

FREIGHT TRAIN

LOCATION: Train

Combat Objectives: 10000, 20000, 30000

This challenge plays like an old side-scrolling beat em' up. Batman enters the back of a runaway train and must defeat thugs while maneuvering toward the locomotive. For the third round, climb the ladder and perform a Takedown on an unsuspecting guy below. After the third round, continue to the last car where a Lieutenant and Black Mask await. Stay behind the Lieutenant while beating him down. After defeating the enemies, destroy the control box on the right to stop the train.

WAYNE MANOR ARMORY

LOCATION: Wayne Manor

Combat Objectives: 10000, 30000, 60000

This challenge begins with regular TYGER Guards, but during the subsequent rounds there are armored guards and plenty of weapons. Toward the end, nearly every guard has a weapon!

END DLC CONTENT!

THE PREDATOR CHALLENGES

The Predator Challenges revolve around using stealth to put down a room full of enemies. The enemies carry guns and are quick to use them. You must use every gadget and skill to clear the room and earn the medals. Three medals are awarded for completing certain objectives. Each room has its own set of objectives and all four characters have a unique set.

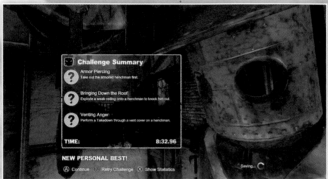

After finishing a room, a scoreboard lists the medals earned and time of completion. For the Ranked Challenges, this information is uploaded to the leaderboard. Select Statistics to list the times at which the actions were performed.

PREDATOR CHALLENGE STRATEGIES

Use all of the tools in Batman's belt to complete these challenges. Quickly move after using a gadget on a henchman, as he will eventually figure out where it came from. Each location has little "extras," such as floor grates, space behind breakable walls and so on. Use it all to your advantage.

Some Extreme Challenge Rooms introduce snipers to the mix. Take them out quickly since they can end things with just a single shot. Use Detective Mode to find their hiding spots. Also, be on the lookout for henchmen carrying the Jammer backpack.

If a sniper is inaccessible at the start, use the Disruptor on the sniper rifle.

Use an REC to disable thugs carrying the Jammer backback.

Some challenges start with a perfect setup to achieve one of the medals, such as in Natural Selection in which two henchmen stand on the bridge to the right—a perfect scenario for getting the Friends Fly Free objective. Use Detective Mode right away to see where the henchmen are—as long as there isn't a Jammer among them.

The objectives for each character are listed below along with strategy for Batman's challenge rooms. Much of the same strategy can be used with the other characters.

PREDATOR CHALLENGE ROOMS

MELTDOWN MAYHEM

LOCATION: Steel Mill Smelting Chamber

BATMAN OBJECTIVES

Smoke Detector: Use the Smoke Pellet to create a smoke cloud and take down a henchman when he panics in the smoke.

Mind Your Head: Knock down a henchman with a Batarang, then finish him off with a Ground Takedown.

Shock Tactics: Shoot a henchman with the REC to make him fire into the air, scaring another henchman.

A lone henchman patrols the lower level at the start. Knock him down with a Batarang and follow that up with a Ground Takedown to get a quick medal. When the others check out the situation, hit one of the enemies in the back with the REC. Lastly, toss a smoke pellet at one at a henchman and take him down when he panics.

BATMAN EXTREME OBJECTIVES

Armor Piercing: Eliminate the armored henchman first.

Bringing Down the Roof: Drop a weakened ceiling onto a henchman to knock him out.

Venting Anger: Perform a Takedown on a henchman through a vent cover.

The armored foe conveniently stands underneath the far Vantage Point. Swing over to the left point and use the Disruptor on the sniper. Now proceed to the next Vantage Point and perform an Inverted Takedown to get the first medal.

Open a vent outside the office and crawl inside. Place Explosive Gel on the weakened floor above the office. Do something to attract attention, then duck back behind the wall. Wait for someone to approach and detonate the ceiling onto him. Lastly, wait behind the office vent for an opportunity to perform a takedown.

CATWOMAN OBJECTIVES

Whipped Up: Perform a Takedown on an enemy above while climbing on the ceiling.

Silence Is Golden: Sneak up behind a henchman and perform a Silent Takedown.

Break Your Fall: Drop on top of a henchman and knock him out on the ground.

CATWOMAN EXTREME OBJECTIVES

Lone Gunman: While climbing on the ceiling, perform a Takedown on a sniper above.

Grate Moves: While in a floor grate, perform a Takedown on a henchman.

Window Pain: Perform a Takedown through a glass window.

DLC CONTENT!

ROBIN OBJECTIVES

Shield Bash: Knock a henchman down with the Shield Bash and take him down.

Over the Ledge: While hanging from a ledge, grab a henchman and pull him over the edge.

What Goes Up: When a henchman climbs to the top of a ladder, send him flying back down.

ROBIN EXTREME OBJECTIVES

Zip Kick Off: Use the Zip Kick to knock a henchman off a walkway.

Have a Nice Trip: Slide into a henchman and knock him out on the ground.

Friends Fly Free: While hanging from a ledge, grab two henchmen simultaneously and pull them down over the ledge.

END DLC CONTENT!

POLICE BRUTALITY
LOCATION: GCPD Building

BATMAN OBJECTIVES

Blast Zone: Explode a weakened wall into a henchman to knock him out.

Knockout Smash: During a Silent Takedown, perform a Knockout Smash to instantly take down the henchman.

Window Pain: Perform a Takedown through a glass window.

At the start, locate the enemy walking along the left wall. Hop down and perform the Silent Takedown, then follow it up with a Knockout Smash. The next two medals take a little more patience. Dodge into the far room and duck under the window. When the coast is clear, place some Explosive Gel on the wall. Make some noise to get enemies near the walls or windows to get the remaining medals.

BATMAN EXTREME OBJECTIVES

Don't Touch That Dial: Leave the henchman with the Jammer backpack until last.

Feet First: While standing on a ledge directly above a target, perform a Reverse Ledge Takedown on a henchman below.

Smash and Grab: Perform an Inverted Takedown from a Vantage Point through the glass ceiling.

There is a great opportunity to get Smash and Grab right from the start. Immediately grapple to the Vantage Point on the right and perform the Inverted Takedown when the opportunity presents itself. For Feet First, get on top of the side rooms directly above an enemy.

Since you need to leave the henchman with the Jammer backpack for last, hit him with an REC to disrupt it. Make sure he isn't near an edge, as you can finish him off. If the Jammer henchman takes the hostage, you can't take him down if anyone else is left to earn all the medals and you can't use the REC on him because he will kill the hostage.

CATWOMAN OBJECTIVES

Whip Into Shape: Trip up a henchman using the Whip and finish him off with a Ground Takedown.

Scare Tactics: Appear out of nowhere to surprise a henchman.

Hit-and-Run: Punch an armed henchman.

CATWOMAN EXTREME OBJECTIVES

Gun Thief: Disarm a henchman with an aimed Whip attack.

Knockout Smash: During a Silent Takedown, perform a Knockout Smash to instantly take down the henchman.

Bullet Proof: Take down all of the henchmen without taking damage.

DLC CONTENT!

ROBIN OBJECTIVES

Bullet Shield: Block a henchman's bullets before performing a Shield Bash, then take them down.

Feet First: While standing on a ledge directly above a target, perform a Reverse Ledge Takedown on a henchman below.

Smash Landing: Smash through a glass ceiling onto a henchman below to take him down.

ROBIN EXTREME OBJECTIVES

Shield Bash: Knock down a henchman using the Shield Bash and then take him down.

Two for Two: Take down two henchmen with two different walls at once using Explosive Gel.

Smoke Detector: Use the Smoke Pellet to create a smoke cloud and take down a henchman when he panics in the smoke.

END DLC CONTENT!

NATURAL SELECTION
LOCATION: Museum Armory

BATMAN OBJECTIVES

Weapon Jam: Use the Disrupter on one henchman's gun and let him try to use it, then take him down (upgrade required).

Aerial Assault: Glide-kick a henchman and knock him out on the ground.

Friends Fly Free: While hanging from a ledge, grab two henchmen simultaneously and pull them down over the ledge.

Wait for the henchman to come down the steps and turn the other way before grappling to the bridge. Hang from the ledge and shimmy over until you can get the Double Ledge Takedown. This gets you the Friends Fly Free objective right away.

From one of the Vantage Points, find a small group of two or three enemies and use the Disruptor on two of them to disable their guns. Now glide kick one and take him down. After a henchman tries to fire at Batman, take him down for the third and final medal.

BATMAN EXTREME OBJECTIVES

Boom Box: Use Explosive Gel to stun a henchman getting a weapon from a Weapons Crate.

Chaos Theory: Perform an Inverted Takedown from a Vantage Point on a thermal henchman.

Deep Impact: Use the Shock Wave Attack on two or more henchmen (upgrade required).

Sneak past the mammoth and grapple to a Vantage Point. Look for the henchman across the room who is scanning another Vantage Point. Once he is done, grapple to that point and immediately perform an Inverted Takedown.

It is a good idea to take out the sniper next. Grapple to the gargoyle at the end of the room that the sniper isn't watching and glide over to the bridge. Perform a Ledge Takedown when he approaches. To get Deep Impact, you need to get two enemies together on the lower level and perform a Shock Wave Attack from one of the gargoyles.

There is a Weapon Crate below a Vantage Point. When the coast is clear, put some Explosive Gel in front of the crate. Now use the Disruptor on a guy and get his attention. When he goes for a weapon, detonate the gel.

CATWOMAN OBJECTIVES

Cat Nap: While climbing on the ceiling, perform a Takedown on an enemy below.

Grate Moves: Perform a Takedown on a henchman while inside a floor grate.

Have a Nice Trip: Slide into a henchman and knock him out on the ground.

CATWOMAN EXTREME OBJECTIVES

Cat Fight: Perform a Beatdown on an armed henchman.

Breaking & Entering: Perform a Takedown through a weakened wooden wall.

Pouncer: Perform a Pounce Attack on a henchman and knock him out on the ground.

DLC CONTENT!

ROBIN OBJECTIVES

Zip Kick: Knock down a henchman using the Zip Kick and take him down.

Blast Zone: Explode a weak wall into a henchman to knock him out.

Knock Knock: Distract a henchman using a thrown Shuriken, then perform a Silent Takedown while he is distracted.

ROBIN EXTREME OBJECTIVES

Snap Flashed: Knock down one henchman using a Snap Flash and take him down.

Smoke Detector: Use the Smoke Pellet to create a smoke cloud and take down a henchman when he panics in the smoke.

Crowd Control: Take down three henchmen at once with one wall using Explosive Gel.

END DLC CONTENT!

END OF THE LINE
LOCATION: Subway Terminal

BATMAN OBJECTIVES

Kick Off: Use the Line Launcher to kick a henchman off an edge and knock him out.

Scare Tactics: Appear out of nowhere to surprise a terrified henchman.

Freeze Frame: Use any Freeze Gadget on a henchman, then take him down while frozen.

From the start, hop over the fence on the left and sneak up behind a henchman. Hit him with a Freeze Blast and perform an Ice Smash Takedown to earn the first medal.

The Kick Off objective is easily achieved on the trains. Find a guy on top of one and glide down to another train. Aim for the enemy and Line Launch toward him. There are many ways to get the final medal, but one way is to jump out of a floor grate directly in front of an enemy.

BATMAN EXTREME OBJECTIVES

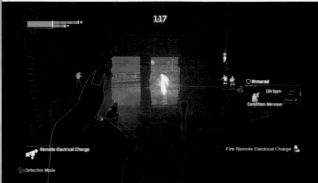

Perpetual Motion: Shoot an armored henchman with the REC and send him over an edge to knock him out.

What Goes Up: When a henchman climbs to the top of a ladder, send him flying back down.

Don't Touch That Dial: Leave the henchman with the Jammer backpack until last.

Since you must leave the Jammer backpack enemy for last, you can't use Detective Mode unless you hit him with an REC. Only do this when he is on the ground to avoid knocking him off an edge and eliminating him too early.

Find a henchman on one of the trains and hit him with the REC to knock him off and get the Perpetual Motion medal. To get What Goes Up, get someone to follow Batman to the top of a train and send him back down when he reaches the top.

CATWOMAN OBJECTIVES

Bola'd Over: Knock down a henchman using the Bolas, then finish him off with a Ground Takedown.

Over the Ledge: While hanging from a ledge, grab a henchman and pull him down over the edge.

Breaking & Entering: Perform a Takedown through a weakened wooden wall.

CATWOMAN EXTREME OBJECTIVES

Whip Into Shape: Trip up a henchman using the Whip, then finish him with a Ground Takedown.

Friends Fly Free: While hanging from a ledge, grab two henchmen simultaneously and pull them down over the ledge.

Grate Moves: Perform a Takedown on a henchman while inside a floor grate.

DLC CONTENT!

ROBIN OBJECTIVES

Shield Smash: Use a Shield Bash to knock a henchman off a ledge.

High Speed Impact: Use a boosted Remote Shuriken to knock a henchman over an edge.

Grate Moves: Perform a Takedown on a henchman while inside a floor grate.

ROBIN EXTREME OBJECTIVES

Triple Snap Flashed: Knock down three henchmen using a Snap Flash.

Fists of Fury: Take down a henchman with a Beatdown.

Bullet Proof: Take down all of the henchmen without taking damage.

END DLC CONTENT!

LOST CITY
LOCATION: Wonder Tower Foundations

BATMAN OBJECTIVES

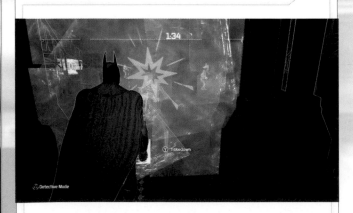

Grate Moves: Perform a Takedown on a henchman while inside a floor grate.

Fall Guy: Batclaw a henchman and pull him off a walkway to take him down.

Breaking & Entering: Perform a Takedown through a weakened wooden wall.

All three of the medals require getting an enemy to the right spot before taking him down. With an enemy on the walkway, stand on the opposite side of an opening from him and use the Batclaw to pull him off.

Make some noise on the lower level and duck behind a weakened wooden wall or into a floor grate. Take down an enemy from one of these positions and then when others come to investigate, get the other one.

BATMAN EXTREME OBJECTIVES

Bullet Proof: Take down all of the henchmen without taking damage.

Switch Hitter: Kick one henchman while on the Line Launcher, then fire the Line Launcher again from the current line and kick a different henchman.

High Speed Impact: Use a boosted Remote Batarang to knock a henchman over an edge.

With an enemy near one of the railings, send a Remote Batarang in his direction and boost it all the way to send him over. With at least two henchmen loitering on the walkway, switch to the Line Launcher and go in one of their directions. Knock him down and launch a line toward another enemy. This can also be done on the bottom floor.

Don't get careless when fighting the other guards. The final medal requires taking no damage! If the hostage is taken, grapple around the gargoyles to the one above him and perform an Inverted Takedown on his captor.

CATWOMAN OBJECTIVES

Caltrop Trip: Knock down an enemy using the Caltrops and take him down.

Round the Bend: Use Corner Cover to hide, then take down an approaching henchman.

Pouncer: Perform a Pounce Attack on a henchman and knock him out on the ground.

CATWOMAN EXTREME OBJECTIVES

Whipped Up: While climbing on the ceiling, perform a Take-down on an enemy above.

Knockout Smash: During a Silent Takedown, perform a Knockout Smash to instantly take down the henchman.

Three Strikes: Punch any three differently armed henchmen.

DLC CONTENT!

ROBIN OBJECTIVES

Snap Flashed: Knock down one henchman using a Snap Flash and take him down.

Fire Hazard: Use a Shuriken on a fire extinguisher and silently take down a henchman caught up in the smoke.

Aerial Assault: Glide-kick a henchman and knock him out on the ground.

ROBIN EXTREME OBJECTIVES

Shield Smash: Use a Shield Bash to knock a henchman off a ledge.

Snap Flash Trap: Place a Snap Flash on a stunned hench-man, then use it to knock down a different henchman.

Grate Moves: Perform a Takedown on a henchman while inside a floor grate.

END DLC CONTENT!

TOP OF THE WORLD
LOCATION: Wonder Tower Observation Deck

BATMAN OBJECTIVES

Fire Hazard: Batarang a fire extinguisher and silently take down a henchman caught up in the smoke.

Confiscated Weapon: Use the Batclaw to disarm a henchman, then take him down (upgrade required).

Mine Your Step: Detonate a mine using the Mine Detonator when a henchman walks over it (upgrade required).

From the start, move along the gargoyles to the next balcony on the right. Drop behind the guard and disarm him with the Batclaw. Take him down for the Confiscated Weapon medal.

A henchman carries around mines and places them on the floor. He announces when one is being set. Watch as he puts it down, then use the Disruptor to blow it up in his face. There are several fire extinguishers inside the Observation Deck, when an enemy approaches one, hit it with a Batarang to create a cloud of smoke. Take down the henchman when he panics.

BATMAN EXTREME OBJECTIVES

Fists of Fury: Take down a henchman with a Beatdown.

Human Cannonball: Shoot an armored henchman with the REC to send him flying back into another henchman.

Cold War: Use the Freeze Cluster Grenade to immobilize three or more henchmen at one time (upgrade required).

There is a fairly simple way to get two medals right away. Grapple around to the right to the gargoyle just past a balcony with a henchman. Wait for another guard to join him and hit them both with the REC. Grapple back to the Vantage Point on the other side of the balcony to avoid detection. The armored henchman with the Jammer backpack comes out to investigate. Toss the Freeze Cluster Grenade in the middle of them to get the Cold War objective.

Move around the Gargoyles until the armored enemy is in between Batman and another henchman. Get the Human Cannonball objective by hitting the armored guy with an REC. Quickly flee the scene or this challenge attempt may end prematurely. Carefully eliminate the guards using Takedowns from the balcony ledges and the floor grates until one guy is left. Finish him off with a Beatdown for the final medal.

CATWOMAN OBJECTIVES

Gun Thief: Disarm a henchman using an aimed Whip attack.

Have a Nice Trip: Slide into a henchman and knock him out on the ground.

Feet First: While standing on a ledge directly above a target, perform a Reverse Ledge Takedown on a henchman below.

CATWOMAN EXTREME OBJECTIVES

Cat Fight: Perform a Beatdown on an armed henchman.

Caltrop Trip: Knock down an enemy using the Caltrops and take him down.

Don't Touch That Dial: Leave the henchman with the Jammer backpack until last.

DLC CONTENT!

ROBIN OBJECTIVES

Zip Kick Off: Use the Zip Kick to knock a henchman off a walkway.

Over the Ledge: While hanging from a ledge, grab a henchman and pull him down over the ledge.

Round the Bend: Use Corner Cover to hide, then take down an approaching henchman.

ROBIN EXTREME OBJECTIVES

Bullet Shield: Block a henchman's bullets before performing a Shield Bash, then take them down.

Round the Bend: Use Corner Cover to hide, then take down an approaching henchman.

Fire Hazard: Use a Shuriken on a fire extinguisher and silently take down a henchman caught up in the smoke.

END DLC CONTENT!

DLC CONTENT!

BLACK MASK
LOCATION: Sionis Slaughterhouse

BATMAN OBJECTIVES

Sonic Boom: Use the Sonic Shock Batarang to pacify a henchman (upgrade required).

Choke Slam: Use the Dive Bomb Tackle to knock down a henchman, then take him out on the ground.

Line Drive: Kick one henchman using the Line Launcher.

The objectives in Sionis Slaughterhouse are straightforward. The trickiest one may be Line Drive, since it can be tough to get a clear shot on an enemy with the Line Launcher.

Toss a Sonic Shock Batarang at the feet of a henchman and detonate it to get Sonic Boom. For Choke Slam, grapple to one of the Vantage Points and pick out a target below. Dive Bomb into the guy to tackle him.

CATWOMAN OBJECTIVES

Gun Thief: Disarm a henchman using an aimed Whip attack.

Cat Fight: Perform a Beatdown on an armed henchman.

Grate Moves: Perform a Takedown on a henchman while inside a floor grate.

ROBIN OBJECTIVES

Shield Bash: Knock a henchman down with the Shield Bash, then take him down.

Zip Kick Off: Use the Zip Kick to knock a henchman off a walkway.

Window Pain: Perform a Takedown through a glass window.

WAYNE MANOR MAIN HALL
LOCATION: Wayne Manor

BATMAN OBJECTIVES

Freeze Frame: Use any Freeze Gadget on a henchman, then take him down while frozen.

Chaos Theory: Perform an Inverted Takedown from a Vantage Point on a thermal henchman.

Domino Effect: Kick three henchmen in one move using the Line Launcher.

There is a great opportunity to get an Inverted Takedown right from the start. Grapple to the Vantage Point at the other end of the mansion. A thermal henchman walks down the steps and pauses below, so knock him out. Find an isolated henchman and use a Freeze Gadget on him, then take him down to get Freeze Frame.

Crowd Control can be a bit trickier, since you need to get three guys next to one wall. You could hold off on the Inverted Takedown and sneak behind the far wall via the vents on the bottom floor. Place the Explosive Gel and head to that Vantage Point. Wait for the thermal henchman to make his rounds back to that point, then get the Takedown. Move to another spot and wait for three of them to congregate to that position and then let them have it.

CATWOMAN OBJECTIVES

Cat Nap: While climbing on the ceiling, perform a Takedown on an enemy below.

Pouncer: Perform a Pounce Attack on a henchman and knock him out on the ground.

Skull Cracker: Sneak up behind two henchmen and perform a Double Takedown.

ROBIN OBJECTIVES

Zip Kick: Knock down a henchman using the Zip Kick, then take him down.

Shield Smash: Use a Shield Bash to knock a henchman off a ledge.

Smoke Detector: Use the Smoke Pellet to create a smoke cloud and take down a henchman when he panics in the smoke.

THE BATCAVE
LOCATION: Batcave

BATMAN OBJECTIVES

Shock Tactics: Shoot a henchman with the REC to make him fire into the air, scaring another henchman.

Weapon Jam: Use the Disruptor on one henchman's gun, let him try to use it and then take him down (upgrade required).

Boomerang Batarang: Knock down a henchman using the Reverse Batarang, then take him down with a Silent Takedown when he looks the wrong way.

Locate the henchman near the Batwing, use the Disruptor on his gun, then drop down in front of him. After he attempts to shoot Batman, take him down. Immediately grapple to the lights. When the others come to investigate, fire an REC at the rear guard so that he scares another with his gunfire. Quickly leave the area.

Pick off the rest of the guards one by one until only one remains. Use the Reverse Batarang to knock him down and drop in behind him. Take him down with a Silent Takedown when he looks the other way.

CATWOMAN OBJECTIVES

Caltrop Trip: Knock down an enemy using the Caltrops and then take him down.

Whipped Up: While climbing on the ceiling, perform a Takedown on an enemy above you.

Hit and Run: Punch an armed henchman.

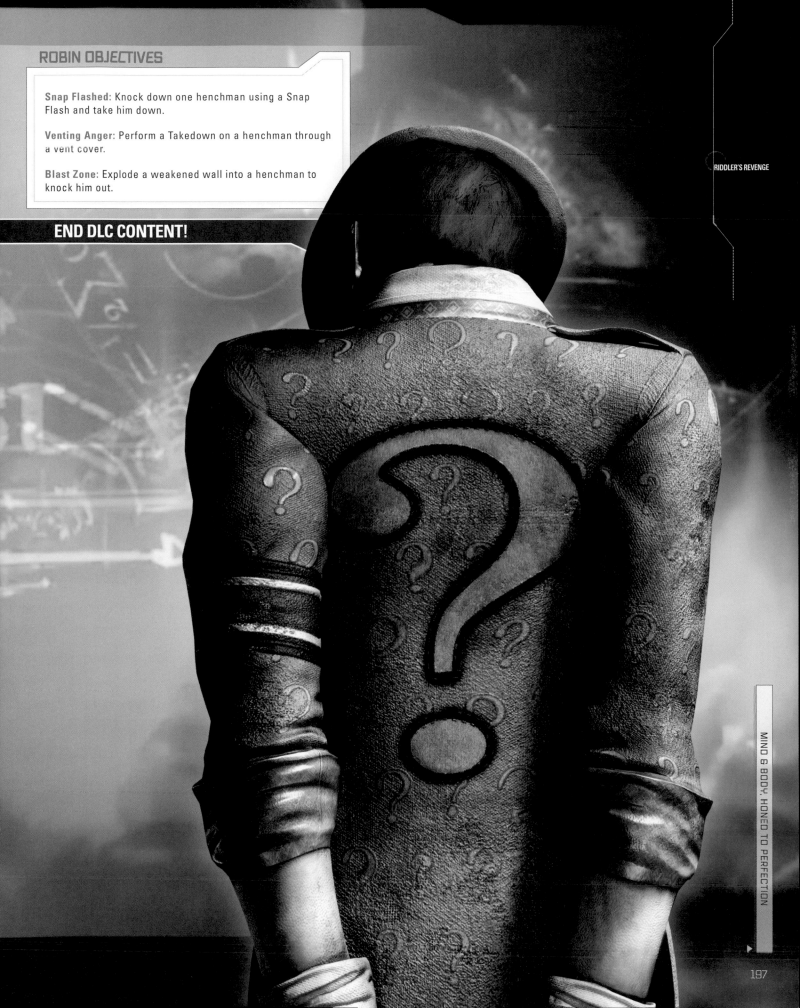

ROBIN OBJECTIVES

Snap Flashed: Knock down one henchman using a Snap Flash and take him down.

Venting Anger: Perform a Takedown on a henchman through a vent cover.

Blast Zone: Explode a weakened wall into a henchman to knock him out.

END DLC CONTENT!

RIDDLE ME THIS, BATMAN

Edward "Riddler" Nigma placed hundreds of Riddles throughout Arkham City. Most of them are in the form of Riddler Trophies, which often require the player to solve some kind of puzzle. There are also Riddles in each area of the city that must be solved by scanning an item or scene. Destroying cameras and certain collectibles also provide credit toward the Riddles.

Disruptor

The Riddles presented in this chapter are listed by areas in Arkham City, including: Park Row, Amusement Mile, Industrial District, the Bowery, the Subway, Steel Mill, Museum and Wonder City. To view which Riddles you have completed, simply select Riddles from the Back Button Menu. Complete a row of Riddles to unlock a piece of concept art or an interview tape. Completing rows of Riddles for the following areas unlock one of five interview tapes from the characters listed here.

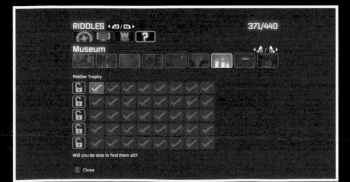

AREA	TAPE FOR EACH COMPLETE ROW
Park Row	Catwoman
Amusement Mile	Mister Freeze
Industrial District	The Joker
The Bowery	The Penguin
Subway	Two-Face

Completing rows of Riddles for the following areas unlock various pieces of concept art.

ROW	AREA	CONCEPT ART UNLOCKED
1	Steel Mill	Sionis Steel Mill: Production Line
2	Steel Mill	Sionis Steel Mill: Loading Bay
3	Steel Mill	Batman in the Steel Mill
4	Steel Mill	Sionis Steel Mill: Furnace
5	Steel Mill	The Joker's house of mirrors
1	Museum	Cyrus Pinkney's Institute for Natural History
2	Museum	Cyrus Pinkney's Institute for Natural History: Mammoth
3	Museum	Zsasz imprisoned
4	Museum	Cyrus Pinkney's Institute for Natural History: Exhibits
5	Museum	The Iceberg Lounge
1	Wonder City	Alleyways of Wonder City
2	Wonder City	Wonder City
3	Wonder City	Lazarus Pit Experimentation
4	Wonder City	Trials in the desert
5	Wonder City	Wonder Tower

Many of the Riddler Trophies unlock concept art or character Trophies, which are found at the Main Menu. For each Trophy, the book lists what it unlocks. For example, if it says "unlocks Challenge Map," then a room is unlocked in Riddler's Revenge in the following order.

Blind Justice
Meltdown Mayhem
Police Brutality
Search and Destroy Campaign
Survival of the Fittest
Natural Selection
Rooftop Rumble
Street Justice Campaign
Hell's Gate
End of the Line
Funhouse Brawl
Offensive Maneuvers Campaign
Prison Riot
Lost City
Top of the World
City Invader Campaign
Combat Expert Campaign
Predator Expert Campaign

Natural Selection [Extreme]
Hell's Gate [Extreme]
Meltdown Mayhem [Extreme]
Midnight Assault Campaign
Prison Riot [Extreme]
Police Brutality [Extreme]
Funhouse Brawl [Extreme]
Hostile Takeover Campaign
Lost City [Extreme]
Rooftop Rumble [Extreme]
End of the Line [Extreme]
Double Jeopardy Campaign
Survival of the Fittest [Extreme]
Top of the World [Extreme]
Blind Justice [Extreme]
Ruthless Vengeance Campaign
Combat Master Campaign
Predator Master Campaign

PARK ROW

RIDDLER TROPHIES

1 Hop over the fence at the west end of the street and look inside the room ahead. Use the Disruptor on the TYGER Sentry Gun to disable it, then go inside to get the Trophy.

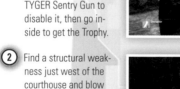

2 Find a structural weakness just west of the courthouse and blow it up, then use the REC on the door.

3 There are four question marks on the roofs to the west of the court-house. You only have four seconds to hit all the switches. Place Explosive Gel on the three switches that are obscured when standing near the Trophy. Detonate them and quickly hit the fourth one with a Batarang.

4 Go to the end of the street northwest of the courthouse and use the Cryptographic Sequencer to hack into the Security Panel (password is ADMITTANCE). Now walk back and pick up the Trophy.

5 Start down the steps leading to the court-house basement and turn around. Use the Batclaw to snatch this Trophy located above the door.

6 While looking to the left of the basement door, throw the Remote Controlled Batarang through the electricity. Turn it around and guide it down the stairs into the closed-off room ahead. Fly it into the fuse box on the wall. This opens the cell door next to Calendar Man; grab the Trophy from within.

7 Find an opening in the wall to the north of Catwoman's apartment. Disable the turret using the Disrupter and blow up the wall ahead. Grab the Trophy and exit the room.

8 Climb to the top of the building, glide to the pad across the way, then kick off the wall and hit the pad from the wall from which you jumped. Kick off again and land on the pad in the center of the floor.

9 Find the three question marks on an upper wall northeast of the courthouse. Place Explosive Gel on each switch and detonate them to unlock the Trophy.

10 A Riddler Trophy sits behind a chain-link fence east of the courthouse. Grapple to the tall building east of the Trophy and locate a pressure plate. Turn to the west, run across the pad, and start to glide. Immediately dive through an open floor below. Use Explosive Gel on the weak point on the floor to get the Trophy.

11 Locate the Trophy on the roof between the courthouse and church. Use Detective Mode to find the question mark switch to the west and hit it with a Batarang.

12 Southwest from the previous Trophy, search for another one on the ground behind a fence. Use a Freeze Blast on the steam pipe to access it.

13 Find the political prisoner refugee camp area. Only a weakened wooden wall protects this Riddler Trophy.

14 There are five question marks on the east wall of the building west of Gotham Casinos. They light up in the following order (numbered from left to right): 5, 2, 1, 4, 3. Time several Batarang throws at each switch as they turn on.

15 Look down to the water southeast from the previous Trophy to spot the next Trophy. Use the Freeze Blast gadget to create an ice raft and hop down to it, then use the Batclaw on the hooks to access the Trophy.

(16) Find the Riddle Ball puzzle on the north side of a building to the northeast of the Bank of Gotham. There are three industrial electromagnets at the end of the cages. Hop to the ledge to

the south to view all three magnets. Aim the REC at the bottom magnet and press the indicated button to send the ball straight up. Press the other button on the upper-right magnet to make the ball enter the horizontal cage. Quickly use the REC on the final magnet to make the ball stay at the goal. Go over and grab the Trophy.

(17) Enter the church and pass through the next door. Look up to the right and grapple to the ledge, then turn and locate a weakened wooden wall. Use the Line Launcher to bust through the wall and find the Trophy.

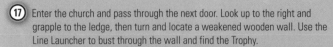

(18) Enter the bottom floor of the belltower in the church and turn around. Use the Batclaw to get the Trophy above.

(19) Use the Cryptographic Sequencer on the security panel atop the church to access this Trophy. The password is ANALYTICAL.

(20) Inside the church, head to the east side and break down the weakened wooden wall on the confessional.

(21) Behind the church, step onto the lighted pressure pad and use the Line Launcher to sail over the red ones. Next, grapple to the upper level to get the Trophy.

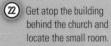

(22) Get atop the building behind the church and locate the small room. Use the REC on the fuse box and the Explosive Gel on the weakened wall.

(23) Find the stairway access at the top of the bar at the end of the street (west of the courthouse). Use the Cryptographic Sequencer on the security panel and use the password CONTEMPLATE.

(24) Enter the alley directly southwest from the courthouse and hop the fence. Slide underneath another fence on the left to procure the Trophy.

25 From the rooftop across the street from the courthouse, run across the pressure plate and grab the Trophy. Or, use the Batclaw to get it from the plate.

26 Grapple to the building to the east of the previous Trophy and access the next rooftop. Turn around and toss the RC Batarang into the vent. Guide it around the turn and into the bottom of the question mark to get the Trophy.

27 From the rooftop southeast of the last Trophy, locate the boarded up roof access. Bust through the wall to get the Trophy.

28 This Trophy sits on the ground southwest of the church. Stand nearby and throw the Remote-Controlled Batarang around the building to the west. On the other side, locate the question mark on the left side and hit the switch to reveal the Trophy.

30 Drop off the roof (from the last Trophy) and cross the street. Locate the cage with two mines and the Trophy. Use the Disrupter (with Mine Detonator upgrade from the "Remote Hideaway" side mission) to detonate the mines and access the Trophy.

31 Jump over the fence that is northwest of the Ace Chemicals building. Use the REC on the shop façade to find the Trophy.

32 Find the car propped up on blocks near the alley to the north of the Ace Chemicals building. Either slide underneath the car to nab the Trophy, or simply use the Batclaw.

29 To the northwest of the Bank of Gotham building, find a pressure plate on a rooftop and a question mark on a wall. Grapple to the closest vantage point on the corner of the bank and glide toward the pressure plate (stay as high as possible). Once directly over it, dive onto the pad. This should make the arrows light up to the question mark. Quickly toss a Batarang at the switch to get the Trophy.

33 Get onto the makeshift wall located down the street from the Monarch Theater. Use the Line Launcher to break through the weakened wooden wall below the Gotham Hardware sign.

34 Enter the alley across the street from Finnigan's. Freeze Blast the steam vent and slide underneath the fence to obtain another Riddler Trophy.

35 Grapple to the Riddler gargoyle on the southeast corner of the building south of the Monarch Theater to open a hatch down to the right. Quickly dive into the opening to nab the Trophy.

36 There are five question marks southwest of the Ace Chemicals building that light up from left to right. The objective is to hit the far right one when it is lit. Wait for the second from the right to light, then throw a Batarang at the right one.

CATWOMAN TROPHIES

37 Return to the destroyed weakened wall west of the courthouse and enter the enclosed area. Now, just leap to the ceiling.

38 Drop down to the south from Catwoman's apartment and locate a cage on the west wall. Use the opening on the bottom to access the Trophy.

39 This Trophy sits on the corner of a rooftop just below an Arkham billboard.

40 This one sits behind the church right above Trophy #21. Step onto the first pressure pad to release the Trophy, then pounce to the ceiling. Crawl to the upper level and leap to get it.

41 This Trophy is located directly above Batman's Trophy #33. As long as the wall is destroyed, hop the fence and pounce to the ceiling to get it.

RIDDLES

1 Perch on the pole hanging over the front of the courthouse. Look south at the bridge down the street while in Detective Mode to spot it.

2 Head west from the front of the courthouse to find Harvey Dent's campaign office.

3 Find Two-Face's Twin Guns on the judge's desk inside the courthouse.

4 Scan Calendar Man in the cell of the courthouse basement.

5 Drop into the cage outside Catwoman's apartment, or walk through the open gate if possible. Scan the window to solve this one.

6 Head up the street from the church toward a fence that blocks access to a collapsed bridge. Scan the Catastrophic Subsidence sign.

7 While inside the church, walk down the hall and turn toward the gurney on the right. Return to the desk to find Aaron Cash's ID and picture.

8 Look on the far west side of the map to see the Confiscated Goods Vault. Go there and scan the door.

9 This one is down the street from the Monarch Theater right before the Confiscated Goods Vault. Look on the northeast corner to find Poison Ivy's plant shop, Baudelaire.

10 After completing the "Mad Hatter" side mission but before leaving the room, scan the Alice in Wonderland book on the table.

11 Run down the street south from the courthouse and grapple over the wall. Just to the right is Hugo Strange's practice.

12 Locate the movie poster outside the Monarch Theater on the north wall. It shows "The Terror," starring Basil Karlo, a.k.a. Clayface.

13 Find the Crime Alley signpost located on either end of the alley near Monarch Theater. Scan one to get the Riddle.

14 Grapple to the top of the Ace Chemicals Building and scan the sign.

SECURITY CAMERAS

HUB

TYGER CCTV RELAY HUB

The hub is located on a rooftop southwest of the courthouse. Use the password is **SURVEILLANCE**.

Hack Device

Cryptographic Sequencer

AMUSEMENT MILE
RIDDLER TROPHIES

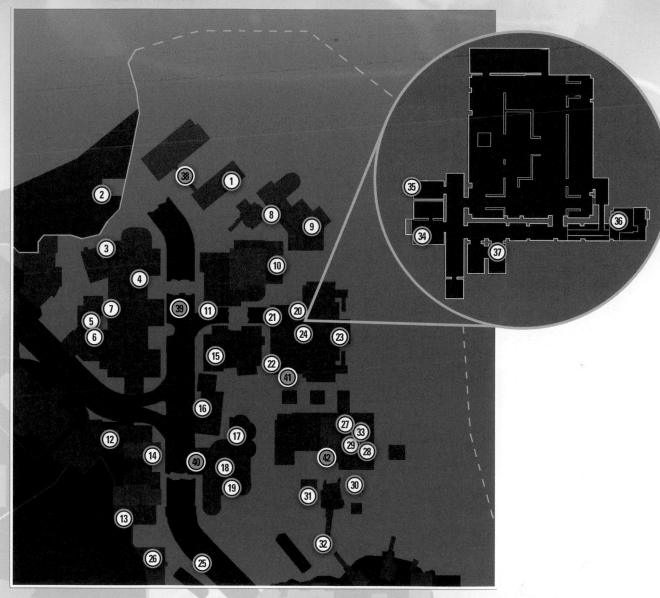

1 Find the roof access on top of the building to the far northeast. Use Explosive Gel to obtain the Trophy.

2 Just to the southwest of the hotel with Poison Ivy, there is a small room along the outside wall. Use the Freeze Blast to create an ice raft and glide down to it. Use the Batclaw to get closer, but don't go inside yet. Use the Distruptor to jam the TYGER turret, then float in and grab the Trophy.

3 From the last Trophy, find the swimming pool on the roof of the building to the south. Dispose of them, look for the weakened wooden wall, and destroy it.

4 Locate the entrance to Gotham Casinos on the west side of the collapsed street. Step into the patio and look to the left to find a pressure pad. Step on it and look the other way. Use the Line Launcher

to break through two weakened wooden walls and land near the Trophy.

5 There are three pressure pads on three different levels west of the casino, all of which must be activated without touching anything but the pads. Grapple to the highest one, southwest of the Trophy, then glide to the pad north of the Trophy and finally south to the final one. At this point, just run over to claim the prize.

6 Drop down a level from Trophy #5 to find another REC puzzle. To solve it, run north along the grating and drop onto a pipe below. Turn around and fire the Line Launcher to the south. Press

the Wire Walk button (note this is a required upgrade needed to obtain this Trophy) to flip to the top and walk along the tightrope until you get next to the electromagnet. Use the REC on it to make it send the ball to the top. Now go back and pick up the Trophy.

7 Grapple to the top of the casino to find a Trophy inside a large cage. Find the openings on each side and slide underneath. The Trophy rotates up and down at a steady pace, so time it so that the Trophy is facing down and grab it. When it rotates up, wait about two or three counts and then slide.

8 Find the pressure plate and the Trophy north of the GCPD Building and next to the dolphin neon sign. Look to the southwest to find three question marks. Create an ice raft using the Freeze Blast

gadget and use the hooks on each side of the question marks to reach them. Place Explosive Gel on each switch and grapple back to the pressure plate. Detonate them to access the Trophy.

9 Higher up on the same building Trophy #8 is another pressure plate and Trophy. Step on the plate and use the Batclaw to grab the Riddler Trophy.

10 Northwest of the GCPD building is a Trophy resting on a platform and a pressure plate on the wall below. Grapple to a nearby high point, such as the roof of the GCPD building. Glide toward the Trophy and dive underneath, then pull up and hit the switch. Immediately grapple through the newly-created opening and grab the prize.

11 While walking the collapsed street toward the GCPD building, look to the left to find another Trophy and pressure plate. Hop down and stand on the plate. Next, look to the west and throw a Remote Controlled Batarang and hit the left or right question mark switch. Immediately release another one, boosting as it approaches the opening. Take out the other side. Toss a third one right at the middle one and boost all the way to get it in time, then pick up the Trophy.

12 Find the six question marks on a wall surrounded by fences across the street to the south of the casino. Place Explosive Gel on the bottom three, then grapple to the west roof. Look down at the puzzle and throw three quick Batarangs to eliminate the top three. Immediately detonate the bottom ones to get the prize.

13 There's a maze with mines behind the Mercey Island Water Co. billboard in the southwest corner of the Amusement Mile area. The Disruptor will only disable two mines at a time, so you need  to find the path to the Trophy with the least mines. To get through the mines unscathed, use the disruptor on the one to the south of the Trophy and the one in the middle of the west side. Crawl inside and go around the live mines to the far corner of the maze. Turn right before the next two mines and grab the Riddler Trophy.

14 Another Trophy is on a rooftop southwest of Gotham City Olympus and three pressure pads. Simply walk across all three to unlock the Trophy.

15 Find the Riddler Security Panel on the rooftop west of the GCPD Building. Use the Cryptographic Sequencer to enter the password DELIBERATE.

16 Land on the balcony below the Gotham City Olympus sign, crash through the weakened wooden wall, and nab the Trophy from inside.

17 Find the pressure pad to the east of the Olympus building that alternates between green and red. Step on when it turns green to get the prize.

18 There is a magnetic ball puzzle on top of the Prawn Shack building. Stepping on the nearby switch opens the left gate and closes the right one. Use the REC on the magnet to pull the ball to the right, then step off and approach the opening in the cage. Once again, use the REC to put the magnet in attract mode. When the ball reaches the opening, grab the Trophy.

19 Grapple to the middle section of the radio tower. The Trophy rests on the north side.

20 Use the REC on the door in front of the GCPD building and use Explosive Gel on the wall to nab the Trophy.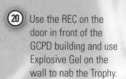

21 From the tall building north of GCPD, use Detective Mode to spot the weakened wooden wall on the north side of the lower level parking lot. Glide down toward it and break through to find the Trophy.

22 Under the southwest stairs in front of the GCPD Building, a Trophy sits inside a small room. Jump to a ledge to the west to access a Security Panel. Look into the room and hack the panel using the password PARKING. Jump back over to collect the Trophy. Note that the Cryptographic Range Amplifier upgrade is required for this Trophy.

23 Run to the back of the police headquarters and glide down to the debris in the water. The Trophy is hanging behind a small archway at the bottom of the building; use the Batclaw to get it.

24 This Trophy is located underneath the staircase in front of the GCPD building. Crawl in from the west side to get it.

25 This Trophy is hanging on the bottom of the drawbridge. Glide down to the barge to the west, then create an ice raft underneath the bridge and use the Batclaw to snag the prize.

26 West of the drawbridge is a Trophy and three pressure pads. Grapple to the building north of the water company billboard, then to some venting to find the first pad. Run south and glide toward a second pad on the wall ahead. Dive and glide to run into it. Push off and glide back north toward the third one. Glide into it and push off again. Grapple to the south building to retrieve the Trophy. You only have seven seconds after hitting the third pad to get the Trophy.

27 Go to the boat shelter southeast of the police station. Use the Freeze Blast gadget to create an ice raft and use the hooks inside the shelter to glide toward the south gate. Use the Cryptographic Sequencer on Riddler's Security Panel to enter the password INTELLIGENCE. Maneuver inside and grab the Trophy.

28 Grapple to the southeast gargoyle atop the GCPD building. Look southeast to spot a cage with red question mark pressure pads. Glide in that direction and begin to dive about half way there, then pull up and glide just underneath the top of the cage. Sail over the pads and pick up the prize.

29 There are vents and question marks behind the Krank Co. Toys sign. Flaps open and close along the right vent, making timing very important. Toss a Remote Controlled Batarang into the right vent just as the first flap rises,

then boost to the right switch. This disables the flaps, so throw another Batarang into the vent and slowly guide it around the left and right turns to hit the second switch.

30 Glide down to a platform south of Krank Co. Toys, face to the north and step onto the pressure pad. This triggers a game with five question marks. Memorize the order in which they light up and then hit each one in the same order. After repeating the first set, a light appears next to the Trophy. After three successful sets, the prize is yours. The sequences appear in the following order (numbered question marks from left to right).

1, 3, 5, 2, 4
4, 3, 1, 5, 2
3, 5, 2, 1, 4

31 To the south of Krank Co. Toys is another platform with three pressure pads and a Trophy. You must press all three pads without landing on anything else. Start on any pad and face the smoke stacks. Grapple

to the top of one and use a Grapple Boost. Glide back around and dive onto one of the other pads. (If you end up hanging on the side of the fence, just drop onto the pressure pad to continue.) Repeat the Grapple Boost technique to land on the third pad, then climb over the fence to obtain the Trophy.

32 Grapple to the north crane and use the REC on the Industrial Electromagnet to make the hook rise out of the water. Use the Batclaw to snag the Trophy from atop the hook.

33 Enter the Krank Co. Toys building and search behind the desk to the right to find this Trophy. Use the Batclaw to get it.

34 Enter the GCPD building through the front or back door and proceed to the front hallway. There are three pressure pads to land on without touching anything else. Grapple to the south ledge and step onto the nearby pad. Turn around and use the Line Launcher on the far wall, then release it to land on the second pad. Turn around again and launch another line back the way you came. At the intersection, look to the right and launch a third line. Just land on the pad next to the Trophy to get the prize.

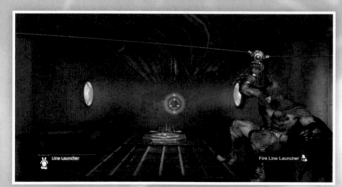

35 Go to the north end of the front hall in the GCPD building. To get the Trophy, you must destroy a fuse box using an electrified Batarang. Run down the hall and head east to reach the stairs near the back entrance. Turn around and toss a Remote Controlled Batarang through the electricity. Guide it underneath the partially opened gate. Continue down the hall around the corner and enter the cell via a small opening at the top of the door. Finish its course into the box to open the door and receive another Trophy.

36 Go to the office below the back entrance to find a Trophy on the desk. If coming from the front, use Freeze Blasts on the steam vents to access the area.

37 Locate the Security Panel east of where the two hallways intersect in the police station. Use the Cryptographic Sequencer and enter CUSTODY to gain entry. Blow up the wall using Explosive Gel to access the cell with the Trophy.

CATWOMAN TROPHIES

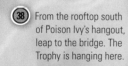

38 From the rooftop south of Poison Ivy's hangout, leap to the bridge. The Trophy is hanging here.

39 From Riddler Trophy #11, jump across the water to the south and run toward the bridge. Pounce to the grating underneath the bridge and move north to snatch the Trophy.

40 Find the roof access on the northwest part of the Gotham City Radio building. Break through the weakened wooden wall to collect the Trophy.

41 Enter the GCPD Building parking garage through the hole used to access Trophy #21. Pounce to the grating above to traverse the gap and pick up the Trophy on the other side.

42 To get this one, you must complete the "Fragile Alliance" side mission. Enter Krank Co. Toys and turn right to find the six TITAN containers. Leap to the ceiling above to get the prize.

RIDDLES

1 Stand behind the billboard on the lower roof west of the casino. Use the REC to lower the shutter across the street, then line up the dot on the shutter with the rest on the back of the billboard.

2 Stand on a high point in the northeast section of Amusement Mile (such as the water tower northwest of the GCPD building). Zoom in to an island to the east and scan. It is Arkham Island.

3 Glide to the building south of Poison Ivy's hideout and land next to the billboard. Look north to spot her containment unit. Zoom in to get a good shot.

4 Grapple to the vent on the east side of the casino and look south to find a Flying Graysons poster.

5 Stand on the southeast corner of the casino roof and peer southeast toward the Gotham City Olympus building. Zoom in to Zeus with a Lightning Bolt and scan it.

6 From Riddler Trophy #21, use the Line Launcher to bridge the gap to the south and look left. Walk up to where it says "Reserved Parking James Gordon."

7 Fly to the northwest gargoyle atop the GCPD building. Look down on the roof to spot the bat signal and scan it.

8 There are lots of crows scattered around Amusement Mile. Find the scarecrow mask in the hay and scan it to solve this Riddle.

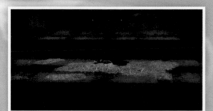

9 Scan the Krank Co. Toys sign located south of the GCPD building.

COLLECTIBLES: JOKER'S BALLOONS

SECURITY CAMERAS

HUB

TYGER CCTV RELAY HUB

Find this hub on the building northwest of the GCPD building; the password is **RECONNAIS-SANCE**.

INDUSTRIAL DISTRICT
RIDDLER TROPHIES

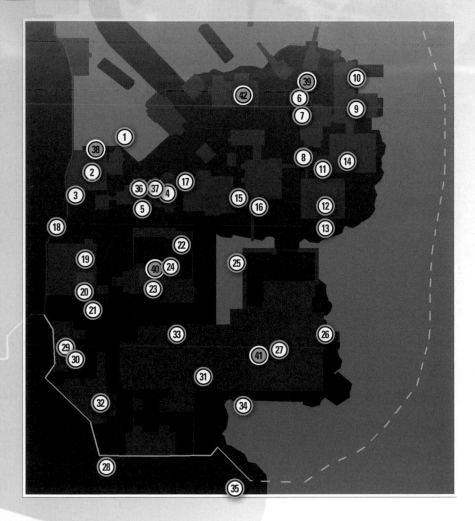

1 Grapple to the crane in the northwest corner of Industrial District and use the REC on the magnet to take down the hook. At the bottom, use the REC again to bring the hook back up. Use the Batclaw to access the Trophy.

2 Hop down off the west side of the crane and use Explosive Gel on the weakened wall. Inside is another magnet and ball puzzle. A magnet sits atop the cage and a motor hangs on the right wall. Use the REC on the motor (up sends the magnet right, down sends it left). Send the magnet to the left and use it on the magnet to attract the ball. Aim to the right and make the motor bring the magnet back. The ball should then drop to the opening on the right.

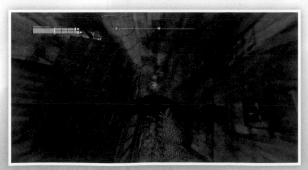

3 Just south of the previous building is another strength test game. Find a high point, such as the two towers to the east. Grapple to the left one and turn around. Glide toward the pressure plate, diving and pulling up to get more height. When close to the wall, start to dive. Maintain plenty of speed and adjust your aim to hit the pad as hard as possible. Detonate the Shock Wave Attack after diving toward the pressure plate. This lights up all the switches; hit the switch with the Batarang.

4 Note that the Grapnel Boost upgrade is required for this Trophy. The two towers to the east contain a locked Trophy with pressure plates on each tower. Look northeast to find a third pad on another

tower. You must glide into all three without touching the ground. Grapple to the top of the far tower and turn around, then glide into the closest pad and push off. Fly around and grapple to another tower and boost to stay in the air to reach another pad. Repeat this for the third pad and collect the Trophy between the towers.

5 Grapple over the brick wall on the south side of Zsasz's hideout to find three pressure pads that flash green in order from east to west. Watch the timing and step on the furthest one as it turns green to disable it. Continue this while heading east and collect the prize after turning them all off.

6 Just south of the eastern crane is a weakened wooden wall. Glide off the crane and break through the wall to collect the Trophy.

7 Locate the destructible wall just south of the previous Trophy. Break through it to find two more similar walls and the Trophy.

8 Two mines and two steam mines block this Trophy, which is west of the gate to Joker's Fun House. Use Freeze Blasts on the steam vents and the Remote Mine Detonator on the mines to reach the prize.

9 Find the roof access with a weakened wall directly south of Riddler Trophy #8. Use Explosive Gel on the wall to reveal the prize.

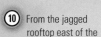

10 From the jagged rooftop east of the cranes, look down to the east to find a big cage. Drop down to the dock on the right and enter the opening. Use the Line Launcher to the north and prepare another line. When the time is right, send a line to the right and use the Tightrope command to jump on top and turn around. Grapple to the platform to claim the Trophy. Use the nearby pressure plate to exit.

11 Find the pressure pad to the north of the Steel Mill in the middle of the road. To the south are two blast doors blocking three question mark switches. The blast doors open when you step on the pad, but immediately start to close.

Quickfire a Batarang to get the middle switch, then toss a Remote Controlled Batarang through the opening. Turn right and send the gadget into the second switch. Boost a third Batarang through the opening and guide it into the left question mark to reveal the prize.

12 Get to the rooftop with the Ferris wheel and grapple to the eastern of the four highest gondolas. Use the Batclaw to snag a Trophy from the car.

13 Dive to the ground south of the Ferris wheel to find another magnet and ball puzzle. Stand on the south side and use the REC on the magnets as follows: attract with left magnet; attract with right magnet; attract with left (if necessary); repel with right; attract with left magnet to get the ball to the opening.

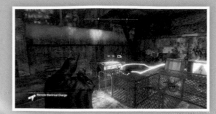

14 From the jagged roof, grapple to a platform on the rooftop to the south. Step on the pressure pad to start a six-second timer. Hop off the platform and use the Batclaw to snag the Trophy hanging below the pad.

15 Locate the pressure pads and lights on the wall in an alley just east of the Otis Flannegan poster. Stepping on the left pad causes three lights to shine, while the right pad turns on five more (these are added to whatever is already on). If more than seven are turned on, the extra digits are lit back up. There are many ways to solve this puzzle, but the method with the least number of presses is: step on the left three times and right pad once (i.e. $3 \times 3 + 1 \times 5 = 14$).

16 Find the mine maze in between a Sionis Industries warehouse and a Joker's Funland archway. There are 11 mines inside, but the Mine Detonator isn't required to solve this Riddle. Crawl inside from the west and turn right, left, right, left. Go east to the dead end and turn left and then right. Go to the east and turn left to claim the prize.

17 From Trophy #15, head up the alley to the north and run around the west building to find a Trophy and Riddler Security Panel. Use the Cryptographic Sequencer and enter PERCEPTIVENESS to obtain the Trophy.

18 West of the tower with the Tricorner Naval neon sign is another hole in the inside containment wall. Use the long-range Cryptographic Sequencer on the Security Panel and enter the password ACKNOWLEDGEMENT. Walk inside to claim the prize.

19 Find the pressure pad puzzle on the rooftop to the south of Riddler Trophy #18. Five pads light up from north to south; time a sprint across as they all light up to get the Trophy.

20 From Trophy #19, drop off the roof to the south to find a pressure pad puzzle. Drop underneath the fencing (if necessary) and stand on one of the pads. Use the Line Launcher (east or west) and land on another pad. Repeat this for the third press pad to unlock the Trophy.

21 Find the crane next to the Subway Maintenance Access. The Trophy sits directly underneath it. Slide underneath the crane, or use the Batclaw to pull the Trophy out.

22 Locate the weakened wooden wall at the base of the Tricorner Naval tower. From a highpoint east of here, glide through the wall and hit the pressure plate on the wall. Push off from the pressure plate and land on the other side of the red pads to obtain the Trophy.

23 Locate the brick wall northeast of the Subway Maintenance Access. Climb over it and examine the south side of the wall; use Explosive Gel on it to claim this prize.

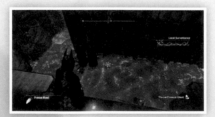

24 From Riddler Trophy #23, run clockwise around the building to find a Riddler Security Panel hidden behind the Duck Shoot counter. Use the Cryptographic Sequencer to enter the password INSIGHTFULNESS to claim the Trophy.

25 Use the Freeze Blast gadget to create an ice raft in the watery area north of the Steel Mill. Use the hook on the east wall to reach the wall. Look up and use the Batclaw on a hatch to drop the frozen Trophy.

26 East of the Steel Mill there is a metal balcony overlooking the bay. Grapple to it and enter the hobo shack to find this Riddler Trophy.

27 Use Explosive Gel on the south side of the smokestack to destroy a weakened wall. Move around the west side of the structure to find an enclosed Trophy. Throw a Remote Controlled Batarang into the air and guide it through the northern opening and guide it into the question mark. You have just four seconds to pick up the prize.

28 Drop to the street and go to the far southwest corner to find a small room in the containment wall. Throw a Remote Controlled Batarang into the left opening and turn it into the switch to disable the electrified floor. Walk in and grab the Trophy.

29 West of the Steel Mill, grapple to the top roof to find a pressure plate, a Trophy, and a roulette wheel of question marks. Step on the pad to make one light up. As they spin in a counter-clockwise fashion, watch where the lighted one stops. Toss a Batarang at that switch to solve the Riddle.

30 Find the weakened wall to the west of the Steel Mill and blow it up using Explosive Gel. Use the REC on the shutter to the left to reveal a pressure pad. Stand on the pad and use the Long-Range Cryptographic Sequencer on Riddler's Security Panel to enter COMPREHENSION. Use the REC again to open the door and grab the Trophy.

31 Behind the Steel Mill, a train sits below a Sionis Industries sign. Stand behind it and use the REC on its AC motor to send it on its way. Climb on top when it stops and use Explosive Gel on the ceiling. Grab the Trophy using the Batclaw.

32 Locate the Trophy hanging from a ceiling inside a garage to the southwest of the Steel Mill. Slide underneath the gate and use the Batclaw to grab the Trophy.

33 Grapple to the northwest corner of the Steel Mill roof and walk to the east to find a weakened wooden wall. Knock it down to reveal another Trophy.

34 South of the Steel Mill in the water is a long cage. The only entrance to the cage is on the eastern side. Grapple to the Steel Mill roof and proceed to the southeast corner. Dive off the roof and pull up, aligning the flight path with the entrance to the cage. Glide through the opening to the pressure pad and collect the Trophy.

35 From the southeast corner of the Steel Mill roof, look southwest to find a small alcove. Glide over there and use a big dive to get some height and distance. Land in the opening to get the Trophy. (You can't grapple to this point, so you must land on the platform.)

36 Enter Zsasz's hideout, look into the right tunnel and use the Freeze Blast gadget to create an ice raft as far in as possible. When the water is down, glide down to it and look up on the left wall. Use the Batclaw to nab the Trophy.

37 After completing the "Cold Call Killer" side mission, stay in Zsasz's hideout and use the switch to create an electric spark underneath the platform. Exit and crawl through the ductwork on the left to land near the Trophy, then look down to the left for the electricity. Throw a Remote Controlled Batarang through the spark and immediately turn it around. Send it over Batman's head into the vent, turn left and guide the gadget into the fuse box to unlock the prize.

CATWOMAN TROPHIES

38 Climb the stairs underneath the west crane and continue to the walkway. Get on the railing and climb down to the underside to get the Trophy.

39 From the spot where you can switch characters, run east to the opening made for Trophy #6. There are three pressure pads inside along with a Trophy on the ceiling. Step on one pad and pounce to the ceiling. Drop onto another pad and repeat until all three are activated. Pounce again to get the prize.

40 From the Tricorner Naval tower, jump down to the rooftop to the south. Dispose of the three armed thugs, then pounce onto the metal ceiling to snag this Trophy.

41 Find the opening just west of the smoke stack that was used to enter the Steel Mill. Walk to the back and pounce to the ceiling to obtain the Trophy.

42 After Batman finds Nora Fries and unlocks the main door to the building, Catwoman can enter. Drop into the ductwork below and follow it to a small room. Pounce to the ceiling for the reward.

RIDDLES

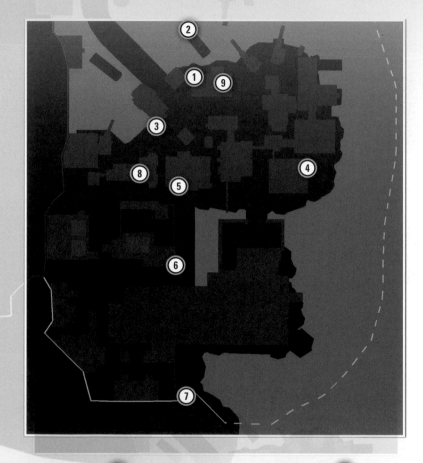

1 On top of the tower at the North Gotham Dock, stand on the east side and look to the west. Line up the dot on the top of the tower with the rest on the far wall.

2 Glide to the barge in the water east of the bridge. Scan the Falcone Shipping logo on the boat.

3 Find Bill's Hotdogs stand east of the crane and scan the newspaper dispenser to the left.

4 Travel to the east side of the building with the Ferris wheel. Find the wall with the Falcone Warehousing and Storage sign and scan it.

5 Look for the Otis Flannegan: Pest Control sign just northeast of the Tricorner Naval Building and scan it.

6 Grapple over the gate south of the Tricorner Naval Building and search for a posed body leaning against a telephone on the right.

7 Proceed south over the Steel Mill from the previous Riddle. Go around the Do Not Enter sign and scan the patched up hole in the southern containment wall.

8 Just after completing the "Cold Call Killer" side mission, stay inside Zsasz's hideout and scan The Broker business cards.

9 After finding Nora Fries in the "Heart of Ice" side mission, return to the warehouse to find Freeze and Nora together.

COLLECTIBLES: JOKER'S BALLOONS

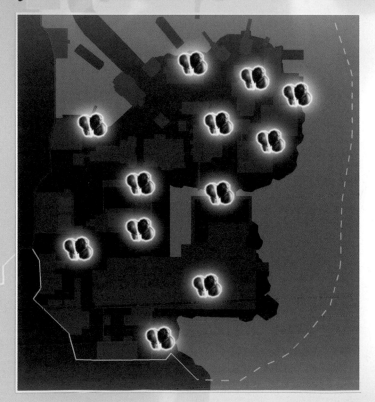

SECURITY CAMERAS

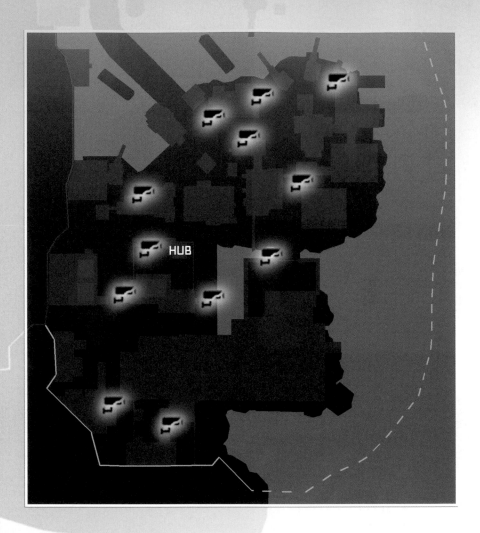

HUB

TYGER CCTV RELAY HUB

This hub is found on the high tower underneath the Tricorner Naval sign; the password is **OBSERVATION**.

THE BOWERY
RIDDLER TROPHIES

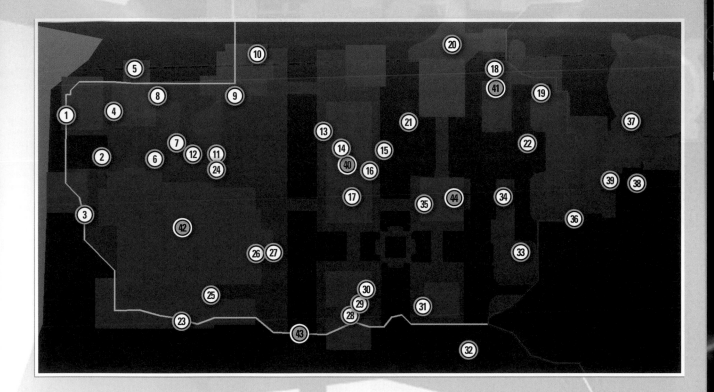

1 Locate the pressure and a trio of question marks in a cage on a rooftop northwest of the Museum. Step on the pad to make the middle mark light up and close the cage. After stepping off, the puzzle is reset.

Place Explosive Gel on all three switches and stand on the pad. Zoom in on each switch as they light up to explode them independently (middle, left, right). Once all three have been detonated, the Trophy is released.

2 There are three pressure plates northwest of the Museum on the ground level. Glide down to one of the western pads; you must activate all three without touching anything else. Use the

Line Launcher to sail to the east one and land on it. Do this again and land on the last pad to solve the Riddle.

3 Throw a Batarang at the first switch on the left. Next, guide a Remote Controlled Batarang through the gap on the far right side of the bars to hit the second switch.

④ Northwest of the Museum, in the narrow alley, use the REC to open the shop façade and discover another Trophy.

⑤ Grapple to the top of the building directly north of the Iceberg Lounge and locate the TYGER sentry gun in the containment room. Don't worry about it now; instead, find the roof access and blow up the entrance using some Explosive Gel. Drop into the vent and follow it to the Trophy.

⑥ This Trophy rests on the back of the horse statue outside the Iceberg Lounge. Use the Batclaw to retrieve it.

⑦ From the Iceberg Lounge entrance, look to the west and spot the tall structure against the wall. Grapple up to it and turn around, then glide off and dive toward the ground. Pull up before touching down and glide over the fence. The Trophy sits in the far-left corner.

⑧ North of the Museum is a small room protected by a Gotham Municipal Network Security Panel. Use the Cryptographic Sequencer to hack into it and enter REFUSE as the password. Step inside to collect the reward.

⑨ North of the Museum is a rooftop with a watertower. Grapple up there to find a Trophy inside a vent. Step on the pressure plate west of the vent to raise gates that block your access to the prize. This also starts a two second timer. Immediately run toward the opening and slide. Batman ends up beside the Trophy, so pick it up.

⑩ From Trophy #9, drop onto the roof to the north to find a Trophy ripe for the picking. Get too close, though, and it closes up. Move away until it unlocks and use the Batclaw to retrieve it.

⑪ Find the monorail car at Platform No.2 just north of the Museum. Climb onto the tall support above to find the Trophy.

⑫ Jump off Platform No. 2 to the west and go around the railing to the right. Drop straight down the pillar to ground level to find this Trophy.

(13) Head north up the road in front of the Museum. Find the Italian restaurant on the corner and use the REC to open its shutter to collect the Trophy inside.

(14) From Trophy #13, grapple to the monorail track and move east. An enclosed Trophy hangs from above, while three question marks dangle on the north and south walls. Hit one with a Batarang and you only get 2 seconds to get the rest. Quickfire three Batarangs in one of the directions, then turn around and launch another three to complete the puzzle. Use the Batarang to retrieve the prize.

(15) Walk along the monorail to the east from the previous Trophy. Find the boarded up wall on the monorail car on the north side. Grapple to a high point

and glide into this wall to get inside.

(16) Drop straight down from the train car from Trophy #15. Hop onto the south end of the west wall and use the Disruptor to detonate the mines between Batman and the weakened wall on the left. Destroy the wall using some Explosive Gel to get the Trophy.

(17) Locate the arches on top of the building south of the Bank of Gotham. The middle arch holds the Riddler Trophy.

(18) Grapple to the big building south of the Ace Chemicals Building, then look down from the east side to find the weakened wooden wall. Dive and glide through the wall to find the Trophy. (This is necessary for Catwoman to find a Trophy.)

(19) From the entrance to the Arkham City Processing Center, hop the fence to the north and follow the path to a Trophy behind a steam vent. Use a Freeze Blast on it, slide underneath the fence, and pick up the prize.

(20) Find the roof access on the rooftop directly south of the Ace Chemicals Building. Use Explosive Gel on the weakened wall and grab the Trophy.

(21) Spray the switch above the dumpster with Explosive Gel. Throw the Remote Controlled Batarang around the corner to hit the switch, then detonate the gel to open the cage.

22 Grapple to the upper entrance of the processing center and examine the wall. Use the Batclaw to retrieve the Trophy from high above.

23 Grapple to the Museum roof and search the middle of the south side to find this Trophy.

24 Follow the stairs on the northeast side of the Museum to Monorail Platform No. 2. Use the Cryptographic Sequencer on the Security Panel and enter METROPOLIS. Enter the car to get the Trophy.

25 Hop the fence on the south side of the Museum and slide underneath the next one to collect another Trophy.

26 Directly underneath the Museum's front entrance at street level, a weakened wooden wall barricades an opening to a shop. Break through it to get another Trophy.

27 Locate the boarded-up room directly above the shop from Trophy #26. Climb onto the Subway entrance and turn toward the room. Use the Line Launcher to break through the weakened wall to collect the prize.

28 Grapple to the rooftop southeast of the Museum to find another magnet and Riddler ball maze. Step onto the pressure pad on the venting to move a couple of gates inside the maze. Use the REC to set the left magnet to attract followed by the same for the right one. Step off the pad and let the ball roll to the left and down one spot. Get back on the switch and repel with the left magnet and hop off to make the ball stay in the middle cube. Repel with the right and finally attract with the left to get the ball to the opening.

29 On the east side of the building, drop down to the walkway below. Go to the south end to find a weakened wall on a shop façade. Blow it open using some Explosive Gel to collect the Trophy.

30 Grapple to the second rooftop southeast of the Museum and look over the west edge to spot a pressure pad on the walkway below. There's another one on the wall above and a third on the wall below. Glide to the opposite wall pad and push off, then soar to the pad on the east wall. Push off again and land on the third pad on the walkway.

31 Grapple to the south rooftop with the watertower to find a Trophy next to some venting. The duct runs into a cage and another connects to a question mark on the south wall. Throw a Remote Controlled Batarang to the west and do a U-Turn; guide it into the vent and then to the cage. Another U-Turn gets the gadget ready for the next vent. Guide it around the left turn and uphill to the switch.

32 Search for the TYGER Inmate Behavioral Analysis Unit door at the south end of the street. Use the Cryptographic Sequencer, with SCRUTINIZE as the password, on the security panel to gain access. Once inside, use the Batclaw to snatch the Trophy from the ceiling.

33 Grapple to the top of the hotel in the southeast corner of the Bowery to find two pressure pads and a Trophy. Climb to the south building to locate a third pad and step on it. Fly down to one of the other two pads and use the Line Launcher in the direction of the third. Drop onto the final plate to unlock the prize.

34 Grapple to the rooftop just south of the entrance to Arkham City Processing Center. Use the Cryptographic Sequencer on the Riddler Security Panel and enter INTELLECTUAL to get the Trophy.

35 Grapple to the top of the building southwest of the processing center entrance and walk around to the west side to find a Riddler Security Panel. Enter BRAINPOWER using the Cryptographic Sequencer to reveal the prize.

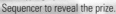

36 Enter the Arkham City Processing Center and stand on the railing. Use the Freeze Blast gadget to create an ice raft in the water and hop onto it. Use the Batclaw on a valve along the south wall to open it up and grab the Trophy.

37 In the main room of the processing center, use the Cryptographic Sequencer with the password PROMOTE on the security panel on the south wall. Use the Batclaw to get the Trophy hanging from the ceiling.

38 Inside the main room of the processing center, grapple to a ledge in the southeast corner. Use Explosive Gel on the weakened wall to get the Trophy.

39 From the main room of the processing center, enter the northeast door. Hit the mirror to shatter it and reveal the room beyond. Use the Batclaw to snag the Trophy hanging from a pipe.

RIDDLE ME THIS, BATMAN

CATWOMAN TROPHIES

40 Located underneath the bridge near Trophy #14. Pounce to the ceiling to grab it.

41 After collecting Trophy #18, hop onto the venting north of the processing center entrance. Climb into the opening and pounce to the ceiling. Use the flip grate to get into the cage above and collect the prize.

42 Find this Trophy on the roof of the Museum just north of the center dome.

43 At the south end of the Jezebel Center, take the stairs down to the landing. Jump south to the balcony to nab the Trophy.

44 Climb to the top of the building southwest of the processing center entrance (look for the big neon GOTHAM sign). The Trophy is on the east side.

RIDDLES

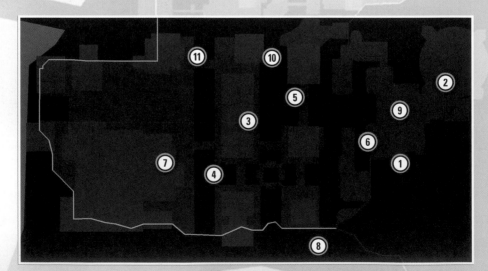

1 Enter the first door inside the Arkham City Processing Center. At the next door, use the Long Range Cryptographic Sequencer to hack into the security panel and enter INTERROGATION. Inside, look back through the middle window and line up the dot below the window with the rest of the question mark on the far wall.

2 Inspect the Wonder Tower from a rooftop in the Bowery. Zoom in if the subject is too small.

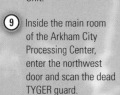

3 Find Sal Maroni's Italian Restaurant on the lower rooftop just south of the Bank of Gotham. It is located on the east side of the building.

4 Locate the Mad Hatter's Hat Shop outside the Museum on the northeast corner of the intersection on the second level. Scan the sign to solve this Riddle.

5 Scan the Quincy Sharp election poster on the south wall of the big building near the Ace Chemicals structure.

6 Search for the plaque commemorating Arkham City on the south wall just outside the second story entrance to the processing center.

7 There are Bruce Wayne "wanted" posters on the right side of the Museum. Scan them to solve this Riddle.

8 In the southeast corner of the the Bowery district is a gate marked as the TYGER Inmate Behavioural Analysis Unit.

9 Inside the main room of the Arkham City Processing Center, enter the northwest door and scan the dead TYGER guard.

10 Just east of the Bank of Gotham is Scarface's Puppet Shop.

11 Find the sign for Jezebel Center on the northwest corner of the Bank of Gotham building. Zoom in and scan it.

SECURITY CAMERAS

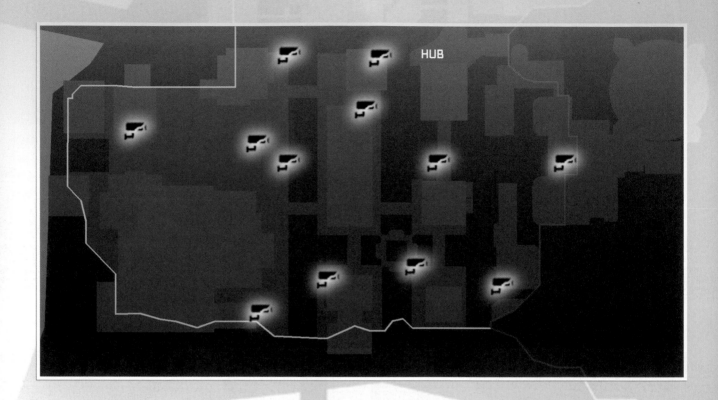

TYGER CCTV RELAY HUB

The hub in the Bowery is found on a balcony of the building located south of the Ace Chemicals Building. The password is **CHRONICLE**.

STEEL MILL
RIDDLER TROPHIES

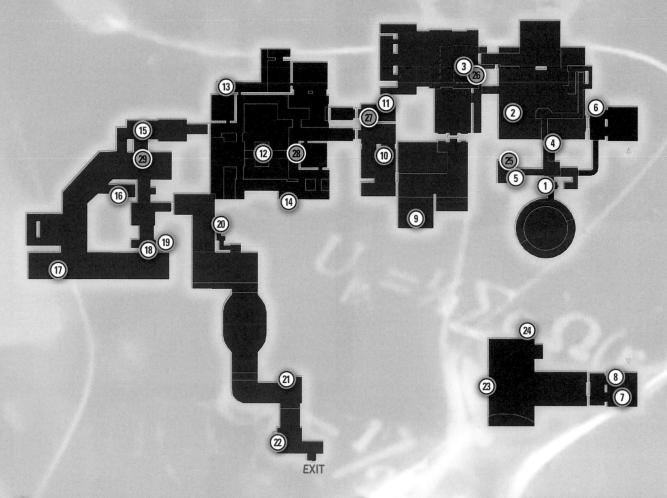

EXIT

1 From the loading bay, drop into the tunnel underneath the floor. Head west and then south to find a tunnel on the left. Follow the tunnel to another room. Crawl under the pipes and use the Batclaw to pry open a valve on the wall to collect the Trophy.

2 Drop into the grating in the middle of the loading bay and crawl to the west. Turn left and look for a steam pipe on the right. Use a Freeze Blast to clear the way and climb up to find the Trophy.

3 Exit the loading bay through the northwest door to find a lift with two Trophies. Use the Cryptographic Sequencer and enter TOUGHEN to gain access to the Trophies. Note that this requires Municipal codes to unlock the cage.

4 Inside the loading bay, fire RECs at the magnet in the back of the room. Attract the crank hook and then repel. Continue to swing it back and forth until it breaks through the fan cover on the south wall. Grapple to the opening to collect the Trophy.

5 From the previous Trophy, walk through the tunnel and drop into the hole. Use the Line Launcher to clear the gap and land on the pressure pad to release the Trophy.

6 Exit the loading bay via the southeast door to access the freight elevator. Use the Batclaw to pull down the valve on the left wall and grab the prize.

7 Drop into the freight elevator shaft and grapple inside the broken elevator on the right to find a Trophy.

8 Look for the breakable floor at the bottom of the freight elevator shaft. Use Explosive Gel on it and drop inside. Move around the equipment to collect another Trophy.

9 In the Assembly Line, drop down and look toward the bumper cars. Use the REC on the magnet to pull the cars away from the vent. Pull the vent cover off the south wall and enter it. Follow the path to another part of the Assembly Line. Exit the ductwork to obtain the Trophy.

10 After pulling away the bumper cars, use a Freeze Blast on the steam pipe on the west side. Crawl underneath the office to find another Trophy.

11 Inside the Assembly Line office, grapple to the platform above and continue to the north ledge. Use Explosive Gel on the wall to collect Trophy.

12 Drop to the lower level of the smelting chamber to the walkway in the middle. Look underneath the big piece of machinery and snag the Trophy with the Batclaw (or slide under it).

13 Access the narrow area to the northwest of the smelting chamber (use a vent on the north wall, or the vent or destroyable wall to the northeast). Once inside, grapple to a ledge on the west side to claim the Trophy.

14 In the smelting chamber, locate the valve on the south wall and use the Batclaw to pry it open and collect the bounty inside.

15 Enter Cooling Tunnel D through the smelting chamber's west door and approach the mine cart. Use an REC on the far magnet to pull (or push) the cart away. Pick up the Trophy hidden underneath.

16 From the mine cart, get on the bridge to the south and create an ice raft below. Use the Batclaw on the vent cover on the south wall to pry it off. Grapple into the hole to retrieve another Trophy.

17 Create an ice raft in the southern part of Cooling Tunnel D and use the hooks to maneuver around the drills. Duck under the wall and scour the ceiling for this Trophy. Use the hook on the left to pull the raft and snag the Trophy using the Batclaw.

18 Create an ice raft in the southeast part of Cooling Tunnel D. Hop onto it and grapple to an upper floor to the south. Collect the Trophy sitting next to the vent.

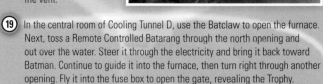

19 In the central room of Cooling Tunnel D, use the Batclaw to open the furnace. Next, toss a Remote Controlled Batarang through the north opening and out over the water. Steer it through the electricity and bring it back toward Batman. Continue to guide it into the furnace, then turn right through another opening. Fly it into the fuse box to open the gate, revealing the Trophy.

20 In Cooling Tunnel B, create an ice raft in the central part and hop on it. Use the hooks to the east to pull the raft over and use a Batarang to hit the question mark on the wall. Grapple to the ledge and pull off the vent cover. Crawl through the vent to find the Trophy.

21 Enter the Steel Mill through the south entrance, follow the path to the water, and drop down. Use the Line Launcher to reach the other side. Using the Cryptographic Sequencer, enter LOGICAL to collect the reward.

RIDDLER'S SECRETS

22 Just before the south exit in the Steel Mill, grapple to a small ledge on the west wall. Use Explosive Gel on the wall to reveal this Trophy.

23 In the Boiler Room, locate the penguins moving past the west wall and use the Batarang to destroy them. Use the Batclaw to get the Trophy.

24 On the north wall of the Boiler Room, use Explosive Gel to access a small room and another Trophy.

CATWOMAN TROPHIES

25 Enter the hole on the north side of the Steel Mill and continue to the Loading Bay. Climb into the hole on the south side, follow it down the hole, and leap to the ceiling prior to the fiery pit. Follow the grating over a fence and collect the reward on the other side.

26 Exit the Loading Bay from the west side and step into the lift that Batman opened with his sequencer. The Trophy is inside.

27 In the west office of the Assembly Line, climb onto the ledge on the north side. Use the flip grate to climb underneath and crawl to another one to the west. Climb inside the cage to collect the Trophy.

28 Enter the Smelting Chamber from the east side and run to the end of the walkway. Climb over the railing and onward to the ceiling below.

29 Climb underneath the drawbridge in Cooling Tunnel D and collect the Trophy hanging below.

RIDDLES

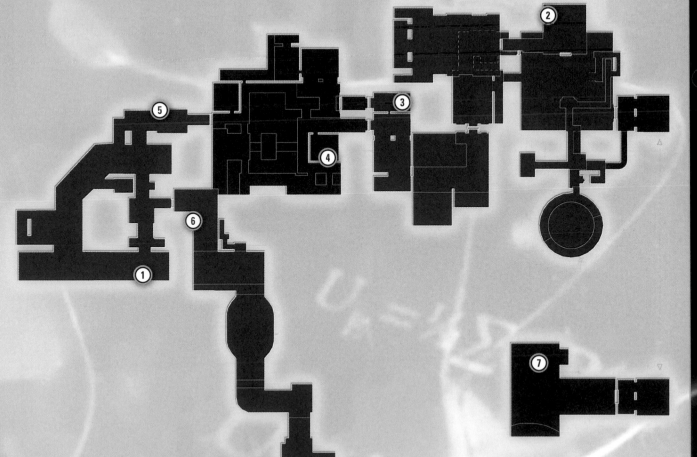

① Create an ice raft in the southeast corner of Cooling Tunnel D and hop on. Pull over to the far wall and peer into the previous room. Use Detective Mode to find a dot on the wall and the rest of the question mark on the far wall. Adjust left and right to line them both up.

② Defeat the enemies in the loading bay and grapple to the manager's office. On the west side, scan Harley Quinn's outfit from the first Batman game.

③ Exit the smelting chamber by using a REC on the two doors on the east side. On the other side of the far wall, locate the backs of the Abramovici Twins. Scan them to solve this Riddle.

4 Enter the office in the southeast corner of the Smelting Chamber. On the south wall, scan Harley Quinn's University of Gotham Degree hanging on the wall.

5 On your second visit to Cooling Tunnel D, Dr. Stacy Baker ambushes Batman. Look for a mallet leaning against the wall next to the Harley head and scan it.

7 Reach the Boiler Room by way of the Loading Bay and the elevator shaft. Look in the northwest area for a small box of Joker's toys and gadgets.

6 After entering Cooling Tunnel B from the northwest door, look on the west wall. Scan the Boyle Cryogenics poster.

COLLECTIBLE: HARLEY HEADS

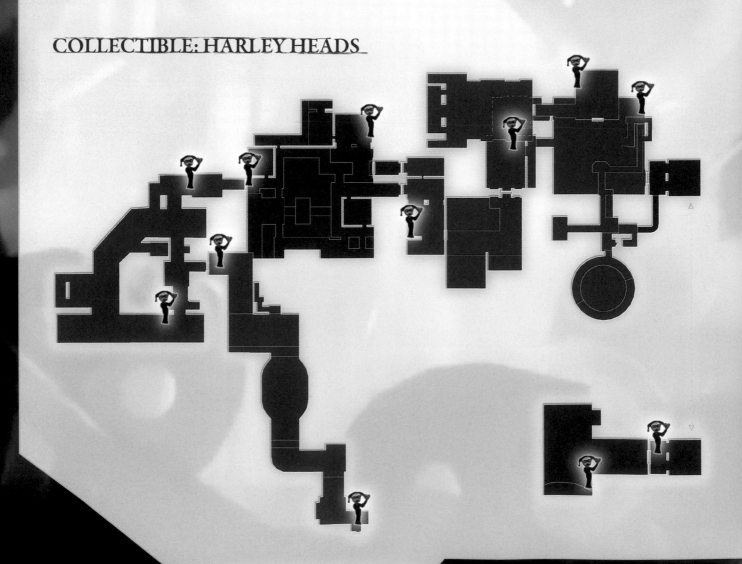

SUBWAY
RIDDLER TROPHIES

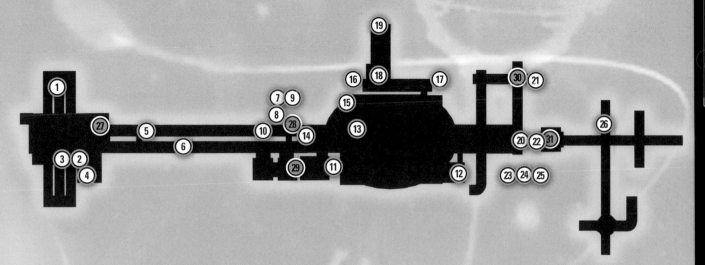

1 Hop over the north gate and take the steps down to the trains on the right. Pry open the vent cover and crawl inside. The Trophy is in the back.

2 Enter the Subway and head to the southeast to find a ticket booth. Use the Cryptographic Sequencer on the Municipal Security Panel and enter TICKETS to collect the reward inside.

3 From Trophy #1, run across the tracks to the grates in the floor. Climb inside and grab the Trophy.

4 Enter the east room after entering the Subway and pull off the vent cover. Crawl to another room and use Explosive Gel on the weakened floor. The Trophy is on the floor.

5 On the east side of the Subway Station is a Security Panel. Use the Cryptographic Sequencer to hack it using the password LOCOMOTIVE. Enter the train on the left to find the Trophy.

6 Run along the tops of the trains. When you cut back into the right line, turn right and look between the two train cars to find the Trophy. Drop down to get it or use the Batclaw to reach it.

(7), (8), (9) After passing the Solomon Grundy mural, hop over the girders on the left and use Explosive Gel on the weakened wall. Crawl underneath the Riddler door to find three Riddler Trophies and a Riddler Security Panel (password: DEADEND). Hacking it causes the floor to become electrified and the door to close. Hack the panel and wait for the Trophies to unlock and door to close. Immediately switch to the Line Launcher and send a line to the far side. Next, use the Tightrope command to get on top of the line and wait for the floor to become safe again. Drop down to collect the bounty.

(10) After passing the Solomon Grundy mural, hop over the girders on the left and use Explosive Gel on the weakened wall. Find the pressure pad on the tracks to the left. Stepping on it lights up three question marks on the ceiling of a train car. Hit one with a Batarang and you have eight seconds to get the other two. Toss a Remote Controlled Batarang into the car and guide it under the boards and into the far question mark. Immediately throw another one and guide it into the middle one. Repeat for the closest mark to obtain the prize.

(11) Grapple to the south gargoyle inside the Subway terminal. Glide to the west and bust through the weakened wall ahead. Collect the Trophy inside.

(12) Break through a weakened wooden wall in the southeast corner of the terminal, then take the steps on the east side to find the Trophy.

(13) This Trophy is hanging from the northwest train car's ceiling. Use the Batclaw to obtain it.

(14) In the terminal, grapple to the ledge below the west gargoyle and enter the small room. Use the Cryptographic Sequencer to enter EFFORTLESS-NESS into the Riddler Security Panel.

(15) Find the room with the fuse box and Trophy in the northwest corner of the terminal. Look at the fuse box through a hole on the east side and use the REC to overload the box. Run up the steps to collect the Trophy.

16 Find the open vents in the northwest corner of the terminal; crawl into one of them to collect another Trophy.

17 Exit the Subway terminal via the door on the north side. Use the REC to open the shutter on the right, then slide into the room and pick up the Trophy.

18 Before proceeding toward Wonder Tower, look straight down from the wooden platform. Create an ice raft as close to the south side as possible. Drop down to it to pick up this Trophy.

19 Before sailing over the water toward Wonder Tower, use the Long Range Cryptographic Sequencer on the Riddler Security Panel and enter INGENU-OUSNESS to unlock a Trophy on the opposite side. Use the Line Launcher to clear the gap and collect the reward.

20 In the east tunnels of the Subway there is a gap and a bridge down below. Use the Line Launcher to clear the gap, or grapple to the west ledge. The Trophy rests beyond the weakened floor.

21 Enter the east tunnels from the Subway terminal and run along the path to find a large gap. Use the Batclaw to pull the Trophy off the far platform.

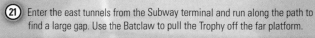

22 Hop onto the bridge railing in the eastern Subway tunnels and create an ice raft below. Use the Batclaw to pull in the Trophy hanging on the east wall.

23, **24**, **25** Use Explosive Gel on the weakened wall south of Trophy #21 to reveal a hidden Riddler death trap. Crawl underneath the door and step onto the pressure pad. Turn around and toss a Batarang at the question mark to unlock three Trophies hanging on the wall. As Riddler starts to count down, he releases gas into two of the six steam vents. First are the far two, so hit them with a Freeze Blast. Repeat this for the middle two next, then move to the other side of the room and hit the final two. Collect the Trophies and leave the room.

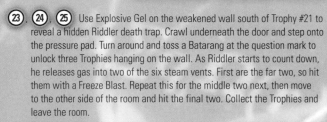

26 At the northeast intersection in the eastern Subway tunnels, locate the Trophy hidden behind bars. Face south and toss a Remote Controlled Batarang down the hall. At the maintenance entrance, turn right and guide it through the electricity. Quickly do a U-turn and bring it back to Batman's position. Guide it into the opening on the cell door into the fuse box. Collect the prize from inside.

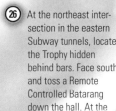
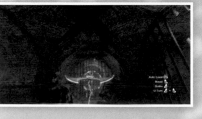

CATWOMAN TROPHIES

27 From the Subway entrance, go down the steps and enter the far. Pick up the Trophy from the table.

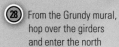

28 From the Grundy mural, hop over the girders and enter the north track. Walk west and pounce to the ceiling. Find the grate and flip to the top, then go east to collect the Trophy.

29 This Trophy hangs above the shutter on the west side of the Subway terminal. Pounce to the ceiling on one side or the other to collect the prize.

30 From the Subway terminal, enter the east Subway tunnels and run around the right-hand turn. Pounce to the grated ceiling and follow it to the next Trophy.

31 Climb underneath the bridge in the eastern Subway tunnels to find this Trophy.

RIDDLES

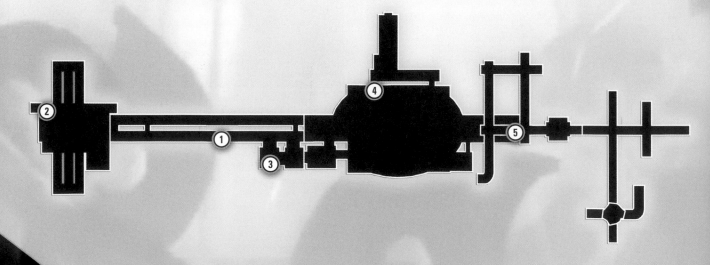

1 After running along the train cars and returning to the right line, drop in between the cars to the east and enter the car behind you. Continue until you see a mirror on the left. Use Detective Mode to line up a dot on the mirror with the rest of the question mark, which is reflected from the right wall.

2 In the Subway Station on the northwest side of the tracks, scan the Vicki Vale Show poster.

3 Drop off the train cars and step up to the mural of Solomon Grundy. Scan it to solve this Riddle.

4 In the Subway terminal on the north wall, scan the Visit Santa Prisca poster to solve this Riddle.

5 In the east tunnels of the Subway, find a gap and a bridge below. Use the Line Launcher to clear the gap, or grapple to the west ledge. Use Explosive Gel on the weakened floor and scan Croc's collar and the bones on the cot.

COLLECTIBLE: JOKER TEETH

MUSEUM
RIDDLER TROPHIES

1 From the Museum entrance, dive through the boarded up window on the left and approach the trio of switches. You have about one second to disable them all. Quickfire Batarangs as fast as possible to complete this Riddle.

2 Walk down the hallway from the start and turn left at the dinosaur. Use Explosive Gel to detonate the wall and collect the Trophy resting on the boxes inside.

3 Inside the Trophy room, grapple to the platform hanging from the ceiling. The Trophy sits in the middle.

4. Before exiting the Trophy room, slide underneath the gate on the left and approach the Trophy. Use the Long Range Cryptographic Sequencer on the Municipal Security Panel on the far wall

and enter TRIASSIC as the password. Pick up the prize before returning to the main hall.

5. Inside the Trophy room, climb onto the Scarface display in the northwest corner and pull the vent cover off the wall. Crawl through the ductwork into the side hallway. Use the Disruptor on the sentry gun to disable it, then collect the Trophy in the next room.

6. Run down the hall after exiting the Trophy room and turn left. Use the REC to open the shutter and pick up the Trophy.

7. After exiting the Trophy room, turn right and grapple to the ledge to the north. Turn around and use the Line Launcher to crash through the windows. Collect the reward on the platform at the end.

8. At the elevator on the south side of the gladiator pit, use the REC to send the empty car up. Place Explosive Gel on the right wall, detonate it, and pick up the Trophy.

9. Hop into the elevator and ride it to the second floor. Walk around the corner and locate the valve on the wall. Use the Batclaw to pry it open, then use it to collect the Trophy.

10. After defeating the enemies in the Gladiator Pit, peer into the west room to find the next Trophy. Toss a Remote Controlled Batarang into the electricity in the northeast corner of the room and bring it back out. Guide it under the left gate and turn right at the displays. Guide it through one of the openings and down to the fuse box on the right. This opens the gate, providing access to another Trophy.

11. After opening the gate for Trophy #10, dive through the window on the right and collect the Trophy. This room also has a fuse box that controls the nearby gate, so these Trophies can be done in the opposite order.

12. Inside the torture chamber, make an ice raft and look for a valve on the east wall. Use the Batclaw to open the valve and use the gadget again to obtain the Trophy.

13 Go to the north door in the torture chamber and grapple to the scaffolding on the left. Turn around and use the Line Launcher to continue south. Start looking to the left to find the Trophy on a platform near the entrance. Fire another line in its direction to pick it up.

14 Use the Line Launcher access the Iceberg Lounge entrance and look into the water in the southwest corner for this Trophy. Create an ice raft and glide over to it. Use the

hooks to get into position if necessary and then pick up the reward.

15 Enter the north door of the Torture Chamber and proceed down the hall. Turn right and use the REC on the shutter to enter a small room. Eight question marks light up in a clockwise fashion; hit one with a Batarang when it lights up. One way to complete this is to blindly Quickfire Batarangs until you hit the one that is lit up. Otherwise, aim for one of the switches and then as the switch that is placed two before this one lights up, let the Batarang fly!

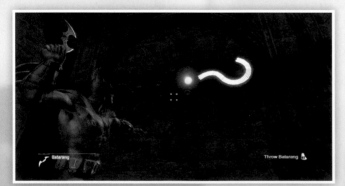

16 Enter the Armory and hop over the railing to the steps below. Continue down to the first floor and run to the displays on the left. Follow the perimeter of the room around to the south side. Open the

grating and enter the ductwork to find the Trophy.

17 From the Armory entrance, run to the right to find a weakened wooden wall. Bust through to collect this Trophy.

18 Move to the northeast corner of the Armory's first floor and use the Cryptographic Sequencer to enter ORNITHOLOGY. Enter the room and obtain the prize inside.

19 Look under the west side of the bridge in the Armory to find a Security Panel and a Trophy. Use the Cryptographic Sequencer to enter the password ARTIFACT, then use the Batclaw to snag the Trophy.

20 Run to the northwest corner of the Armory on the bottom floor. Enter the open vent, fire a Freeze Blast at the steam pipe, and pick up the Trophy behind the wood pallets.

21 Locate the War Room down the south hallway from the Torture Chamber. Look inside the display to find this Trophy inside a treasure chest.

(22) Move to the northwest corner of the War Room and toss a Freeze Blast at the steam pipe. Crawl inside and retrieve the Trophy behind the bookcase.

(23) Enter the Iceberg Lounge after completing the Museum and run down the hall to the east. Use the Mine Detonator to remove the mines below the gate on the right. Slide into that room to collect this Riddler Trophy.

CATWOMAN TROPHIES

(24) Exit the Trophy room and turn left at the intersection. Assuming the shutter is open, go on inside. Leap to the ceiling and enter via the flip grate to get the Trophy.

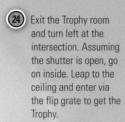

(25) Go into the Torture Chamber via the east door and descend to the bottom. Move north to find a flip grate; enter the cage above to collect the Trophy.

(26) From Trophy #25, pounce to the ceiling and use the grating to move west and then north. This Trophy hangs just ahead.

(27) Use the grated ceiling to reach the north door of the Torture Chamber and continue down the hallway to the Armory. Proceed to the right and stop before the bridge, then leap to the ceiling to collect a Trophy.

(28) This Trophy is on the display case in the northwest corner where Batman found Mister Freeze's suit.

RIDDLE ME THIS, BATMAN

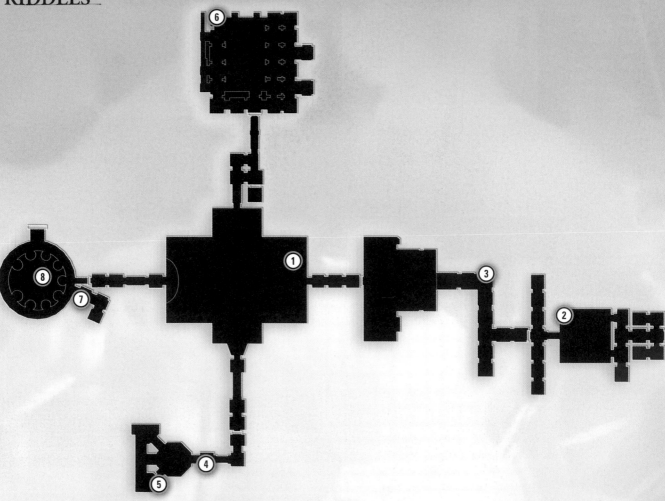

① Just inside the east side of the Torture Chamber, use the Line Launcher on a side wall and use the Tightrope command to get on top. Enter Detective Mode to find the question mark on the far wall and the dot on the post. Walk along the wall and adjust the camera to line them up.

② From the entrance balcony, run down the right-hand stairs and scan the Scarface puppet display.

③ After leaving the Trophy Room, turn right at the intersection and continue to the north end. Scan the portrait of Penguin and his parents to solve this puzzle.

4 Run down the hall south of the Torture Chamber but just prior to the War Room and examine the display case on the left. It contains two hyenas with hats on; scan it to complete this Riddle.

5 Enter the War Room and run to the south side behind the gate. If the nearby Security Panel has been hacked, simply walk through the left opening. Scan the poster of the Abramovici Twins.

6 On the first floor of the Armory in the northwest corner, scan the display with the three skeletons.

7 Enter the Iceberg Lounge and enter the east hallway. Scan the mannequin with the top hat to solve the puzzle.

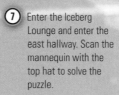

8 Locate the cop holding Penguin's umbrella gun in the middle of the Iceberg Lounge. Scan him to solve the Riddle.

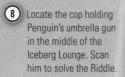

COLLECTIBLE: PENGUINS

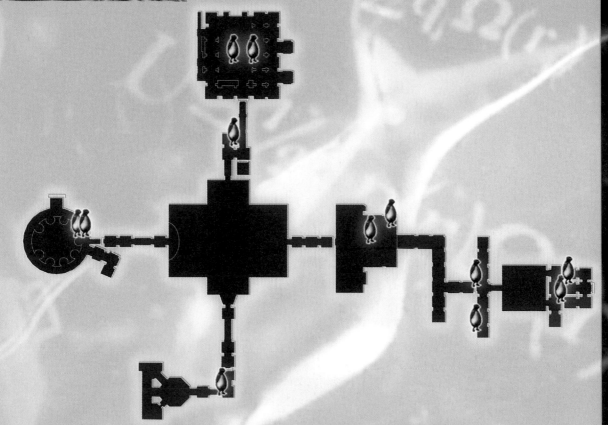

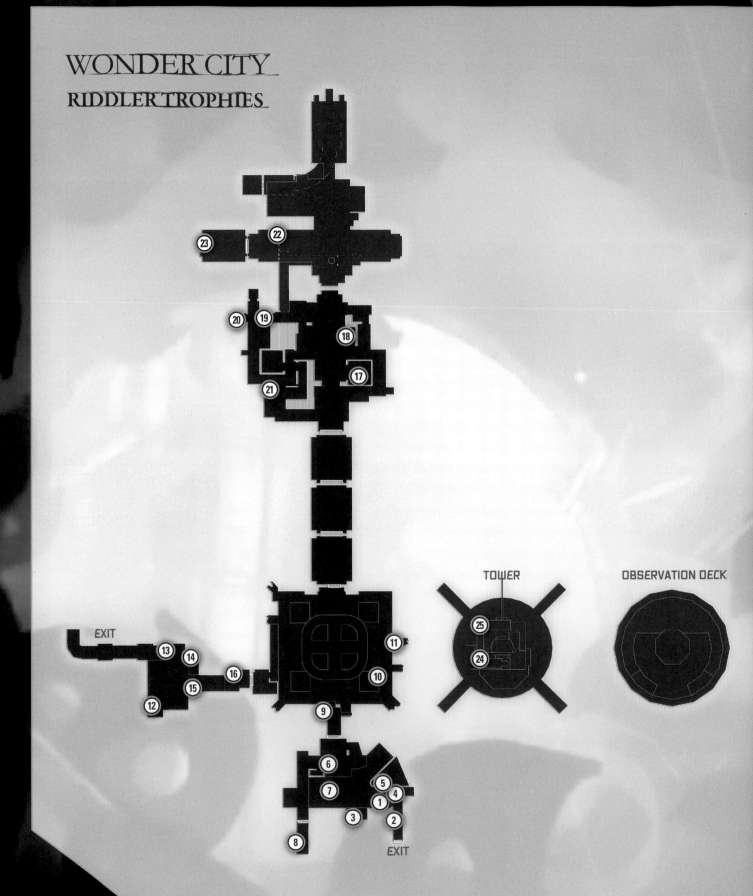

WONDER CITY
RIDDLER TROPHIES

TOWER

OBSERVATION DECK

EXIT

EXIT

1 From the entrance to the southern collapsed streets, walk down the hall and grapple to a ledge on the left to find a Trophy.

2 Go to the lower floor and face the entrance. Freeze Blast the two vertical steam pipes to reveal a grapple point, then climb it to access the Trophy.

3 Turn left after the first two Trophies and use the Line Launcher to traverse the gap to the west. Halfway across, look to the left and fire another line to reach the Trophy.

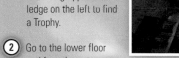

4 Hop down to an ice raft, then turn and grapple to the upper ledge. Perform a Grapnel Boost to burst through the wood. Use the Batclaw to retrieve the hanging Trophy.

5 This Trophy is hanging on the south wall in the room at the end of the starting hall. Stepping inside the room causes the Trophy to become locked. So, leap through the glass and use Explosive Gel on the left window to create an opening. Leave the room and use the Line Launcher to the west. While passing over the water, send another line to the right-hand platform. Look through the broken window and use the Batclaw to obtain the Trophy.

6 From the platform used to retrieve Trophy #5, turn around and grapple to the next floor. Use the Batclaw to pull in a Trophy hanging on the ceiling.

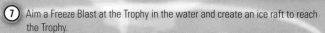

7 Aim a Freeze Blast at the Trophy in the water and create an ice raft to reach the Trophy.

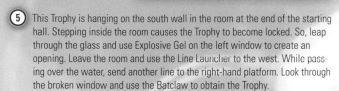

8 Use the Line Launcher to reach the ledge west of the water, or walk around the side of the room. Use the Cryptographic Sequencer and enter FORTIFICATION to hack the Security Panel. Take the short hallway beyond the door heading south and use the Batclaw to retrieve the Trophy from the ceiling.

9 Drop to the south side of the Wonder Tower Foundations walkway. Use the Cryptographic Sequencer on the Security Panel to enter ARMAMENT and snatch the Trophy.

10 Drop to the bottom floor of the Wonder Tower Foundations and search the southeast corner to find a Trophy sitting next to the floor grates.

11 Run to the east side of the walkway and look for the destructible wall. Use Explosive Gel to bring it down and collect the prize inside.

12 The next five Trophies become available through the Processing Center once TYGER codes have been obtained. Use the Freeze Blast to create an ice raft and use the Batclaw to retrieve the Trophy to the south.

13 Use two Line Launches to reach the northeast platform and Trophy #14. Turn and fire a Batarang at the rope holding up a frozen Trophy to knock it down to the water. Create an ice raft and glide down to receive this prize.

14 Grapple to the northeast platform used to reach Trophy #13 to get this one.

15 Climb down the ledge that runs along the east wall to find another wooden platform. Look southeast and use the Long Range Cryptographic Sequencer on Riddler's Security Panel to enter CEREBRAL.

Target the Trophy using the Batclaw to pull it in.

16 Hop into Underhill & Davies Books at the east end of the collapsed streets and use Explosive Gel on the floor. Enter the hole and look at the ceiling. Toss a Batarang at the Riddler switch to collect the nearby Trophy.

17 In the main section of Wonder Avenue, run north through the middle of town and turn right after Wonder City Jewelry. Look for a room on the second floor and grapple to it; a pressure pad and Trophy wait inside. Step on the pad and face north. You must activate three pads without touching anything. Use the Line Launcher and land on the pad in the far corner. Turn left and use the Line Launcher again to sail into the far building. Release the line and land on the final pad. Return to the original room to collect the Trophy.

18 Drop to the street and look for Billingham Butchers on the north side. Slide into the small opening just to the right to find another Trophy.

19 Enter the Adamson & Stjernberg Drugstore on the north side of Wonder Avenue and use Explosive Gel on the far wall. A locked Trophy sits inside. connected to a Riddler Switch on the west

wall. Exit the building and fling a Remote Controlled Batarang into the open window to the south. Guide it through the building and through another window to the west. Continue to the north into the alley and locate the switch on the right; hit it to release the Trophy. You have nine seconds to retrieve it.

20 Enter the west alley (the one with the Riddler Switch for Trophy #19) and look for a weakened wooden wall on the west side. Bust through it and collect another reward from Riddler.

21 From the entrance to this section of Wonder Avenue, turn left and head north to find a baby carriage. The Trophy is inside the carriage.

22 Cut through the Drugstore, but this time continue north down the ramp. Use the Disruptor to detonate the mine and slide under the bars to collect another Trophy.

23 After emerging from the "secret corridor," turn to the left and proceed to the end of the street. Use a REC on the motor in the ground to open the doors and continue inside to collect the prize.

24 Ride the elevator to the observation deck. Hop onto the ledge to the left and climb down to the ledge. Shimmy along the ledge past where you can drop to a platform below. Around the corner, climb up and collect the Trophy.

25 Climb up the tower and glide through the elevator shaft. Walk through the cage and turn around. Grapple to the top of the cage and follow it around the corner for another Trophy.

RIDDLES

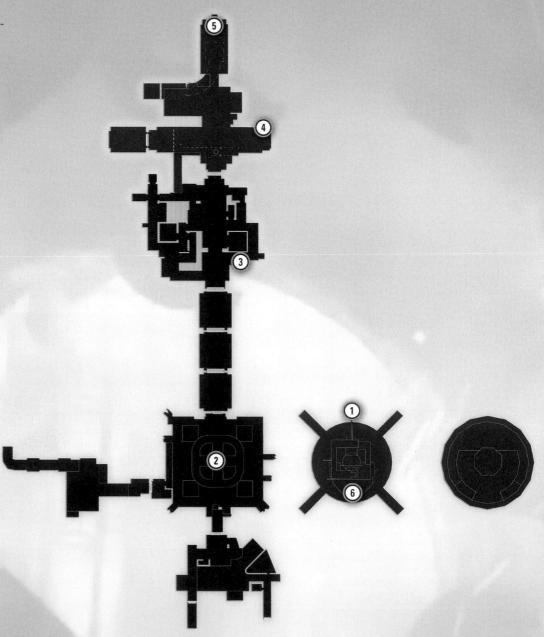

1 Climb the exterior of the Wonder Tower and glide across the elevator shaft to the platform below. Walk onto the pole and tip-toe across the wire to another pole on the north side. Enter Detective Mode and look at the tower. Jump to the north and scan the question mark while falling.

2 Enter the Wonder Tower Foundations and drop to the bottom floor. Scan the globe located below the elevator.

3 Enter the main area of Wonder Avenue and head to the southeast side. Scan the sandwich board about Wonder City.

4 After emerging from below to the Chamber of the Demon, run to the far right and look for the Solomon Grundy wanted poster. Scan it to solve this Riddle.

5 In the northern section of the Chamber of the Demon where the secret stairs appear, scan the two Rā's al Ghūl statues.

6 Ride the elevator to the top and scan the Gotham City view plate next to the railing.

COLLECTIBLE: DEMON SEALS

PHYSICAL CHALLENGES

The final screen of Riddles is for Physical Challenges. Complete the following to work toward unlocking the last of the Riddler rewards. Each row unlocks the following:

ROW	CONCEPT ART UNLOCKED
1	Catwoman
2	Two-Face
3	The Joker
4	The Penguin
5	The Riddler

NAVIGATIONAL CHALLENGES

CHALLENGE	TIP
Glide for over 150 meters without using the Grapnel Boost upgrade.	Find a high tower and glide off the top. Dive and pull up to gain speed while flying between the buildings.
Glide for 250 meters (Grapnel Boost upgrade is allowed).	Grapple to the top of a high building and boost off to stay in the air. Remember that the Grapnel Boost is permitted in this challenge.
Perform a vertical dive for over 50 meters.	Glide off a high tower and dive all the way to the ground.
Perform five consecutive line launches without touching the ground.	With so many buildings in the city area, it's quite easy to attain consecutive line launches.
Glide for 30 meters while maintaining a height of less than 5 meters above the water.	Dive toward the water and pull up just before impact. Now hold the glide as close to the water as possible.

COMBAT CHALLENGES

x22

RIDDLER CHALLENGE COMPLETE
Achieve a x20 combat combo

Saving...

CHALLENGE	TIP
Achieve a x20 combat combo.	Use the Critical Strikes and Special Combo Boost Upgrades to complete this challenge. Keep up constant attacks and take advantage of Counter opportunities.
Use 3 Quickfire gadgets in one combat encounter.	This needs to occur in an encounter, not a combo. Start by quickfiring three gadgets to complete this one.
Achieve a x5 variation bonus in one combat encounter.	Mix up your moves during an encounter. This is a great technique to learn for Riddler's Revenge.
Aerial Attack off a stunned enemy into another (3 required)	Cape Stun a foe and double-tap the Evade button. While running into the enemy, simultaneously press the Attack button and press the Movement button in the direction of another enemy to jump off and land.
Use the Slide to trip an enemy (3 required).	Slide into unsuspecting enemies, or work it into a combo.
Perform a Beatdown to finish an enemy (5 required).	Perform a Beatdown on the final enemy. This is the easiest enemy to achieve this on, because there are no distractions.
Counter an enemy projectile (3 required).	When an enemy picks up an item, wait for the Counter lines to appear, then press the Counter button.
Hit an explosive object with a Batarang before it is thrown.	When an enemy picks up a fire extinguisher or barrel, Quickfire a Batarang to make it explode in his hands.
Take out 2 enemies at once with the Glide Boost Attack.	From the rooftops, find two enemies standing next to each other. Glide Attack one foe and boost into the two of them. Make sure they are far enough away that you can complete the move.

GADGET CHALLENGES

CHALLENGE	TIP
Use a Combo Batarang in combat (10 required).	Quickfire Batarangs during combos to achieve this challenge.
Perform a Batclaw Slam (5 required).	Use the Batclaw to pull an enemy toward you and immediately hit him to perform the slam.
Use the Quickfire REC during a combo (5 required).	Quickfire the REC during a combo.
Use the Quickfire Explosive Gel during a combo (5 required).	Lay down Explosive Gel using the Quickfire command and detonate it to knock the enemies down.
Use the Quickfire Freeze Blast during a combo (5 required).	Quickfire the Freeze Blast during combos. This is a great way to take an enemy or two out of the fight.
Use the Smoke Pellet to disorientate enemies into attacking each other.	Toss a Smoke Pellet in the middle of a group of enemies and they may start attacking each other.
Finish a fight with a Combo Batarang (3 required).	Continue to Quickfire Batarangs while fighting the final enemy of an encounter.
Use the REC to get an armed enemy to fire his weapon and surprise at least one other nearby enemy.	While perched on a Vantage Point, look for two thugs scouting together and hit the back one with an REC.
Use the REC to force an enemy to hit another enemy (3 required).	When facing a group of enemies, Quickfire the REC into the group.
Use the REC to blast one armored thug into any other thug.	Line up an armored thug with another enemy and hit him with the REC.
Use the Freeze Cluster Grenade to immobilize three or more henchmen at one time (upgrade required).	Find three enemies who are standing together and toss a Freeze Cluster Grenade in between them.
Use the Freeze Blast to freeze an enemy then a Batarang to knock them down.	Follow up a Freeze Blast with a Quickfire Batarang during a fight.
Perform a Grapnel Boost Takedown.	Use Detective Mode to find an enemy roaming close to the edge of a roof and grapple to him. While grappling, engage the Grapnel boost to automatically perform the Takedown if close enough to the enemy.
Use the Reverse Batarang to knock down an enemy.	It may take more than just a Reverse Batarang to knock an enemy down, but keep at it.
Kick an enemy while riding on the Line Launcher (3 required).	Aim the Line Launcher toward a group of unaware enemies to make Batman kick as he passes through them.
While riding on the Line Launcher towards an unaware enemy, use the Takedown attack to drop down and knock him out.	Find an unsuspecting enemy in the distance and get on his level. Line Launch at him and press the Takedown button when available.
Catch a Remote Batarang.	Throw the Remote Controlled Batarang and guide it into Batman's hand.
Fly a fully boosted Remote Batarang into a thug and send him flying through the air.	Aim the Remote Controlled Batarang at an enemy and boost all the way in.

INVISIBLE PREDATOR CHALLENGES

CHALLENGE	TIP
Use the Freeze Blast to freeze an armed enemy before taking him out.	Use the Freeze Blast on an armed enemy and then press the appropriate button for a Takedown when prompted.
Use the Smoke Pellet to disorientate an armed enemy and follow up with a Takedown.	Throw a Smoke Pellet at a nearby enemy and perform a Takedown when given the opportunity.
Disarm an enemy using the Batclaw Disarm (3 required).	Use the Batclaw on an armed thug. He may dodge the attempt, so keep trying.
Use the Disruptor to jam the gun of the last armed enemy in an area, then get him to fire at Batman.	Leave one armed enemy for last, then use the Disruptor to jam his gun. Make sure he sees you and attempts to fire before taking him down.
Use the REC to temporarily disable a backpack Jammer device.	Find an enemy with the jammer backpack and use the REC on him.
Take down an enemy using the Sonic Shock Batarang.	Toss a Sonic Shock Batarang at an enemy.
Perform an Inverted Takedown from a Vantage Point.	Hang from a Vantage Point and perform the takedown on an enemy below when prompted.
Perform a Knockout Smash (5 required).	Sneak up on an enemy and perform a Silent Takedown. DO the Knockout Smash when the text appears.

CATWOMAN CHALLENGES

CHALLENGE	TIP
Use Caltrops to stun an enemy (3 required).	Toss Catwoman's Caltrops at an enemy to stun him.
Perform a Special Combo Whiplash and Special Combo Whip Trip in one combo flow.	During a long combo with a group of enemies, perform each special move when the opportunity arises.
Complete one Claw Climb using at least 8 separate leaps without missing the timing for a single jump.	You need to find a tall building to make all the leaps, plus all the button presses must be spot on. The Tricorner Naval tower in Industrial District is a good place to get this one.
Perform a pounce attack (3 required).	From a rooftop, find an enemy below and perform the pounce attack.
Use the Quickfire Whip Attack during combat (3 required).	Use the Quickfire Whip Attack during an encounter.

TROPHIES/ACHIEVEMENTS

For those who like to unlock Trophies/Achievements, we have it covered! This section contains a listing of all the game's achievements and a brief description on how to unlock them all. The Trophies/Achievements are divided into gameplay categories for convenience.

MAIN STORY

Play through the main story to unlock the following awards. There's no way to miss any of them. Note that if you don't complete the Catch Achievement/Trophy before completing Watching in the Wings, you must get it on another playthrough.

 I'M BATMAN
Put on Batman's suit.

 ACID BATH
Stop Two-Face from finishing his trial.

 SAVIOR
Rescue the medical volunteers.

 COMMUNICATION BREAKDOWN
Destroy the Penguin's three transmitters.

GLADIATOR
Be the last man standing after the fighting in the arena.

 WRECKING BALL
Defeat a powerful enemy boss at the bottom of the museum.

 LOST AND FOUND
Uncover the secret of Arkham City.

 SAND STORM
Defeat a powerful assassin.

 HIDE AND SEEK
Outsmart a brilliant scientist.

 GHOST TRAIN
Survive a massive battle in a makeshift train station.

 FREEFALL
Stop Protocol 10.

 EXIT STAGE RIGHT
Complete the main story.

SIDE STORY

It's not required to complete the side missions to finish the game. To get the awards for these, you must find each mission and see it through to its conclusion. All of these are covered in their own chapter!

 FORENSIC EXPERT
Locate a gun for hire (Shot in the Dark). Complete the investigation in the three victims and search for Deadshot's stash in the northeastern part of Arkham City.

 CONTRACT TERMINATED
Complete Shot in the Dark.

 SERIAL KILLER
Complete Identity Thief.

MYSTERY STALKER
Find Azrael and complete "Watching in the Wings."

 DISTRESS FLARE
Find Bane and start "Fragile Alliance." He's inside a building with a flare on its roof; it's on the eastern side of town

 BROKEN TOYS
Complete Fragile Alliance. Destroy all the TITAN containers in the city and in Bane's hideout.

 RING RING
Answer a ringing phone in Arkham City to start "Cold Call Killer." Ringing phones can be found in any outdoor district of Arkham City. Listen for a ringing sound, turn on Detective Mode and pick up the phone.

DIAL Z FOR MURDER
Complete Cold Call Killer.

STOP THE CLOCK
Complete Through the Looking Glass.

BARGAINING CHIP
Complete Heart of Ice.

AR KNIGHT
Complete all eight Augmented Reality Challenges.

FULLY LOADED
Collect all of Batman's Gadgets and Upgrades. This requires considerable leveling. You also need to complete the side missions "Remote Hideaway" and "Hot and Cold." To get the points needed to purchase these upgrades, seek random battles on the streets of Arkham City. Fight with as many gadgets and styles as possible to raise your bonus experience as well.

AGGRAVATED ASSAULT
Stop all Acts of Violence in Arkham City (there are 16 prisoners to save; 15 plus Jack Ryder, or 16 through the course of the game). This involves rescuing a number of political prisoners who are being attacked throughout the region. Look for pairs of men on the street and listen for the sounds of intimidation. Break up the fights to save each prisoner.

IQ TEST
Start Enigma Conundrum, at the church. Scan the church organ to trigger this.

CONUNDRUM
Rescue the 1st hostage from the Riddler, in Enigma Conundrum.

MASTERMIND
Rescue the 2nd hostage from the Riddler, in Enigma Conundrum.

PUZZLER
Rescue the 3rd hostage from the Riddler, in Enigma Conundrum.

INTELLECTUAL
Rescue the 4th hostage from the Riddler, in Enigma Conundrum.

BRAINTEASER
Rescue the 5th hostage from the Riddler, in Enigma Conundrum.

GENIUS
Rescue the final hostage from the Riddler, in Enigma Conundrum.

CHALLENGES

BRONZE REVENGE
Obtain 24 medals on the original Arkham City ranked maps (as Batman). You can't embark on this before unlocking those maps, so collect Riddler Trophies. The more maps you unlock, the easier it is to get medals.

SILVER REVENGE
Obtain 48 medals on the original Arkham City ranked maps (as Batman). This requires much more skill in combat because you need to average a silver rating on all of the maps. Fight with the longest possible combos and train in an active defense. Don't take any hits because they're too costly to your ratings.

GOLD REVENGE
Obtain all 72 medals on the original Arkham City ranked maps (as Batman). Find all the Riddler's Trophies. Once you have access to every ranked map, practice each one in turn. Instead of shifting between maps, pick one or two maps at a time and master them.

CAMPAIGN BRONZE
Obtain 28 medals on the original Arkham City campaigns (as Batman).

CAMPAIGN SILVER
Obtain 56 medals on the original Arkham City campaigns (as Batman).

CAMPAIGN GOLD
Obtain all 84 medals on the original Arkham City campaigns (as Batman).

FLAWLESS FREEFLOW FIGHTER 2.0
Complete one combat challenge without taking damage (as any character). Choose one of the earlier challenges, as they tend to be less aggressive. Don't fight to get a gold; instead, use counters aggressively and stay at range to make the most use of gadgets.

EXPLORATION

 TWICE NIGHTLY
Beat the Main Story on Normal or Hard Mode, then play through New Game Plus and beat that, too!

 GOTHAM BASE JUMPER

Climb to the top of Wonder Tower below the security center. Leap off and circle the tower five or more times. Get as high as possible before doing this, as Batman can only drop so far before he rescues himself.

 PAY YOUR RESPECTS
Find Crime Alley and pay respect for a full minute and a half. Crime Alley is in Park Row. It's located east from the courthouse and west from the church.

 STORYTELLER

Calendar Man is in the jail cells below the courthouse (in the back of the building). Hear his special stories by walking into the cell area on specific dates. Changing your system's date is a good way to get this done without waiting for months on end.

The special dates are as follows:

New Year's Day; Valentine's Day; St. Patrick's Day; April Fools' Day; Mother's Day; Father's Day; Independence Day; Feast of St. Roch; Labor Day; Halloween; Thanksgiving; Christmas. Visit Calendar Man on the dates circled on the calendar.

 CATCH
Look for Azrael on the rooftops of Arkham City. Throw a Remote Batarang at him during the "Watching in the Wings" side mission.

 50X COMBO
This can be accomplished in any play mode and with any character. It's easiest to practice in the various challenge rooms, because those fights are often quite involved. Otherwise, look for encounters with a considerable number of enemies. When Batman knocks down almost all of his opponents, use a Beatdown on the last person while everyone gets back up. This makes it easier to pump his combo higher without wasting any time.

 PERFECT FREEFLOW 2.0

Perform a perfect combo including all of Batman's combat moves in any play mode.

 GADGET ATTACK
Use five different quickfired gadgets in a single fight. This isn't possible until later in the game, after getting the Freeze Blast. Don't even try to fight when you want to unlock this. Just switch between the REC, Explosive Gel, Batarang, Batclaw, and Freeze Blast. One hit with each is all that it takes.

 PERFECT KNIGHT— DAY 2

Complete every challenge in the game! Collect all the Riddler Trophies to get every challenge. Complete all the side missions, upgrade all gadgets, complete New Game Plus, and run through the challenge maps. This leads to 100% completion of the game and unlocks the Trophy/Achievement.

CAMEOS! FINDING SPECIAL CHARACTERS

There are several hidden characters who are stuck in Arkham City. This section reveals how to find them all. Follow the instructions below to uncover these unique peripheral characters.

JACK RYDER CAMEO

1. Enter the streets directly north of the Ace Chemicals building.

2. Travel west through the streets toward a group of thugs.

3. Knock out the thugs who are beating up a helpless.

4. Talk to Jack Ryder, the victim of the attack, several times.

5. Complete the side mission "Shot in the Dark."

6. Talk to Ryder in The Mad Hatter alley.

ERNEST RAY & DAVE HIGGINS

1. Find the political prisoner camp in Arkham City.

2. Search west of that position for two prisoners near the courthouse.

3. Talk to the prisoners hiding in the alley.

IAN BALL

1. After exiting the courthouse early in the game, walk to the political prisoners on the west side of the building.

2. Talk to the prisoners hiding near the fire barrel.

GCPD POLITICAL PRISONER

1. After leaving the steel mill for the first time, travel to the GCPD building

2. Defeat all of the armed thugs surrounding the area

3. Get on the roof to the west of the GCPD building

4. Talk to the outcast near the loud speakers.

CALENDAR MAN

1. Search the courthouse basement.

KILLER CROC

1. Late in the game, enter the Subway Maintenance Access area via the Industrial District.

2. Walk to the northern side of that area.

3. Throw a Remote Batarang through a damaged gate and hit a button on the other side.

4. Killer Croc emerges and greets Batman.

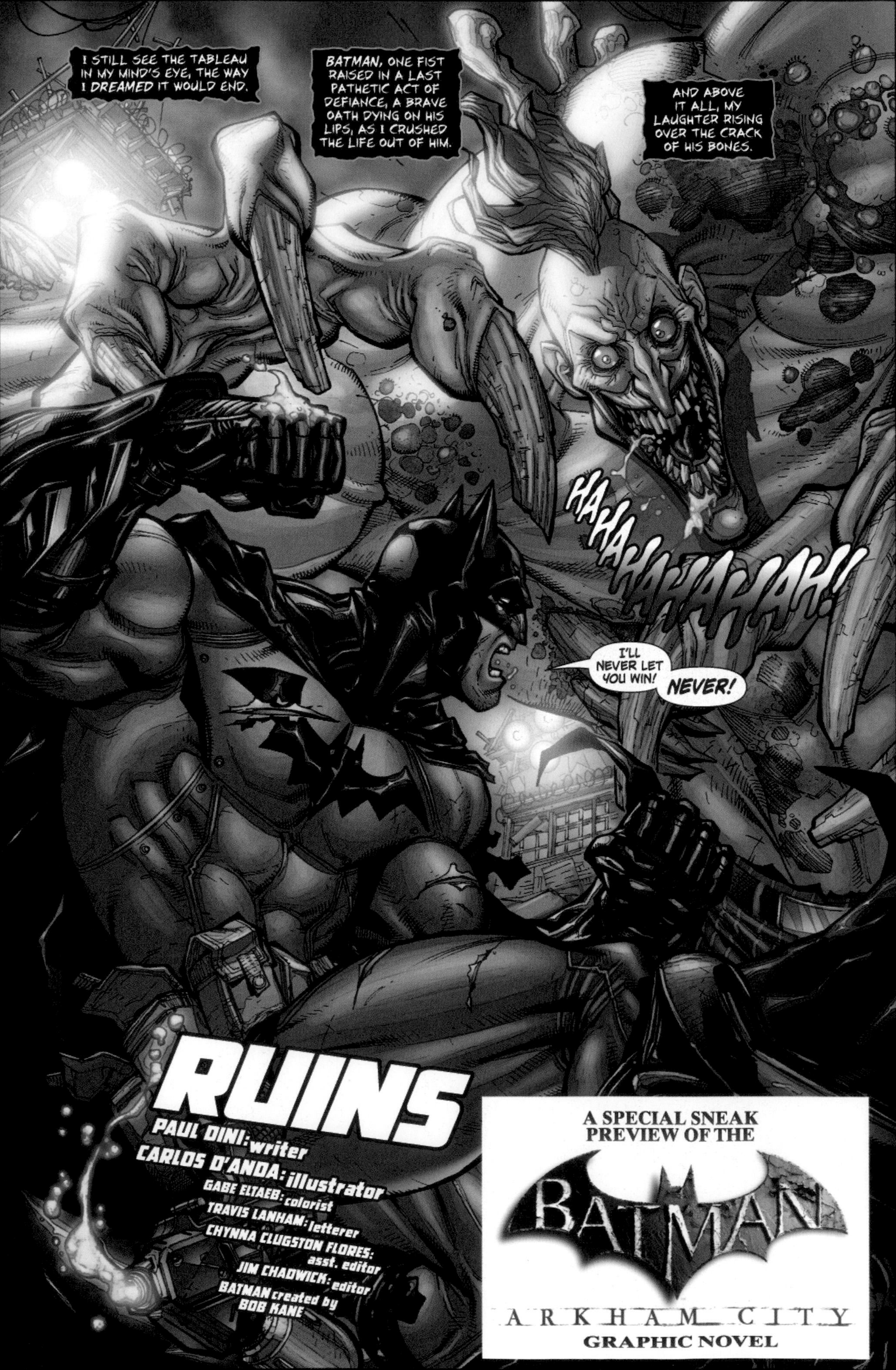
I STILL SEE THE TABLEAU IN MY MIND'S EYE, THE WAY I DREAMED IT WOULD END.
BATMAN, ONE FIST RAISED IN A LAST PATHETIC ACT OF DEFIANCE, A BRAVE OATH DYING ON HIS LIPS, AS I CRUSHED THE LIFE OUT OF HIM.
AND ABOVE IT ALL, MY LAUGHTER RISING OVER THE CRACK OF HIS BONES.
HAHAHAHAHAHAH!
I'LL NEVER LET YOU WIN!
NEVER!
RUINS
PAUL DINI: writer
CARLOS D'ANDA: illustrator
GABE ELTAEB: colorist
TRAVIS LANHAM: letterer
CHYNNA CLUGSTON FLORES: asst. editor
JIM CHADWICK: editor
BATMAN created by BOB KANE
A SPECIAL SNEAK PREVIEW OF THE
BATMAN
ARKHAM CITY
GRAPHIC NOVEL

Discover what happens between the hit videogame,
BATMAN: ARKHAM ASYLUM and the upcoming sequel,
BATMAN: ARKHAM CITY!

BATMAN
ARKHAM CITY

A hardcover
graphic novel collection
of the **acclaimed**
Limited Series

Written by
PAUL DINI

Art by
CARLOS D'ANDA

OCTOBER 2011

INCLUDES **5** BONUS CHAPTERS
Previously available
exclusively online!

IN STORES
OCTOBER 18th

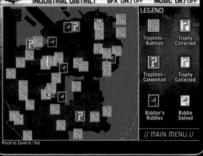

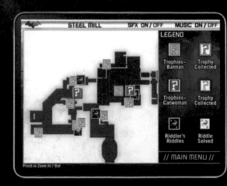

OFFICIAL STRATEGY GUIDE

Written by Michael Lummis & Michael Owen

ISBN: 978-0-7440-1316-0
Printing Code: The rightmost double-digit number is the year of the book's printing; the rightmost single-digit number is the number of the book's printing. For example, 11-1 shows that the first printing of the book occurred in 2011.
14 13 12 11   4 3 2 1
Printed in the USA.

BRADYGAMES STAFF

PUBLISHER
Mike Degler

EDITOR-IN-CHIEF
H. Leigh Davis

TRADE AND DIGITAL PUBLISHER
Brian Saliba

LICENSING MANAGER
Christian Sumner

OPERATIONS MANAGER
Stacey Beheler

CREDITS

TITLE MANAGER
Tim Cox

BOOK DESIGNER
Carol Stamile

PRODUCTION DESIGNER
Tracy Wehmeyer

AUTHOR'S ACKNOWLEDGEMENTS

I'd like to thank Michael Owen for teaming up with me again on this project. We had a blast! Praise to Tim Cox for many hours of work getting all our materials together and melding it into a top rate guide. Special thanks to everyone at Rocksteady Studios and Warner Bros. for wonderful support and giving us such an amazing game to work on. I can't wait for the retail release so I have an excuse to play it again! —*Michael Lummis*

Thanks to Leigh Davis for giving me the opportunity to work on the guide for this incredible game, to Tim Cox for fixing all of my mistakes and putting together an awesome guide, and to Michael Lummis for once again being a great guide writing partner. Huge thanks to everyone at Rocksteady Studios for making an absolutely amazing game and all their support. Most of all, I would like to thank my wonderful wife, Michelle, for her patience during this busy time and for putting up with my virtual absence. —*Michael Owen*